KISS ME AGAIN

KISS ME *Again*

an invitation to a group of noble dames

BRUCE KELLNER

Turtle Point Press New York

© 2002 by Bruce Kellner

LCCN 2001 132391

Publisher's Cataloging-in-Publication
Kellner, Bruce.
    Kiss me again : an invitation to a group of noble dames /
by Bruce Kellner. — 1st ed.
        p.   cm.
    Includes bibliographical references.
    ISBN 1-885586-24-8
    1. Kellner, Bruce—Friends and associates.   2. Women and literature—
United States—History—20th century.   3. Women authors—
20th century—Biography.   4. Women artists—Biography.   I. Title.
PS3561.E3923Z4685   2002   813'.6
                                        QBI01-700780

Design and composition by Wilsted & Taylor Publishing Services

Sources and permissions are located on pages 295–296 and constitute an extension
of the copyright page.

FOR *Betsy*, ANOTHER NOBLE DAME

A holy parcell of the fairest dames. . . .
That euer turn'd their eyes to mortall views.

WILLIAM SHAKESPEARE

In 1891, Thomas Hardy published *A Group of Noble Dames*, a volume of his admiring biographies of a countess, a marchioness, a duchess, an honorable, and several ladies. Now I have written about some other noble dames, but with one possible exception no blue blood flows near their veins, and their pedigrees don't grow from family trees. Nor do these affectionate homages march in symmetry, either in form or in content. Some embrace whole lives; some touch on only a few years; some are more autobiographical than others.

My acknowledgments account for published and unpublished sources from which I have employed material. I have edited some letters considerably to delete extraneous or repetitive information, but others appear without so much as a comma altered because I wanted to preserve their eccentric charm. I've changed a few names and left out a few others. Anybody brave enough to recognize an ancestor masquerading as somebody else may be right.

CONTENTS

$\mathcal{A}$RDEN

*A*rden and I lie next to each other on top of one of our grandmother's patterned Joseph's coat of many colors quilts, its bright and zany shapes spilling over the day bed. We are supposed to be having our afternoon naps. High backed chairs have been placed against the edge of the bed to keep us from falling out, or to create the illusion that we are in a private room or perhaps an oversized crib and therefore immune to whatever our mothers are doing or saying at the big table just a few feet away. When we tire of peering at them through the spindles of the chairs' backs, straining to hear their whispered chatter, Arden unfurls a strand of her long yellow hair from its curl and holds it high above our heads. Then she bites it in half and gives half to me. Then we bite our halves in two, then those halves into fourths, then eighths, and so on, trying not to giggle, to see who wins by getting the smallest piece.

Arden was my first cousin, my first friend, and my best friend—the only child of my mother's older sister. As a physical presence I remember her clearly still at three, at four, at five, at ten, as a teenager, as a wife, as a mother, in early middle age, and then at forty-seven, dying of the cancer that little by little fed on her body. She defied death for ten years and faced it with an im-

3

placable serenity. As an emotional presence she seems always to have been in my life, and without exaggeration I believe that no day has passed since her death when I have not thought about her.

I was born in March and she in October; in between, her mother had come to help my mother for several weeks after I was born, and since our mothers spent the ensuing summer together, Arden and I always pretended—and even half-believed—that we had known each other since her conception.

When we were children and initially aware of each other in some sequential history—that is, when we first began to reckon time by events and associations—she had honey-colored sausage curls of prodigious length—dimmed from the carroty orange of her infancy—and a mouthful of silver braces and rubber bands, and toe shoes, and an imagination that could leap with my own. Our relationship developed over such a long period of time that our sense of loss was physical as well as emotional when we married, she several years before me, and drifted into the separate worlds that spouses and children demand. She was my alter ego, far more, indeed, than I was hers, although I know that I was crucial in her life too. She knew me better than anyone else, ultimately knowing everything about me and not being surprised when eventually I confided in her a catalog of deeper fears and compulsions than I have ever shared with anyone else. Sometimes for only the most fleeting of reasons I think about her on a regular basis that marks time's passing from day to day. I have never read many books without wondering how she would have reacted to them, not books for my teaching so much as for my private pleasure; I have rarely seen a play or a ballet or a movie without pausing over what her response might have been; I know I write nothing without her eyes on the page. Now, twenty-five years since her death, I still miss her inconsolably and can still weep if I think about her too deeply.

During my early years, my mother and I journeyed west from Indianapolis and, later, from Louisville, first alone and then with my sister, to spend our summers in Kansas with relatives. Arden was only seven months younger than I, so almost from the beginning we were part of each other's lives. But since we were separated most of the year we were not together long enough to weary of each other, and to develop a sibling's rivalry. My earliest memories of her are connected with our grandparents' farm in Enterprise, and with the basement in her family's house a few miles away in Abilene. Her parents moved to the basement during the summers to escape Kansas's scalding heat. It was not finished in the manner of latter-day "recreation rooms" or "family rooms," but it was spotlessly clean and practically furnished with a stove and a refrigerator and a sink. There was a bathroom, a storeroom for exploring, a playroom for children, a bed for naps, and a huge table with many chairs. I could draw its dimension with fair accuracy even now, but I could not do that for any of the six successive houses I lived in with my own family. Arden's parents had an electrified Victrola attached to their console radio. We played *Rio Rita, A Cottage for Sale, Swamp Ghosts, Chloe, My Angel*, Moran and Mack as *The Two Black Crows*, Rudy Vallee singing *I'm Just a Vagabond Lover* and Madame Ernestine Schumann-Heink singing *Trees, Is She My Girlfriend? Howdy-ow-dow*, and dozens of other 78 rpm records her parents had accumulated during the late Twenties and early Thirties.

Arden's father called us "house apes" because it was difficult to get us to go outside to play, although we did go to the Abilene swimming pool a few years later, and we spent a lot of time together on our grandparents' farm. Sometimes we went up the street to play with a poor little rich boy in a huge house, a late child ignored by his parents and older siblings, or we spent long afternoons in the Abilene Public Library, or spied on a neighborhood hermit lady who talked to birds in her backyard, but all that was somewhat later. Inevitably, time blurs and memory's calendar cannot ever be entirely accurate.

Arden began to take dancing lessons when she was about four years old and soon enough was up on her toes, in satin bodices over her chunky torso, with stiff net tutus fanning out from her hips, or in tight, fringed panties and spangled midriff blouses, and little caps of bunny fur over her toes before she impaled the satin slippers with her pointed feet, lacing them up with lengths of ribbon. For tapping, she wore black patent leather shoes with round toes and floppy bows over the instep and big silver quarter-moons over the heels and toes of the soles. There was a pair of red toe shoes with fitted metal cups over the ends too, so that while dancing to *Dizzy Fingers* or *Nola* she could switch her bottom and bounce her curls and dimple in spite of her mouthful of silver and then clump around *en pointe* during a tap-toe number. I thought she was wonderful.

During the summer between our birthdays when I had just turned four, and she was about to be four, we went with our mothers to Colorado for a vacation, and the surviving photographs that record our stay there are clear moments in my memory. We had cherry pie on Mount Evans; whoever took the photograph snapped us from the distance, but I still taste the thick red sauce, and we are eating it with our fingers. Arden and I pose, standing on a stone water fountain near Echo Lake; the water runs freely from an open spigot next to her, and I can still hear its uneven flow, a trickle, a gush, two trickles, a gush, a trickle, two gushes, that makes us try to guess what comes next. Arden and I stand with my mother at our cottage, where the entrance is at the top of a short flight of stairs, and the space below its porch and the ground is covered over by latticework, and even in this sepia snapshot the latticework is green and my mother's dress is tan, trimmed in pink. I see these instants in time, not because of their photographic images, fading now in old albums, but because they are locked in my head. The context is clear, the posing, our mothers cajoling us to smile, our joy in being together.

There are other images too, not preserved by the camera but as true as today is or tomorrow will ever be:

At our grandparents' farm we dress kittens from the barn in doll clothing, outside between the house and the farmyard, never inside. No animals are ever allowed inside, although we beg to bring in the kittens. Once we go with our grandfather when he pitches a rock-weighted gunny sack full of newborn kittens over the side of the bridge into the Old Smokey River. Why were we allowed to witness this horror? I do not recall that either of us cried over the incident, although we both loved cats.

In the cellar under the house there are dozens of old movie magazines that we pore over and cigar boxes we build houses from. Once we dig for treasure or the bones of the escaped black slave who is supposed to be buried there. We do not play often in the cellar because it is damp as well as cool, and the single overhead light bulb is, perhaps, only fifteen watts.

Our grandmother recites for us: "Seevuh nanzy rahpotzee, da lam ont, ewsse dine?" This is in French, and it has something to do with a lame ant.

In the front parlor where nobody goes very often, we pump songs from the player piano, shaking this uncle's wattles, that aunt's pompadour, the bugle beads on my mother's dress, and other silvered photographs of family members that adorn the top. Gingerly we touch the artificial rose, its red so deep as to look black, in a jar of pampas grass. Its color comes off on our fingers, just as it had long ago when our grandmother blushed her cheeks with it before her wedding. We know all those stories, all the songs too: *Hello Central, Give Me Heaven; Lay My Head Beneath a Rose; Some Day All Things Will Be Different.* Arden cries when our grandmother sings *Redwing*, and I cry when she sings *If I Only Had a Home.*

In the henhouse I gather eggs, first poking at the hens with a wire blanket beater to get them off their nests. Arden is afraid of chickens, so she stands back and holds the basket. But I love their feathers, their poking heads, their staring round eyes that seem to see nothing, their cozy waddles. Also, I like to throw out a handful of corn into a fairly small space near the henhouse, and when a great group of those clucking biddies are pecking contentedly, I sprint with a whoop into the center of them and send billows of feathers flying up in a cackle that frightens and delights us both, though Arden watches only from the distance.

In the cow barn we pour mounds of feed out for each of the cows and then when they have lumbered into their stalls we lock them in with wooden stocks worn smooth and polished by time. After the milking and processing, we join our grandfather in his model-A Ford for the milk deliveries from his small dairy, carrying up the chilled bottles from the morning's draw and returning with empties. We are rewarded with a nickel each that he can ill afford.

These farm chores are less fascinating for Arden than for me. I come to them on summer holidays as to rides at an amusement park; she endures them more regularly around the calendar, as her parents make frequent trips to Enterprise from Abilene, and she is lonely, wandering around the farm alone. But she adores our bald, banty rooster of a grandfather. I am a little afraid of him, as I am of all men, but she sees him frequently and I do not. We both love our grandmother, who blows out eggshells for us so we can make puppet heads of them. She calls us "kiddies," plays her ocarina for us, bakes huge sugar cookies called "gems." Once or twice she makes the table talk for us, since she believes firmly that she communicates with the other world, calling out, "Spirit of Columbus! Are you with us?" And the table knocks. It really does. And all this happens all at once or over and over again when we are three or six or nine or in between—an unblemished, blurry Garden of Eden where no snakes lurk.

Often, when Arden and I were on the farm with time to kill, we practiced on the player piano or pretended to practice, since we'd started taking piano lessons together, Arden's having begun when she was still eight and when I had just turned nine. Sometimes, we crossed the road to a neighbor's house to play her elaborate parlor organ, its oak casing always polished but never otherwise touched, for the owner—a little wizened woman who gave us unsweetened Lutheran cookies—did not play. I cannot recall how we first got ourselves invited; probably our grandmother arranged it to get us out of the house. The organ's dozen or more stops—vox humana, trumpet, violin, flute—all wheezed in much the same tone, it seemed, as we pumped away to play our modest duets, and we tired easily, bored by our own limitations at the keyboard or suffocated in the airless summer heat, so we never stayed long. More often we explored the barn loft where two workhorses lived below, Tom and Babe with one eye between the two of them, or the pasture with its cottonwood tree hanging over a pond where we were warned never to wade, and we never did.

I do not recall falling into the cow tank where goldfish the size of brook trout swam up to feed from the muzzles of the cows, but Arden always remembered vividly how she ran to get our mothers who pulled me out. Similarly, Arden never recalled getting the terrible cut on her forehead when she was bucked from her fat black and white pony, Patsy, but I remember my own fear of the blood that spilled onto her yellow curls and streamed over her terrified expression and lay in puddles before it soaked into the parched earth of the farmyard. That was later though.

By the time Arden and I were eight or nine, we had begun performing a sort of extemporaneous theater to entertain ourselves, described clearly enough for us by its attendant two-edged verb, "Let's play." As we didn't go to the movies often we must have picked up such seductive vibrations elsewhere, probably from the comic strips, in part at least. We were both addicted to comic strips, like *Tillie the Toiler*, *Boots and Her Buddies*, *Jane Arden* and, later, *Brenda Starr*. Arden loved *Brenda Starr* and I loved *Terry and the Pirates*, both of which, in retrospect, were often sexually charged. "Let's play," one or the other of us would say, putting a significant period afterward. I suspect that Arden may have said it more often than I did, although I was always more than willing and surely never refused the invitation. All my life, I have been all too eager to make public suggestions and all too reticent to make private ones. Probably that says more about me than I dare probe.

After Arden's or my "Let's play," the succeeding sentences laying out the circumstances for the drama would come rapidly and always agreeably, with some considerable embroidery: "You be the dancer and I'll be the director," or "I'll be this mean girl in the office and you be the manager who wants to fire me," or "Let's be enemies in war and I'll be this spy you don't know about until you fall in love with me and then I can get you to give me the secret documents." Whatever the variation, the improvised plays that followed went on at length. Arden was much engaged with horses, so frequently our scenarios were western: She would be a cowgirl pony express rider and I would be a postal clerk; she would be an Indian princess and I would be a scout. Sometimes there were intimations of sadomasochism in these adventures, tying each other up for torture, although only in pantomime and never ever physical. Inevitably, our plays involved a great deal of embracing and kissing.

Why, as puberty approached, we did not slip familiarly into bed for sex, I have no idea. Perhaps because we were too close; perhaps because the bond we felt precluded it out of some unspoken sense of incest; perhaps because sex itself was real and our games were not. Or perhaps it was something more latent in me. I was a sissy, as my father and some relatives and schoolmates reminded me, though Arden never did. We both knew about sex, or at least about its clinical fundamentals: My father had explained it to me when I was nine, as if it were a road map, with some neighborhood dogs turning it into an illustrated lecture, and Arden's mother had given her a book to explain it with bee pollen and flowers at about the same time, but we did not discuss what we knew. We never exchanged gender roles in our plays or moved beyond kissing, and our kisses never advanced past our closed mouths pressing against each other. Kissing was kissing, and we did not readily connect it with anything more intimate. Sixty years ago, of course, children on the cusp of maturity were somewhat more innocent, because there was no television, and because advertising was still decorous. When we talked about all this in later years, Arden and I agreed that we had lived in Eden rather longer than most.

Nevertheless, a single sexual experience—which we ourselves thwarted—occurred when we were eight or nine. I have no way now of tracking down an exact summer, for we often went to our grandparents' farm for family reunions. The incident is still quite clear to me, and so is the sullen, nineteen-year-old son of my mother's younger sister's second husband by his first wife, who made an extraordinary suggestion to Arden and me. He was sitting on the swing that hung from a tall tree in the center of the farmyard, quite far down from the house, in the broad space flanked by the chicken coop and the workshop and other out-buildings. Arden and I frequently swung each other giddily high there, but this boy sat barely moving. He was lanky and dark-haired, and he was smoking a cigarette. He sang a song for us:

> There's a skeeter on my peter, St. Marie,
> There's another on my brother, can't you see?
> There's a dozen on my cousin,
> Can't you hear them skeeters buzzin'?
> There's a skeeter on my peter, St. Marie.

Then he asked us if we'd like to see if there were any skeeters on his peter, unfastened his jeans and pulled out his penis, bouncing its heft in his hand. It was stiff and red. "No skeeters," he laughed. "You got any skeeters on yours?" Then he asked us to come into the henhouse with him so he could look at us without our clothes on, and maybe play some game he knew, and promised to give us each a nickel. We ran away. We never mentioned the incident to each other for nearly thirty years. When we did, our memories of it were identical.

In 1940, when I was ten years old and Arden was about to be ten, our parents took a two-week vacation in Colorado together. My sister and I stayed with our grandparents, but Arden stayed in Abilene with her other grandmother. We were furious at the unfairness of this arrangement. All three of us, our parents had decided, would be not too much responsibility but too much work. Arden's other grandmother was an oversized personage, not a person, an intimidating monolith with thin lips and hair dyed dead black. She had no humor about her, and she sighed a lot. Only once during those long two weeks did she drive Arden down to Enterprise—a fifteen-minute distance at most—and then she sat on the front porch with her white hat on and her white gloves on and her white shoes crossed at her ankles, with her white purse over her arm, and waited in silence while we played. We could not play, we could only mourn our separation.

When Arden and I were about twelve, she no longer wanted to dramatize our fantasies, and perhaps that accounts for our not having slept together. I can still recall my pang of regret the first summer that she did not say, "Let's play." A summer's absence had intervened; the war had called a halt to casual motor trips; gasoline and tires were at a premium. Her parents had driven to Kansas City to pick us up after our train ride from Louisville; she and I were in the back seat of the car with my mother and sister; Arden was sitting next to the window, I was sitting next to her, and I kept waiting, but she didn't whisper it to me. I had my first wet dream that summer; Arden menstruated that summer.

Still, there were other pastimes. We were regular swimmers at the local pool, she being much the better, but we took lessons together. Encouraged by her, I jumped off the second diving board, terrified, and she, with a promise from me of a hundred-dress trousseau for a favorite Brenda Starr paper doll, dived from the same great height. Paper dolls were important to us. Boots, from *Boots and Her Buddies*, with her eyes closed, fat legs together, one hand up behind her head, was Arden's favorite, so I supplied her with a lot of homemade dresses. A redhead from *Tillie the Toiler* and a more extensive wardrobe got burned up, however, because, we left her and her outfits scattered on the basement table, despite repeated warnings. Arden's mother threw them all into the flames of a little black stove where she burned trash. Boots, at least, survives, filed away with all of our letters.

Arden and I only started to write regularly to each other while we were in college, but as children we wrote extended notes when we had spats in the basement, and one or the other of us would grandly stomp off into the bathroom and lock the door. Then our communications passed through a knothole, just big enough for spying or for slips of paper folded into thin strips. One or two each way was usually sufficient.

Arden was responsible for having sparked my first interest in reading, for I had had little encouragement to read at home. I cannot recall any actual discouragement, but my parents did not themselves read for pleasure, nor did they read to me, nor later to my younger sister. Books simply did not figure into my family life as they did into Arden's. She was read to regularly by her mother, and when I was there for the summer I got in on these sessions as well. Arden had a set of books called *The Book House* from which we were read to endlessly; I had a set of books called *Junior Classics*, which I did read around in but without much enthusiasm. I had a few other books, but Arden had a whole library, or so it seemed to me, and the impressive matching size and uniformly colorful jackets on the Nancy Drew books made me long for a library of my own. Approaching puberty, we got hooked on Nancy Drew mysteries, after which we moved immediately on to best-sellers from the Literary Guild, to which her mother belonged, and devoured a good many historical romances and dangerous modern novels. I still remember reading and rereading the passage in Somerset Maugham's *The Razor's Edge* when Sophie, down on her luck in Paris, was in the sexual thrall of a gigolo and announced to her friends, "God, can he screw!" How we pored over that line and felt hot. Then, in one of Frank Yerby's novels, we discovered that "her raspberry nipples stabbed his mahogany chest," steamy prose in our limited anthologies. It moved us on to a varied bibliography.

Had *The Book House* and all the other books in her private library belonged to anybody else I would have been jealous, but they belonged to Arden, so I didn't mind. How can I explain that? Once, seeing *Wuthering Heights* with Merle Oberon and Laurence Olivier when we were about ten, I registered exactly what Cathy meant when she cried, "I *am* Heathcliff!" Arden and I held each other's hands and said nothing, but I knew that she knew too.

None of which is to suggest that we did not argue. We argued endlessly and fought bitterly. Those were terrible times for me. She would close her lips over her buck teeth and braces as tightly as she could and grow steamingly silent; I would grow equally but coldly silent. And then we would pretend to be fascinated with whatever we were doing singly, but not for long. I think we never distrusted each other or misjudged each other's motives; we respected each other's talents and fed from them in mutual satisfaction. Arden and I were never in competition with each other and at the same time we were always in competition with each other, but it was so mutual that there was never on either side a shred of envy. I dare say other cousins or friends or even siblings have shared similar relationships. I have never heard of one.

Perhaps Arden's premature death has led me to romanticize our early life together; I doubt it. When I think now of us from my first recollections to, say, our early teens, I think of Bruce-and-Arden: my name came first when our parents referred to us because of the rhythm, not for any pecking order. After that, of course, the relationship inevitably changed. We began to date, and our interests surely diverged by the time we graduated from high school, but I believe our devotion never changed, nor our need for each other. I needed Arden more than she needed me, and that was true until her death, even with over ten years to get used to the idea that a part of my life was going to pass that she would not share.

Arden's faith in God remained steadfast and unquestioning until she died; her death only reinforced my hunch that if God is at all aware of me, he is a practical joker and therefore beneath my contempt. Throughout her long acquaintance with cancer, Arden remained convinced of God's mercy and that somehow we would all live happily ever after, just as we'd both known we would when we were children.

On the farm we had a playhouse, an abandoned chicken shed, five or six feet high at its taller end. Built as a lean-to, it then sloped to perhaps four feet at the lower end, high enough for us to stand upright. There were windows, at least there were two openings covered over with slats, and in the middle of the room there was a floor-to-ceiling post. Furnished with cast-offs from our grandparents' cellar and whatever we rounded up on our own around the place, it seemed opulent. We constructed a cardboard wall to divide the shed in half, and I painted a mural on the side that faced what we called the entrance hall; the other half was bedroom, kitchen, bathroom, living room, sometimes more exotic locales—and the two spaces were about the same size. We used the entrance hall only for entering, but it was as spacious as the rest of the house. In retrospect, is that not some strange metaphor for Arden and me?

When we were sixteen, Arden and I peroxided our hair, starting out with forelocks and before the end of the summer going all the way. Hers was movie star blonde; mine was a sort of copper, unevenly streaked with nearly white patches because I'd used straight bleach here and there. As we both had a lot of hair, it was difficult to miss us. Our parents shook their heads in disbelief, and back in high school that fall so did our classmates. Was it our last joint venture? I think so.

After that, we saw each other less frequently, although Arden sometimes trained into Kansas City for a play or a musical comedy on tour when I was ushering at the Music Hall and could sneak her in free, even if the preposterous hats that she insisted on wearing threatened to give us away. But busy high school schedules and going away to college and getting married and having children all got in the way in time.

One Thanksgiving at the farm—in our late teens then, home from college for the first time—Arden and I walked down to the playhouse, by that time long abandoned. It looked much the same as it had during our childhood, but so much smaller than we remembered it. We did not go inside that day but stood instead on the wet November ground and looked at the house where for half a dozen years we had once been married, with many children, or we had been adversaries in battle, or royal lovers abandoned to wolves by the wicked queen, or barricaded in our homestead under attack by Indians. We always lived happily ever after. In the early evening gloom when we made that final visit, we stared on our childhood and held hands. I wept, but not only because I have always been an easy weeper.

For the next thirty years we met when we could: quick family visits, an overnight with me when I was teaching in the midwest, a few weekends together either with Arden's husband and children in Kansas or with my wife and my children in the East, a coincidental holiday in London. Once, when we'd met by pre-arrangement for a picnic at the Washington, D.C., zoo, we realized more or less simultaneously, but without saying anything about it, that our children were all together and having a good time. We squeezed each other's hand.

During the intervening years before those encounters, however, we had exchanged poems, confided our love lives, traded books, and simultaneously encouraged and suffered through each other's arcane—and we thought intellectual—enthusiasms, beginning with mine for Gertrude Stein, whose work almost nobody read then, and Arden's for Henry Miller, on whose suppressed works she'd done independent study in the rare book collection at the University of Kansas. If not the first, we were among the first of our generation to take these writers seriously. Once we wrote a scholarly paper together, via the postal system, about Gertrude Stein's use of Daniel Webster's actual speeches in her opera *The Mother Of Us All.* I was in the navy then and Arden was still in college, and simultaneously we were writing endlessly about the variations in Henry Miller's prose, depending on his subject matter. Later, we were both involved in amateur theater, I directing plays at a small college in New York State and she acting and singing in local productions in Kansas. We traded books back and forth all the time. There was always much to write about, and we never stopped writing. Probably our letters to each other could double as diaries, but I have never had the courage to reread many of them.

In 1969 Arden was diagnosed with breast cancer. "Why you?" her mother lamented, and so did I, and Arden said, "Why not me?" During the ensuing years, that meant surgery, chemotherapy, cobalt treatments, radiation, and then the destructive drugs that had to follow. After her radical mastectomies, when she and her husband were en route to Europe for a holiday, I took a train into New York to see her—and to see the angry, tidy scars. I had not wanted to look; she wanted me to. She got cross when I cried. Three years later, when the cancer had spread, I flew out to Kansas for a long weekend. We played duets, regaled her children with stories of our naughty childhood, talked into the night. She had cheated death with her breast surgery, although little by little her body had continued to fail her, and she did not expect to live long after that visit. It depressed her when she realized that she would never know her grandchildren.

During the next three years, there were several periodic recoveries, periodic relapses, culminating in April 1977 in a degeneration of her neck so that her head had to be held in place by a complicated metal brace that she was advised not to remove. (So she went home and took it off to have a shower.) Her motor control dwindled, and her weekly injections gave her one or two good days in exchange for four or five bad ones. Long before, I'd urged her to smoke marijuana, said I'd get it for her, good safe Colombian, risk sending it through the mail if necessary. I'd been told on good authority that it was remarkably successful in some cases as a pain mask, but something in Arden's character refused the suggestion, perhaps its illegality, perhaps knowing how many healthy heads it had scrambled.

In May the cancer had traveled to her hips, in June there was blockage in her jugular vein. Then she was on a last round of chemotherapy that could induce heart failure or a stroke. "It wouldn't be a bad way to go," she said. During that last spring, Arden prowled the house at night with insomnia, in great pain some of the time and in some pain the rest of it, moving heavy pieces of furniture around, like an incipient mother waiting out her delivery with impatience, while her husband and children slept. She herself snatched sleep when she could, in a recliner chair. For her comfort, the house was kept at about fifty-five degrees, and everyone wore sweaters—even in the dead heat of a Kansas summer—and often Arden would simply nod off, or leave in the middle of a meal to take a nap or a cold bath. But she was determined to live to see her eldest son married that summer, even though she spent her days merely trying to get comfortable for brief periods at a time. "Surely death must be a wonderful release," she wrote during that final bout with chemotherapy. "I'm talking practically—not wistfully!" If it were a choice between dying quickly and decaying slowly, she'd joyfully embrace the former.

Knowing that she could not live long after that, I proposed to my mother that I fly out to collect her in Kansas City and that we then drive out together for the wedding. Why should I wait until I would not see Arden again when I could see her again?

"That's better than Decadron," she laughed when I called to tell her I was coming, high and wide on drugs which in turn must have begun to destroy her vital organs, plus massive doses of Seconal in her attempt to get some sleep. Only the plans for the wedding held her together, physically as well as emotionally.

The wedding itself was lovely, Arden in yellow chiffon floating down the aisle on her younger son's arm. The congregation stood for her. Childhood friends came from Abilene whom I'd not seen in forty years, kids we'd played with long ago. Arden held court at the reception, too weak to walk about, her thinning hair hidden under a chic cloche to remind me of the extravagant hats she'd always fancied.

Even aware of how gravely ill Arden was, I was not entirely prepared to cope with saying goodbye, as I knew we would have to do when I left, a final goodbye. When friends part, they do so on the assumption that they will see each other again, even when age or illness besets one or the other of them: Arden and I knew that in this case our goodbye could only be our last one. My mother and I stayed over an extra day after the excitement had died down and the newlyweds had left on their honeymoon. Arden's husband and I washed one of their cars in the driveway, in a mixture of sunshine and drizzle, and just in the middle of that, a double rainbow arched above us, brilliant against a thick gray sky. I ran to the house to get Arden for it.

"There we are, Bruce! They're there because we're here!" she said, and I had to work hard not to cry, for Arden had always made fun of my easy tears, and although they would at that point have been borne of joy, they would have betrayed my anguish too.

That last night I said I intended to wake up at two AM and join her during her customary late night prowl, which usually began about that time, and I did, without the aid of an alarm clock. Arden was shoving some cabinet or other from one place to another in the big family room at the back of the house that she and her husband had bought years before. They'd suffered there through their second child's early disabilities, patterning him through years of patient exercise so that he could grow up to play baseball, write a sports column for the local newspaper, get married, and hold a job. Then they'd gone through Arden's long recovery after a third child's dangerous birth: it had so nearly killed Arden that her husband and her parents had been summoned into her hospital room to say goodbye because her death was so imminent. Then they'd lived with the long disease that had finally done its worst.

We talked until some of the others in the house began to rouse, about five hours later, and we said goodbye in the early dawn of our last day together. We'd spoken at length about death and her absolute conviction that an afterlife lay ahead for her. Arden believed in no saints and angels flying around, nor in immortality's taking a recognizable form. "Whatever it is," she said, and she laughed, "it won't be more of the same, but don't ask me for any details."

She knew of course of my equal conviction that nothing lay ahead but rot in the earth. We did not speak of that, and I tried hard to question it myself at that point. We talked instead about ourselves, about how extraordinarily lucky we were to have had each other for so long. It had not been long enough for me, and I said so, bitterly. I wanted more: I wanted her to be here when two books of mine—already contracted for in the summer of 1977—were published, for my first book had been dedicated to her, and I valued her opinion beyond any other. That was selfish of me, she said, because I was thinking about myself and not about us, and I knew what she meant. Whatever we had had together, it was going to suffice, she said, and I pretended she was right.

Actually saying goodbye was harder than I had anticipated, for I'd thought Arden and I had faced that demon by ourselves under cover of night's giving way to day a few hours earlier, but the physical moment of separation was as painful to me as the loss of a limb must be, or a body's organ, or a breast. Grief may have a common core but nobody's own sorrow translates into another's approximation. I could not let go of her hand.

The drive back to Kansas City began in agony, and twice I told my mother I wanted to stop and return, if only for a few minutes. By the time we'd reached the turnpike, perhaps forty miles north, what I had already known became clearer as the distance between us stretched out.

I would never see Arden again.

I had stomach cramps, my head pounded, my skin hurt me, I could not stop crying, and I could not see the road. We stopped the car so that my mother could drive, so that I could vomit. Perhaps at Thanksgiving, I thought, or Christmas, I might fly out again. I knew she would not live that long.

When Arden died four months later I did not weep at first, and my true concern was for her husband and their children. I had written every few days since our parting in July, although toward the end Arden could not read without the aid of a strong magnifying glass, and I telephoned her weekly, although she spoke little because the drugs had taken over, and she was not always fully in command of her head.

"Call me when you get home," I said, as she prepared to enter the hospital for what would prove to be the last time, and she replied that she really wished she could call to tell me where the services were and where to send the flowers. Arden laughed about that, but the humor lay in the shadow of our gallows.

Later, when her best friend had gone to the hospital for what proved to be a final visit, Arden seemed to be sleeping deeply. She sat with her for a while and then prepared to leave, but Arden's great blue eyes flew open and she was suddenly animated and smiling.

"Oh! I danced all night last night!"

"Did you, Arden?" her friend said. "I'm so happy for you!"

But Arden had already gone back to sleep.

In the first days I was somewhat mad, I think, unable to speak or control myself. I walked out of my classes or meetings without warning; I was remote with my wife and children; I stumbled badly during lectures. Then my closest colleague on campus saved me, I think. One afternoon in the faculty coffee room, she had said something about Arden, and I broke down completely, more so than I might have done with someone to whom I felt less close. She took my shoulders into a vise-like grip and said, "Look here! Your grief *is* going to abate, but you are *never—ever*—going to get over this, not if you cry until your heart breaks."

That was twenty-five years ago, and she was right.

Some Teachers

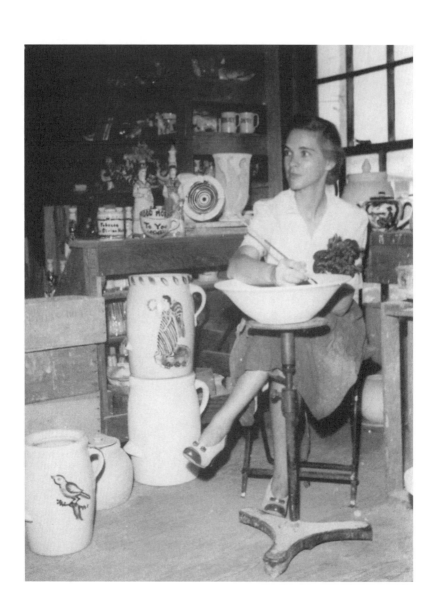

*T*he teacher used to say, "That's good for your age," when I drew pictures in kindergarten, but whatever "that" was marked the end of it until the fifth grade, because Greathouse Elementary School in St. Matthews, Kentucky, didn't offer any art classes in its regular curriculum. Then, when I was ten years old, a blonde whirlwind blew into my life after school, two afternoons a week, to give lessons to a few of us.

Mary Alice Hadley came to Greathouse to supplement her income as a potter by offering art classes two afternoons a week to a small group of students—I think there may have been ten or twelve of us, no more—while she was honing her own designs and working out of the Louisville Pottery Company. It produced no dinnerware itself at that time, but she and the owner had come to some agreement that allowed her to use his facilities. Then, when the business changed hands in 1944, she found herself summarily dismissed, so she opened her own pottery company. Examples of her early work suggest the successful direction she took to become one of the leading pottery designers in America. Even after her tenure at the Louisville Pottery Company, it reproduced some uncomfortably similar patterns but without giving credit where credit was due. As an independent potter, Mary Alice Hadley's distinctive "M A Hadley" on every piece she produced followed soon after my art lessons under her guidance.

We met in the cafeteria after school had let out, to paint with big brushes and colored powders mixed with water, on huge sheets of heavy gray paper—oatmeal paper, we incorrectly called it—while Mary Alice Hadley moved among us. She was bright and pretty, with enormous turquoise eyes and a generous mouth, and her heavy honey-colored hair coiled into ropes at the nape of her neck. She marched when she walked and she laughed when she talked, and I loved her at first sight.

She encouraged us to paint without drawing first, to sketch with color, to fill the page, to let the paint laugh all over it. Later, she got me into the Louisville Art Center for Saturday classes with a group of kids a few years my senior. I was probably pushing my luck at twelve, for teenagers can be cruel to their immediate juniors; but Mary Alice Hadley had already given me a visual way that allowed me to hold my own: decorative primarily, cheerful, stylish, and very probably in conscious imitation of the distinctive look of M A Hadley pottery. Subsequent art teachers certainly left their mark on me too—sometimes scarring, sometimes not—but no one else so strongly affected my work.

Mary Alice Hadley gave up giving private lessons when she went into business for herself. A set of dishes she had decorated with ships and whales for use on the boat that she and her husband, George, took out on the river during the weekends was the beginning of the Hadley Pottery Company, but her celebrated logo—a dashing, rearing blue horse with a flying mane and tail—appeared at about the same time as a second pattern, and during the ensuing years she added her Pear and Grape, her American Bouquet, and her Farmyard, although she should not be held responsible for some of the chintzy patterns the company began to issue long after her death. Today her pottery, each piece signed in glaze, "M A Hadley," is handled in several pricey shops across the country, and what began as a small and special enterprise has become big business.

When I was in the eighth grade, long after the art lessons had stopped, I went to see the old building, not yet completely renovated, from which the Hadleys were running a full-time business. Things were makeshift and less than organized, except for a huge rolltop desk for paperwork. A few of Mary Alice Hadley's paintings hung on the walls, bright and sunny oils and watercolors, and there I first saw that unforgettable, beautiful blue horse, proudly prancing across various surfaces.

Some years after my family had moved to Kansas City, I visited the Louisville factory during a summer holiday and got a full tour of the place by the lady herself. The old brick building on Story Avenue had by that time been completely transformed to house an impressive enterprise. There seemed to be dozens of employees, though perhaps time has swelled their number in my memory. In any case, I watched a girl decorating plates with glazes in Mary Alice Hadley's original designs, saw the huge kilns where they were fired, and the long trestles holding finished work, bowls, cups, plates, platters, tiles, casseroles in various patterns, plus a number of other ceramics, and more of them yet in the seconds showroom where less than perfect but still wonderful pieces sold cheaply.

Mary Alice Hadley had not changed at all and seemed as young and pretty as ever, the big ropes of yellow hair, slightly snarled as usual, still clinging to the nape of her neck like loaves. It was a happy day: she gave me a big Toby mug she had done herself—a second of course, but a beauty—so I would remember her, she said.

Mary Alice Hadley died a few years later, still young, at the height of her creative powers. Someday, perhaps, someone will gather together an exhibition of her paintings, as charming in their own way as her pottery designs.

I would cheerfully loan the Hadley that hangs above my desk. It is not signed, but the style is unmistakable, and it is painted with powdered colors turned magically by water into paint on the sheet of oatmeal paper on which I'd been laboring. It was to be a picture of a number of passersby in front of a dress shop window: husbands and wives, children, a lady with a dog, all drawn tightly in pencil and then painted with feeble colors. Mary Alice Hadley paused to look, cocked her head, shook it back and forth.

"No, Bruce!" she cried. "Loosen up! Have some fun!" And then, dipping brushes successively in several colors, she painted four mannequins, each dressed in chic 1940s attire, in my shop window. I was ready to give up pencils forever. The colors have surely faded with time; the memory has not.

If Mary Alice Hadley was responsible for introducing me to Art, Julia Reubelt was responsible for introducing me to Letters. I think she was not very old, but she looked ancient. Six feet tall and slat thin, a rat's nest of no-color hair in a small knot, purse-lipped, she seemed iceberg cold. She wore a pince-nez on a slender gold chain, attached to a modest brooch on her bosom either fallen or disguised by the pleats that her entire wardrobe seemed to feature. She terrified me even from the distance of the seventh grade, so I longed to be assigned to Mrs. Bimford's homeroom. We all longed to be assigned to Mrs. Bimford's homeroom. There were two sections of every class, and we spent the summer in suspense. She looked like a movie star. Her brunette pageboy had style and her clothes had chic, even if she did wear thick-lensed glasses. Besides, she had really spectacular breasts, and since breasts had begun to bud on the various objects of our affections in class, such matters were important. The boys talked about that a lot and stared hard at Ann Blackshear because she didn't wear a brassiere and seemed to have filled out in advance of the other girls. That phrase just wasn't adequate for Mrs. Bimford's panoramic view, so we called her twin mountains her chabobbas, after a line in a popular song: "Chabobba, chabobba, chabobba, and jah-lah-wah cookulla goomba," and we longed to gaze at the landscape all through the eighth grade, especially at the blackboard when she raised and lowered her arm. Such activity carried considerable significance. We called her "Mrs. Bimford's," with a built-in possessive apostrophe, no matter how many times she corrected us, and even some of the girls knew why.

I was assigned to Miss Reubelt, however, only saw Mrs. Bimford's during math class once a day. I learned to like to read seriously because of Miss Reubelt, and almost everything I know of grammar and rhetoric came from her, largely because she was so ruthless about it. But I came to find grammar an enchantment when oddly angled lines snaked across the blackboard to diagram sentences, and I never outgrew shifting parts of speech from one to the other just to see how far the gears would shift. Also, Miss Reubelt persuaded me to recognize the wisdom of her decisions as they contradicted my own: to read *Treasure Island* instead of *Captain from Castile* or whatever the Literary Guild selection was, month by month.

I never quite outgrew my fear of her. She spoke in a little-girl voice that caught me off-guard, making some especial point, pausing, and then suddenly widening her eyes to stare laser beams through me or whomever else she happened to be addressing. Certainly my age had something to do with my response; I was ready to learn, and Miss Reubelt was the first school teacher from whom I ever really retained anything. Multiplication tables and spelling hints do not apply here, memorizing poems, parsing sentences, measuring the lengths of rivers are beside the point, though doubtless such ground rules made possible my response. Under Miss Reubelt I learned to care about learning, and by the end of the eighth grade it was easy to ignore Mrs. Bimford's inflated mammaries. Besides, once a day for an hour of math was sufficient.

In 1978, I called on Miss Reubelt when I went back to Louisville for an academic conference, and I took her a copy of my first book. She seemed to me the same, but I wasn't frightened any longer, and we had a happy visit. I saw her again two years later, by which time she had aged a great deal and was obliged to use a walker, but her stare was as penetrating as ever, though I knew then that it was borne of passionate interest, and I knew absolutely how proud she was.

For the year before my family moved to Kansas City, I attended a county school in Anchorage that covered kindergarten through twelfth grade, since there was no high school to follow Greathouse Elementary in St. Matthews, then merely a Louisville suburb. Getting there was part of the pleasure, and we had a choice of two ways to make the journey. An ancient train ran between St. Matthews and Anchorage, with green plush seats, panelled mahogany, and brass bric-a-brac, and on arrival, the conductor pulled the gas lamps down from the ceiling to extinguish them. Alternatively, there was a bus crowded beyond capacity with kids singing dirty songs and smoking. That year is surrounded in a rosy glow, in part from the transportation, in part because of another English teacher, another art teacher.

Gladys Rowe was as sour as grapes out of season and frequently given to sharing them when she was crossed in class, a marcelled, gray-haired grass widow with high spots of rouge on her cheeks to off-set a permanently down-turned mouth. We spent the larger part of most classes learning grammar and spelling, but now and then we got on to literature. Mrs. Rowe liked *The Rime of the Ancient Mariner* a lot. Her strangled voice was caught between a southern muffle and a hill twang, and she liked to read aloud, pointing a finger, rolling her eyes, striding about the room, on her short sturdy legs, then suddenly stopping cold:

> He hoooooooooldzem, wutha glitteren' ahhhhhh!
> Thuh weddin' guest—stood still!
> An' lessens—lakka thre-uhrs chaaaaaald!
> Thuh Marner!—hathees willllllllll!

She stood on her chair to be the albatross, and later, when the boat in Coleridge's poem lies on a becalmed sea, thanks to Mrs. Rowe's passionate reading, we longed for the bell so we could get to the water fountain, not because we were eager to leave her class:

> Wowter! Wowter! Everwhurs!
> An alllll thuh boards—did shrrrrrrrrink!
> Wowter! Wowter! Everwhurs!
> Ner inny dropptuh—
> drrrrrrrrrrrrriiiiiiiiiiiiiiinnnnnnnnnnnkkkkkkkkkkk!

Each of us was required to memorize fifty lines, and some of us, inspired, went on to learn more, reciting for each other, our pronunciation correcting each other's pronunciation to match Mrs. Rowe's own and our dramatic gesturing encouraged to emulate her performance. She stood in the back of the room behind us, with her arms folded and nodding her head in approval as, one by one, we recited for each other. Did we read anything else? I recall no other assignments, no other selections, although the size of the textbook was formidable. Mrs. Rowe and Miss Reubelt came from different planets, but they could have given lessons to Strunk & White, the University of Chicago Style Sheet, and the Modern Language Association in the mechanics of writing.

Millie Kalb taught art, ballet and tap, and perhaps some music at Anchorage. She looked just like Tillie the Toiler, sat on the desk, short skirts above her pretty knees, kept time with her Joan Crawford shoes doing little kicks in the air, and talked with the same Eastern Kentucky twang that had afflicted my now nameless fifth grade teacher who said perry-meter and divva-shun. They had been classmates in college, and when Miss Kalb discovered that connection between us, I became a favored member of her Art I class. Art II, Art III, and Art IV all did the same things at different hours of the day, depending on what took her fancy, and each fairly small class had a mixture of students from all four years.

Miss Kalb's fancy included, during my single year under her guidance, papier-mâché, oils, watercolors, sketching, and tempera (meaning poster paint), always in rotation. We got a lot of experience in doing what a later generation would call its "own thing," but Miss Kalb's leaned toward the casual, although we didn't know that then, and I think she was neither very bright nor very talented. She dismissed a number of other painters as outdated—her own work had a certain vulgar charm, like romantic magazine illustrations—and she showed us pictures in books to prove it. Rembrandt was "a good drawer" but he only liked to paint old men. Renoir's women were "fat," and she did not approve of nudity. She really hated the Post-Impressionists and Cubists, although at the time I knew only that from her point of view "modrun art" stunk. But she liked a lot of fashion illustrators, and she really liked Jon Whitcomb. For a time we all practiced drawing his dewy-eyed blondes and pretty servicemen who advertised various products in magazines.

When Miss Kalb disapproved on aesthetic principles of some creation or other in class, she pronounced it "downright tacky." I think "tacky" became the most crushing criticism of the year. Miss Kalb was about twenty-one years old and had not yet finished college. She was working on her degrees in both art and music during the summers, she said, sitting on the edge of her desk with her knees crossed, swinging her strappy high heels, and urging us on to greater feats for the art exhibition she planned in the spring. It never came to be because she got sidetracked.

When we moved on to tempera paint a little later in the semester, Merle Hellebusch and I did simultaneous paintings which so inspired Miss Kalb's always active imagination that she forgot all about the exhibition. Merle was a sophomore, my first friend at Anchorage, and my only competition in art class. We bonded, I think, because we saw right through Miss Kalb. Merle had a thick Georgia accent and a languid manner she'd interrupt with a clucking laugh that I can still hear. Our paintings had nothing to do with each other until Miss Kalb got hold of them. Mine had a gigantic female head, with heavily painted eyelids and a big red mouth, a cigarette in a holder and smoke that turned into dancing wraiths, Medusa-like blue hair that flamed upward, turning into skyscrapers, and champagne glasses bubbling about her in the air. Merle's painting, partly filched from a color photograph in *Esquire*, was of a man with a wolf's head, dressed up like a Damon Runyon stud, dancing with a sexy woman in a chartreuse turban, a lemon-yellow blouse cut low, a pink skirt slit right up to her crotch, mesh hose, and lots of jewelry.

I think our pictures were supposed to be impressions of George Gershwin's *Rhapsody in Blue*. Miss Kalb frequently put records on the phonograph and urged us to paint away the hour. She was ecstatic over our efforts and decided that Merle and I should paint a scenic drop—about twenty feet high and fifty feet long—for her spring dance recital. She was determined to have no ordinary evening of grade school girls dressed up like swans and the oldest students routined into some usual jazz-tap number. Miss Kalb would mount a production—of *Rhapsody in Blue*.

Merle and I must have worked the better part of the spring semester on that backdrop, and I regret that no photograph was made to commemorate its completion—or do I? Memory is almost always kinder than truth. At one point Miss Kalb encouraged me to dance the role of the wolf. Wisely I demurred, choosing to watch the performance from the auditorium. There must have been a whole series of kiddie numbers first, since Miss Kalb was obliged to teach classes for the lower grades too, but only after the intermission have I any recollection of the evening. Had I seen rehearsals? I must have. Probably I thought it was very grand, or at least part of me must have thought so.

The long-playing record had not yet been manufactured in 1945, so the three scenes of our *Rhapsody in Blue* corresponded to the length of three 12-inch 78 rpm sides, each about five minutes long. When the curtains parted, that backdrop looked very murky, big and impressive, but murky: To the right, my huge blue-haired lady floated in space and filled it, the skyscrapers streaming out from her head in many directions; a sidewalk corner ran past her chin and, angling upward, continued all the way to the other side of vast expanse of canvas where, under a painted lamppost, Merle's giant dancers embraced.

During Side One, a tall blonde girl named Joyce, a star pupil and a senior, posed *en pointe*, surrounded by lesser satellites, all of them dressed up for *Les Sylphides*, and then performed a kind of standard Ballet Russe de Monte Carlo opener, pure and pretty. When the record ended, the curtains swished shut and we sat in the dark until Joyce had changed out of her tutu and into her wolf outfit.

Then somebody turned the record over, the curtains opened, and there was Miss Kalb all dolled up like Merle's shady lady. She looked, well—downright tacky. I guess that was the general intention. I had never seen a burlesque show, except in a movie called *Lady of Burlesque*, but Miss Kalb did everything except strip and rather more than Barbara Stanwyck had managed. Black curls bouncing and hips rolling, she strutted back and forth and tossed off a bump that shook the balcony. Then Joyce slinked on wearing the clothes Merle had painted for the guy's outfit: a purple zoot suit with a reet pleat, a black shirt, and a pink tie. To crown this ensemble, she wore the papier-mâché wolf's head we had all worked on in art class. Joyce and Miss Kalb did a cross between an apache dance and a *pas de deux*, striking an imitative pose now and again in front of Merle's couple. At the conclusion—only as far off as the end of Side Two—Miss Kalb was up on her toes, one leg stretched out behind her. Joyce had hold of her free foot and walked her around in a circle and then let go. Miss Kalb threw her arms into the air with such abandon that she should have fallen down, but the curtains rushed closed a second time and we never knew.

There was applause, though hardly enough to bridge the gap until Joyce got back into her white costume for Side Three. While the corps de ballet—those half a dozen girls from Side One—ran around toward the rear of the stage, waving their arms over their heads, Miss Kalb and Joyce engaged in a kind of contest: Sacred and Profane Love vying for power at opposite ends of a bedsheet, dyed blue, that had been cut up into fourths and sewn into a very long strip. At one point, Miss Kalb threw herself on the floor, stage right, one mesh-hosed leg posed like a pin-up girl's, and extended an arm toward Joyce with a flourish and a big smile. Joyce did some arabesques. Then, posing in fifth position with one arm out, she deferred to Miss Kalb, who spun around before she did the splits. At the finale they were both on their knees, more or less praying to my skyscrapers, while the corps de ballet did some fast turns and then ran around them in a circle. Side Three ended with the whole cast *en pointe*, or pretending to be. Everybody applauded. Merle and I took a bow. Miss Kalb, so we later heard, got reprimanded by the principal for flashing so much thigh.

My brief tenure at Anchorage came to a close when my family moved to Kansas City at the end of my freshman year. Southwest High School was vast and intimidating, and most of the teachers are now as blank as their blackboards were at eight AM, but art classes gave me some respite from the loneliness outsiders inevitably suffer.

Flora Wright, crippled either by arthritis or a stroke, could not draw or paint herself, but her art classes gave me the best discipline I have ever had, including what I got in the navy. The sophomore year was given over entirely to pencil, charcoal, and pen and ink. (I had missed out on the Miss Wright's freshman year in basic design, painting glamour girls and fashion models, bunnies, and backdrops for Miss Kalb instead.) The junior year pushed ahead to watercolor and tempera. The senior year devoted itself to ceramics and oils. Somewhere along the way we did etchings as well.

Miss Wright was as close to a fascist as anybody I have ever encountered. Overenthusiastic ideas were destroyed with an uncompromising "no"; anything remotely sexy met with an impassive stare that could curdle the paint on the paper; in our Art Honor Society meetings—a national organization she had founded years before—she let us know fairly clearly who was to be president, who was to be vice-president, who secretary, right on down to the master-at-arms, usually a well-meaning boy in whom she recognized no talent. As a rule, Miss Wright did not like boys, so she begrudged a gifted one named Bruce Hartwigsen membership into her National Art Honor Society, although Bruce later ended up as a distinguished member of the art faculty at Yale. Also, Miss Wright was anti-Semitic. Rita Copaken was the most talented student in class, also the most imaginative, but we were never able to elect her as president, although Mary Lou Ulery and I—Miss Wright's pets—tried hard. Under her married name, she later became a successful sculptor in the Midwest, and author of *Rita Blitt: The Passionate Gesture*, a remarkable book about her evolution as an artist. Everybody in the organization had an office, however, even if new ones had to be invented. In the spring, when we did our annual show, the judges—teachers and administrators from other schools in the city—knew whom to vote for, thanks to Miss Wright's expert steering. There was a Best in the Show award and a Best Figure-Drawing award and a Most Improvement award: three years in a row we knew who would win before the judges even got a look around. Miss Wright wrote me a letter of recommendation for some art scholarships that conceivably contributed to my failure as an artist as much as my modest talents did. What reputable art schools would have been encouraged to invest—in "a healthy chap from a good Christian home" who "plays only classical music"?

One year in college as an art major was enough to set me straight, but I've never regretted my false start. Learning from Miss Kalb what *not* to do may have been as valuable as learning from Miss Wright what *to* do, and Mary Alice Hadley's touch is pervasive in the mix as well, helping to determine the direction in which my tastes and my talents might travel. My pleasure in the sentimental and the tacky notwithstanding, there is certainly as much of Miss Wright's teutonic formalism and Miss Reubelt's insistence on exactitude in the whole cloth of me as there is of Miss Kalb's cheerful vulgarity and Mrs. Rowe's hammy declamation, even if it turns up only in the fringe. My professional paths—and to a considerable degree my avocations too—began with these "noble dames."

$\mathcal{A}$MANDA M. ELLIS

*T*he first time I saw Amanda M. Ellis, she was speeding along in second gear—she always drove in second gear—behind the wheel of her 1937 yellow Oldsmobile coupe, a long dark blue crepe scarf flying from the brim of her Garbo hat out the side window into an October breeze. I'd heard about her: a stout spinster with electric blue curls, perilously high heels, and ridiculous hats. That was in the fall of my freshman year at Colorado College in 1948; in the summer of 1968 I saw her for the last time. She was then recuperating from one of the frequent bouts of illness that beset her during the last twenty-five years of an active life; but she was as full of plans and enthusiasm for her work as she had always been. When the news of her death reached me, one of my personal eras had come to an end, for Amanda Ellis did as much for me, maybe more, to establish a point of view toward my career than anyone else during the intermittent periods of my academic training.

Amanda Mae Ellis—she loathed her middle name and never used it, although she never abandoned the initial—graduated from Colorado College in 1920, Phi Beta Kappa, Delta Gamma, Queen of the May, a pretty girl with great dark eyes, slender as an aspen, demure as wild violets: an old-fashioned coed with rad-

ical views about education. She went on to the universities of
Iowa and Illinois as both student and instructor and then returned to her alma mater in 1927 as an assistant professor. She
retired—thirty-nine years later—as full professor and writer in
residence. The latter title had been created in desperation by an
administration sorely in need of a compassionate solution to the
embarrassment she had become.

By that time, Amanda Ellis had written a dozen books, published many articles, raised money to renovate the old music auditorium on campus (before it began to crumble under the stress
of the students' practice sessions on the second floor), started a
children's theater, founded the county library, served as vice-
president of the College English Association, and was paid hom-
age by the Millinery Institute of America, for which she unwittingly served as a walking advertisement and advocate under the
weight of her extensive collection of extravagant hats. More importantly, she had stimulated and delighted and challenged and
infuriated a remarkable number of students during her years in
the classroom, including me.

She came into my life and I into hers—a year after I'd first seen
her on the campus, always under one of those hats—when as a
sophomore I enrolled in her popular Twentieth Century Literature course in drama. Subsequently, I took the second half of the
course, devoted to novels, and then before I graduated managed
to sign up for her courses in Chaucer and in Middle English. I
wish I had been able to take her course called Prose Fiction, but
schedule conflicts prevented that.

In Twentieth Century Literature, Bertolt Brecht was as unknown to Amanda Ellis as he was to the House UnAmerican Ac-
tivities Committee in the late Forties; so were Jean Anouilh and

Jean Giraudoux and even Luigi Pirandello. Does anybody read Maxwell Anderson and John Galsworthy today? Elmer Rice? The Sidneys, Howard and Kingsley? Probably not, but we did, and we were introduced, too, to Thornton Wilder's *The Skin of Our Teeth*, pretty advanced fifty years ago, and Tennessee Williams's *A Streetcar Named Desire*, pretty racy. So was Eugene O'Neill, and I believe we must have read a dozen of his plays and at least that many by George Bernard Shaw. For the first time, I began to think seriously about what I was reading and perhaps to think in the language of writing. I'm told that something akin to that happens in learning a foreign language; a point comes when suddenly you begin to think in another language. I began to think in my own language and to realize that just maybe there was more to comedy than quick laughter, more to tragedy than easy tears.

But Amanda's classes were never strictly academic. (I never called her Amanda until she asked me to, several years later, but we always referred to her as Amanda when we spoke of her, and it is now difficult not to think of her as Amanda.) She liked to sprinkle her lectures with anecdotes, and her students always looked forward to the first meeting after the Christmas holidays, because she would have just returned from New York with fresh news of a round of plays she'd seen. I still remember her moving account of a daring and upsetting new play called *Death of a Salesman* that occupied an entire period, and another given over to the Maxwell Anderson-Kurt Weill musical play *Lost in the Stars*, based on Alan Paton's South African novel about apartheid, *Cry, The Beloved Country*. My roommate, Richard Rutledge, and I dragged in his big phonograph so we could play the recordings from *Lost in the Stars*. He had had the course the previous

year and had persuaded me to enroll, and then we both returned
for the fun of it the next year. How many other teachers could
make a similar claim for popularity? Maybe we attended for the
anecdotes; maybe it is inevitable that they remain more vivid
than the plays we read.

I believe—after many years of teaching—that students probably remember little of what we tell them of dates and places,
facts and figures, even of interpretation and analysis; but they
may retain a kind of excitement through the personalities of the
people who taught them. That was true for me with a young poet
named Alvin Foote who taught me freshman English, usually
hungover, during his single year at Colorado College; with William Blakely, a nervous and erratic psychologist; with George
McCue, a dyspeptic fellow who taught Old English and history
of the language; with Amanda M. Ellis.

In Amanda's medieval literature courses there were no theatrical tales to punctuate the ones under consideration from Can-
terbury, but we went to class faithfully anyhow because we liked
it, despite the difficulties in translating. I have always attributed
the plus on my B to a tactful summary of "The Miller's Tale," delivered extemporaneously in class, because the girl to whom the
selection had been assigned simply burst into tears of embarrassment when Amanda called on her. I believe the expression I
used to describe the especial circumstances on which the joke
in Chaucer's story turns was "passed wind." Suzie Beer—always
one of Amanda's strongest supporters—congratulated me after
class but claimed I could have carried that off with a little more
style had I said "dropped a rose."

Amanda took none too secret credit for herself when Suzie and
I had begun to date the previous semester, after coinciding in her

Middle English class. We were, after all, two of her pets. We had coincided in Louis Knapp's somnolent Shakespeare course as well, but I believe he took no notice.

Amanda's courses in Middle English and Chaucer did not draw the large enrollment of her Twentieth Century Literature class that always sprawled out in a huge classroom. We met instead—about ten of us—around a table in Amanda's office in Hayes House, the charming late Victorian clapboard manse that sheltered the English department and its various battle stations, secret encampments, and spies. I believe I began to develop a sense of time because of Amanda, during that Middle English course—an awareness that the world did not start to spin the day I was born—largely because so much of the literature foreshadowed what later periods usurped as their own, although I hardly realized that for a long time.

Amanda's third regular offering, Prose Fiction, seemed to alter its content from year to year, even as late as the last time she taught it. In 1966 she added John Cheever's *The Wapshot Chronicle* to her regular standbys. "I've never taught the latter before," she wrote me that May, for we had corresponded intermittently since my graduation over a decade before, "but I liked it a lot and the students seemed to. How much new material there is on Hemingway, Dostoyevsky, D. H. Lawrence, and Proust! I just spent $140 for new books. . . ." (That was of course $140 over thirty years ago. Multiply by ten.)

Off-campus, Amanda was much the same as she was on-campus. She demanded a certain amount of attention from those who cared to offer it: running errands for her, for instance, in the Yellow Flash, as we called her little Olds—she was herself a terrible driver—later replaced by the Green Hornet, a 1951 Chrysler purchased when her novel about Elizabeth I, called *Elizabeth, the Woman*, was published by Dutton in 1951. Sometimes she needed a gentlemanly arm in treacherous weather, and even in the best of weather in later years. Sometimes she commandeered us for chores around her office when books or bookshelves needed shifting. But the rewards for the attention could be agreeable. Lunch or dinner in the tavern at the Broadmoor Hotel was a semi-regular Sunday occurrence for Jerald Ketchum, Richard Rutledge, Hugh Wass, and me. We used to encounter her there, at her regular table, and sometimes joined her, always Dutch (though she never complained when our visiting parents picked up the check). Amanda used to make a ritual of telling us what we ought to have, or telling the waiter what she thought we ought to have, and then ordering herself a hamburger with a poached egg on top. Invariably, she introduced us to the waiter, herself included.

"Would you like to know who we are? I am Miss Ellis, and this is Mr. . . ." The pudgy hand would extend into space while she searched her head to tell us apart. Even in later years, when she knew us very well indeed, she continued to call Jerald and me by each other's names now and then.

Amanda actually lived at the Broadmoor in those days, in a pink and aquamarine suite, surrounded by hundreds of books. I think it must have been in the fall of my junior year that she telephoned one Sunday afternoon to invite some of us out for a new drink she had just invented. That we were all underage seemed not to have occurred to her or to us. She welcomed us in at the door of her apartment, wearing a hat, and didn't remove it for the entire time we were there; it stayed on, I believe, through the potation as well as dinner to which we escorted her afterward. She ushered us in and then poured out a dark red concoction that tasted like cough medicine.

"What's in this, Miss Ellis?" one of us asked politely but with some concern that we all shared, if only through sly glances at each other.

The recipe followed: "Two parts orange juice, one part port wine, one part Southern Comfort, one part rum"—there was a pause—"and some gin."

"How much gin, Miss Ellis?"

She cocked her head and clucked aloud and winked at us. "Just enough to hold it together," she confided and offered a second round.

On other occasions we were rewarded variously. Amanda dragged some students backstage with her in Denver to meet Katharine Hepburn who was then touring in *As You Like It*. Amanda had written in advance to prepare the way, advising the actress of a dramatization of her novel, *Elizabeth, the Woman*, which had miraculously managed to make the *New York Times Book Review's* best-seller list for one week. The Bryn Mawr twang that came from the dressing room queried, "Ellis? And who *is* Miss Ellis?" There was a muffled reply that Amanda decided was an invitation, because she tottered in to talk about *Elizabeth, the Woman* as a perfect vehicle. Katharine Hepburn came out with her, shook hands all around, thanked everybody for coming, and then disappeared. Her eyes never left Amanda's hat.

In front of the Chief Theatre in Colorado Springs, with two or three of us in tow, Amanda accosted Albert Dekker, who had just completed an exhausting performance as Willy Loman in the national touring company's production of *Death of a Salesman*. "Would you like to know who we are?" she said, rather than asked. Dekker looked alarmed. Amanda adored celebrities and, as she at least looked like one herself, nobody seemed to mind. We didn't.

I remember her officiating in pink lace—and for once without a hat—at the punch table, raising money for the Fine Arts Center adjacent to the college. I remember her baptizing her ample bodice with champagne at a post-performance party for the entire company of the visiting Ballet Theatre. I remember Amanda's stories about her seven summers as social hostess on the Holland-American line, although she resembled less a games mistress than anyone I have ever known; about her chagrin at dining in Paris on *tête de veau* when the waiter sliced right from the snout in front of her; about a failed romance during the Twenties—we never learned his identity—when, young and very much in love, they ran across the Champs Élysées at dawn, sprinkled by late-autumn snowflakes. Also, I remember somebody else's story—by that time several years old—about her sudden transformation from school marm to plus-size fashion plate during the early Forties.

Photographs reveal Amanda to have been good-looking and willowy in her twenties. In her late thirties, iron gray hair in a bun, thick-soled sensible shoes, and tailored suits had transformed her into an *Alte Mädchen in Uniform*, a conventional old maid. Then Amanda underwent gynecological surgery, and by the time I first saw her she looked very different from those earlier photographs. Many years later, she confided in me, although I do not know why, that she had had a complete hysterectomy before she was forty. Amanda was about five feet three inches tall; she weighed two hundred pounds, perhaps a little more, a little less, from time to time. As if to compensate for her losses, she swathed her girth in diaphanous dresses and loosely tailored suits, tinted her hair blue, and adopted full makeup, the latter doubtless in an attempt to disguise a faint five o'clock shadow. I believe she was reasonably happy most of the time, and always happy with the figure she cut around town.

Amanda was vain about her appearance, and she never appeared in anything less than high fashion—at least for Colorado Springs—so it is not surprising that she was more hurt than insulted when a local department store invited her to model clothes for stout ladies in its annual style show. Her hats, of course, most clearly identified her: Sonni, John Frederick, Lily Daché, or Mr. John. Under their great variety, her tinted coiffure darkened slowly from a Forties blue when I was a freshman, to a Fifties brown, to a Sixties midnight black. If the hats began for me with wide felt brims and gossamer veils, I remember best a white straw the size of a turkey platter, on the underside of which grew an incredible garden of artificial flowers in virtually every color of the palette. She had seen it in a cosmetics ad in a magazine and had promptly ordered it from Lily Daché—for $300. That was just about the cost of a semester's tuition at Colorado College when I was a freshman. Once, during a New York holiday, in a black Napoleonic felt cascading with plumes, Amanda was escorted to dinner by some former students. The restaurant was jammed and the waiting line long, but the head waiter took one look at the lady and ushered her right in to a table that miraculously appeared. She always looked as if she ought to be somebody.

Amanda lived a gay and frivolous and elegant life off-campus, but she loved academic life equally well and, despite the parade of beautiful hats that accompanied her from one world to the other, she approached the latter with a scrupulous scholarship. It was mitigated, of course, by the kind of good nature and sense of humor that chalk-dusted academics will never understand and always resent. In an English department rife with internecine warfare, Louis Knapp, the chairman, was scared of her, I think, but impressed by her publications; George McCue and Frank Krutzke made life especially miserable for her, sometimes sacrificing students in their attempts to undermine her. Were they jealous? Young instructors were encouraged to steer clear of her for fear that association might taint their tenure tracks. Plenty of English majors found her impossible to deal with; others were unswervingly loyal, even after she had begun to fail. The hockey players liked her because she was always good for a C in Freshman Composition to keep them eligible to play, even if that entailed a good deal of one-on-one tutoring for her.

Time would prove everybody's worst fears correct—whatever they were—but the acrimony of her colleagues had to have hastened Amanda's intellectual and emotional and physical atrophy. She was ill all too often: shingles, an ulcer, intestinal troubles. On these occasions, rather than cancel class, she would call one of her minions into the hospital—Suzie Beer more than once—to pick up a lecture that Amanda would have written out in her sprawling holograph to be read aloud.

Before I graduated, her decline had begun to show itself more than a little. This covered a period of seven years, since I had dropped out of college for a four-year stint in the navy during the Korean War. By the time I returned to complete my degree Amanda had lost none of her charm but much of her acumen. Classes sometimes began late because it took her so much longer to get from her car to her second-floor office, although once ensconced at the head of the table she was in full command again, and her lectures could be informative and amusing, even riveting on occasion—when she wasn't sidetracked by inanities, gossip, paranoia.

A whole class period could sometimes lapse into irrelevancies, not often but often enough to register that all was not well. In my final semester she seemed to be easily distracted. I remember her taking up nearly a whole Chaucer class to eat some luscious grapefruit that Suzie had brought back from Phoenix after the Christmas holidays. We'd arranged everything in advance to hold class in the Commons, flatware and napkins out, and we were to meet there. Suzie had even cut the grapefruits in half for us, and then we waited. Miss Ellis had forgotten. Somebody went to her office to help her hobble over, by which time the fifty minute period was pretty well shot, and then she proceeded to give us a lesson in how to segment grapefruit. Suzie at least could remember a happier occasion in the Prose Fiction course just a year before when Amanda had convened class for breakfast at a Colorado Springs restaurant called the Copper Kettle so they could all discuss the food passages in Thomas Mann's *Buddenbrooks* while filling up on a heavy *Deutsche Frühstück*.

Some of us tried to pretend that all was well, covering as best we could for vagaries in the classroom, forgotten assignments, repetitions. Yet on a day following some embarrassing occasion Amanda would be in absolute control, and brilliant, with her wit as intact as her remarkable ability to recreate Chaucer's world. Nevertheless, when the year ended, I was relieved. During those that ensued, her continued physical failings only complicated an early encroaching senility.

Toward the end of her tenure at Colorado College—a decade

hence—her tastes grew more eclectic, her appearance more garish, her reliance on helping hands more pronounced, her bouts with illness more serious. Also, her enrollments dropped sharply, although she still maintained a roster of satellites and acolytes and continued to enchant plenty of students even if others dismissed her as merely eccentric. She spent a lot of time in the classroom recounting the plots of musicals she'd seen instead of serious plays. She grew indulgent in assessing freshman themes, more impressed with her students' originality than with their scholarly research, especially if they were hockey players—or so I was told. Still, she continued her independent research, but when a new book appeared, the interviewer for the college bulletin poked gentle fun at a volume of Turgenev reposing next to Betty Friedan's *The Feminine Mystique* on Amanda's bookshelves, as if academics dipping into pop psychology were somehow unworthy. It was time to quit long before she was obliged to, but perhaps her colleagues had edged the clock forward.

Even before her academic career concluded, Amanda had to forego participating in graduation processions, which irritated her emotionally as much as the marches had irritated her physically. In earlier years, she seemed to sail but actually waddled down the aisle of the chapel, in pain at the pace required of her, mortarboard cocked back behind a dizzy abundance of curls, black gown flying out on either side of her sturdy trunk, and her master's hood slightly off one shoulder, rather like a stole, usually a clump of artificial flowers inserted in her waistband. I think my graduation ceremony, in the spring of 1955, may well have been her last appearance in an academic procession.

Elsewhere she moved at a slower pace, tottering along precariously on high-heeled pumps or other footgear complicated with straps and platform soles. In later years she took to a cane, but to my knowledge she never abandoned her stiletto shoes until the end. Richard Rutledge once observed, perhaps with more truth than he intended, that like the ballet dancer in *The Red Shoes*, when the slippers came off, she would die.

"Heels, you know, are much better for my weak ankle," she explained in perfect seriousness when I berated her for wearing them. I think she believed it. She had fallen more than once, most seriously down a flight of stairs at the Broadmoor many years before, and one of her ankles had healed improperly.

In 1957, Suzie Beer and I drove down from Denver—where, during our on-and-off-again romance, we were having a post-graduation reunion over the Thanksgiving holiday with friends —to take Amanda out to lunch. Having fallen in and out of love with each other more than once when we were seniors two years before, we'd remained fast friends, so it seemed like a good idea. Suzie wore a huge hat in honor of the occasion, a great white wool coal scuttle, very chic, very noticeable. Amanda's was bigger— or perhaps it only looked bigger because of its multiple feathers. "That's a cute little hat too," she observed of Suzie's chapeau, without the slightest malice.

I did not see Amanda for five years after that. When we met again she had failed fearfully. At the annual college picnic she had contracted a severe case of poison ivy that somehow got into her bloodstream. Other complications made for a long recuperation on baby food and several kinds of pills. "What a way to spend a summer!" she wrote, ". . . all told I'm a walking drug-store." At the same time, she underwent some further difficulties in the English faculty over course content in a second section of her beloved Twentieth Century Literature being offered by another member of the department. He'd included some plays she'd never even heard of, and she was in considerable distress.

At the age of twenty-five, Amanda had faced down the entire College English Association convention in a passionate speech that radically altered some old ideas about freshman composition in America—a plea for rhetoric in context rather than grammar rules in isolation—but at the age of sixty she could not easily accept any change in much of anything. "Ellis morale *Low* but not conquered," she wrote to me during an evening meal at the Broadmoor, where she was "all dressed up in an aqua velvet suit, a hat you'd love (a large aqua with an enormous plume of ostrich). The costume raised my spirits. As Mehitabel said to Archie: There's plenty of fight in the old girl yet—but, I'm always a lady—what the hell, Archie," she concluded, quoting one of her favorite books, Don Marquis's *archie and mehitabel*, in which a cockroach types the adventures of an amorous cat.

At the same time that these various ailments and affronts were afflicting her, she was at work on a new book. "I wish to write a biography of Dorothy Wordsworth," she had written long before, at the close of 1956. "I've never gotten over the idea I have to write about her. . . . I wish it to be like Elizabeth, a book that's alive." In truth, her successful 1951 novel, *Elizabeth, the Woman* wasn't very good. It had followed a number of earlier publications with more distinguished pedigrees: an *Atlantic Monthly* prizewinning critical survey of the history of English literature, for example, and multiple editions of her *Representative Short Stories*. But before the Wordsworth book reached completion, she devoted herself to some longtime interests in a series of enormously successful paperbacks about Colorado history, legends, and folklore. Later, she revised and rewrote them as part of a big book entitled *The Strange, Uncertain Years*. There was even a television script under Amanda M. Ellis's signature on *The Twilight Zone*, but her activity did not deter her physical deterioration. Despite brief periods when she rallied, her letters were as often filled with news of her health as with news of progress on the Wordsworth book. Amanda wrote in a sprawling, often illegible longhand, later transcribed into type for her. By November 1963 she had completed five chapters, but "It's been hard going, that book." Nearly a decade before, I'd known that everything else had become hard going as well.

A few years later, the administration had tried to ease her out with a trumped up appointment as "writer in residence," which cut down on her classroom schedule. She was finally forced to retire in 1966, and none too soon. Still, after thirty-nine years, the tug was considerable. "I'm retiring," she advised me in May of that year. "The mandatory age for retirement here having been 68 on April 30. I'm told I look younger than I did years ago," she added to bolster her spirits.

It was the first time she had ever admitted to her date of birth. Once, during my sophomore year when I happened to see her driver's license, she was quick to tell me that the dates were all wrong. Then I remembered the 1957 reunion lunch with Suzie Beer, when Amanda suddenly asked how old we thought she was, and Suzie looked at me as if to say, "It's *your* turn." I offered in desperation an early fifties suggestion. "Late forties," Amanda countered with a wink and a confidential smile. She was then fifty-nine.

"When the students were told I was retiring," she wrote, "to my amazement, tears came into the eyes even of the boys. I'm told that's a tribute but it was more than I could take. . . . Then said one boy, 'You mean you can't ever teach here again?' I said, 'Oh, I'll have an office on the campus and I don't intend to do nothing. I'm not that old!' and laughed. But no laughs or smiles came. Then I turned to our class work."

The year before her retirement, Jerald Ketchum and Richard Rutledge indulged her worst fantasies during a three-hour lunch date in New York. Other department members were out to get rid of her, she said, and she urged them to petition the college to intervene for her. The day before, my wife and I had taken her to breakfast and got an apparent preview of what Jerald and Richard were in for. Margaret, who had never met her, was understandably alarmed as soon as Amanda emerged from the elevator, despite my advance warnings. But I was not prepared either when she appeared, supported by a bellhop on one side and her cane on the other, bent over so far that her face was obscured, and not only by the plethora of feathers on her hat. She could no longer stand entirely upright, although her fat little feet were still stuffed into high-heeled shoes. Her former bulk, so much like an old-fashioned refrigerator with a bubble coil on the top, had become pear-shaped, her makeup a travesty: heavy pancake, smeared lipstick, jet-black eyebrows she had borrowed from Groucho Marx, and hair to match. Once seated, however, she seemed to be much the same, and for a while she chatted amiably with us. Only later did she descend to the grim reports of her treatment by the English department. Often enough before, I had urged her to take early retirement and get out of the unpleasant situation that was guaranteed to get no better. But the college had made her "writer in residence," she crowed, requiring only a half-time teaching schedule. I knew that she could never admit to the truth about that assignment, nor had I the heart to say anything about it. Not surprisingly, she waited until she was forced to quit.

Before she had to face that reality, however, her new book was published: *Rebels and Conservatives: Dorothy and William Words-worth and Their Circle*, the reviews of which, she wrote, were "fabulous so far." They weren't bad, and neither was the book for a friendly ramble about the lives of the subjects, but curiously it appeared without a single footnote or source, just a long bibliography and therefore largely useless to scholars. Unless they took Amanda's word for it. She'd have liked that.

She was back in the hospital not long afterward for some serious surgery, but she cheated death a little longer. We all wondered if she'd ever got around to drawing up her will, for she often made avowals regarding her possessions and felt strongly about how they were to be distributed. She used to refer to this table, that lamp, her silver, her china, and who would receive this and who would receive that. Jerald Ketchum was to have first choice of her library, I second choice, and she wanted its residue to go with her papers to the Colorado College Library for an Amanda M. Ellis Collection, where she planned to leave the bulk of her estate. Once she half-seriously suggested that her hats were important enough to warrant a museum.

Amanda died intestate. Death, like age, frightened her. So long as she did not acknowledge either of them, they could not happen. "There's life in the old girl yet," she said plenty of times, echoing one of Mehitabel's favorite lines to Archie. And, just as often, "How do I look?"

After her death, the Colorado College Library took some of her papers and some books; later I learned that everything else was reduced to cash at auction, in Denver, including all those hats. They went to strangers for next to nothing, more or less as jokes.

My final encounter with Amanda occurred when my wife and I stopped for a visit in Colorado Springs in the summer of 1968. We had hoped to take her out to lunch, but she was again just out of the hospital—this time because of a stroke and resulting high blood pressure. She moved with great difficulty and, despite an incredible weight loss, she looked not so much thin as wasted. Her cheeks were sunken, her black hair was now white at the roots, but her lipstick was still red and her eyes were bright. She could only hobble from one chair to another with difficulty. Her high-heeled shoes had finally given way to a pair of comfortable, homey carpet slippers.

Amanda's housekeeper of many years, black, patient, middle-aged, efficient Birdie, prepared lunch for us in the apartment in town to which she'd moved some years before. Much earlier she'd given up her residence at the Broadmoor, but almost everything looked familiar: the little love seat on which Amanda had sat so many years before to sip that unpotable cocktail she'd invented, her crossed feet swinging, not quite touching the floor; the walnut secretary that held various editions of her own books; the framed painting of the dust jacket illustration for *Elizabeth, the Woman*; her extensive library shelves—all against walls of rosy pink and deep aqua, still her favorite colors.

Amanda seemed genuinely interested in my first book, scheduled to be published a few months later, and she was full of plans for a new book of her own, this time about three old favorites: Eleanor of Aquitaine, Joan of Arc, and Heloïse; and for a trip to Europe to do research in the fall, or as soon as she felt well again. I knew she would never leave that house except to be hospitalized, although she lived another year.

Amanda had always punctuated her speech with a little clearing of her throat, a tiny gravelly sound that could indicate anything at all: pleasure, discomfort, inquiry, anger (although I never witnessed significant anger), hesitation, pride, helplessness, embarrassment, gratitude. It was something we'd always known of, that little catch in her throat, and more than once we'd made gentle fun of it. Now her voice was reed-thin, and the gravel moved restlessly in everything she said.

At some time during that last afternoon, the milkman came to the door. Birdie answered his ring, but Amanda insisted on seeing him to place the order herself.

"Would you like to know who we are?" she said genially, beckoning him into the room, and we had a nice chat.

Amanda seemed almost as reluctant to see him go as if he had been an old friend, and I wondered how many of those "500 students" who "remembered me this Christmas" in 1958, as she had claimed in a letter then, had forgotten her by 1968.

The day was hot, the apartment was as close as a vault, and even though there were vestiges of Amanda's old wit, I was eager to escape, promising to send her a copy of my book when it came out, promising to write to her, and I did that, once or twice, and sent a Christmas card—I think. And then I too forgot.

ALICE B. TOKLAS
(AND GERTRUDE STEIN)

*A*lice Toklas survived for twenty years after the death of Gertrude Stein, a period that began in loneliness and ended in loneliness. In between she made a sufficiently full life for herself, writing two cookbooks and a memoir, several articles, many letters, and becoming for me a brief and treasured acquaintance, so that ultimately her memory need not be entirely dependent on the achievements of her more celebrated friend.

First, however, Gertrude Stein, a four-rose general with an army of one marching behind. Alice Toklas established that order long ago, and no one ignores it. Alice Toklas brings up the rear.

I met her first through her voice, by way of Gertrude Stein's imitative prose when in 1946 at the age of sixteen, I discovered *The Autobiography Of Alice B. Toklas* included in *Selected Writings of Gertrude Stein*. A Friday afternoon stop at the New Books shelf in my high school library had already become a habit by the time I spied that stout beige book and then saw the frontispiece of two elderly ladies chatting in a garden—one of them had a large nose, the other one had a crewcut—followed by six hundred pages of tight type. The memory is as fresh now as it ever was: I thumbed from back to front, from front to back, and lit on this:

Nearly all of it to be as a wife has a cow, a love story. All of it to be as a wife has a cow, all of it to be as a wife has a cow, a love story.

That was the first paragraph, so I read the second one:

As to be all of it as to be a wife as a wife has a cow, a love story, all of it as to be all of it as a wife all of it as to be as a wife has a cow a love story, all of it as a wife has a cow as a wife has a cow a love story.

It went right on down the page like that, a broken record that knew its own grooves pretty well and when to get stuck and when to go on playing. I flipped around to find some classy nonsense that made me smile: descriptions, called *Tender Buttons*, of household props like petticoats and red roses and potatoes and chicken—there were four about chicken, one dense, one smutty, one impenetrable, one funny—and chairs, tables, breakfasts, handkerchiefs. I flipped again, this time to "Sweet sweet sweet sweet tea," which I somehow knew right away ended with "sweetie," although I have never had a strong ear or eye for puns. Maybe that poem turned up several flips later—time would prove there was as much of Gertrude Stein to forget as to remember—before I turned the page to find "Toasted susie is my ice-cream." I spent the rest of the weekend alarming my parents with snippets of what seemed to be patent foolishness or at least a typesetter's nightmare, but by Monday I knew it had all been somehow touched by my own fairy godmother's wand.

How many others first read *The Autobiography Of Alice B. Toklas* through to the last page before discovering Gertrude's Stein's surprise in her last line? I got to it on Sunday afternoon. All day long, she'd dropped names across the pages I had never heard before. I had read little current literature at that point, having progressed instead from Nancy Drew and the Hardy Boys to histori-cal novels put out by the Literary Guild.

The explanatory sections in *Selected Writings of Gertrude Stein* were nearly as baffling as her *Tender Buttons*—to this sixteen-year-old, anyhow—but I liked just about everything, including the gossipy babble about the end of the book about the French Occupation and the G. I.s, and all for the same reason: none of it was like anything I'd ever read or even thought about before, and its variety seemed endless. Then a few months later I heard a Sunday afternoon radio broadcast of the truncated version of an opera by Gertrude Stein with music by Virgil Thomson, called *Four Saints In Three Acts*. It was not like anything I'd ever heard or even thought about before either, not at least on those Saturday afternoon broadcasts from the Metropolitan Opera House that I'd been listening to for as long as I could recall.

But then I took a two-year vacation from Gertrude Stein, stashing her away somewhere on my head's hard drive, after those initial encounters. School got in the way, I suppose, and be-ginning to try to write, and then getting ready to go away to col-lege. Two years later I was en route to campus for the first time, when I heard a radio program called *Author Meets the Critic*, de-voted that afternoon to a new book called *When This You See Re-member Me: Gertrude Stein in Person* by W. G. Rogers. The animos-ity of one of the critics and the joking derision of another were surprising, but they persuaded me to buy the book the next day, and then I read it during the three-hour wait at registration. I wonder now how many freshmen put their time to such good use during their own inescapable stone-age lines every September. I purchased Yale's recently released *Four In America* too—bewil-dering biographical speculations about Ulysses S. Grant as a religious leader, Wilbur Wright as a painter, Henry James as a general, and George Washington as a writer—and discovered a riveting paragraph that will serve anybody in search of a key into Gertrude Stein's treasury:

> Clarity is of no importance because nobody listens and nobody knows what you mean, nor how clearly you mean what you mean. But if you have vitality enough of knowing enough of what you mean, somebody and sometimes and sometimes a great many will have to realize that you know what you mean and so they will agree that you mean what you know, what you know you mean, which is as near as anybody can come to understanding any one.

Also, I bought my own copy of the *Selected Writings*; and by the end of my freshman year, I had built up a fairly good shelf that included *Geography and Plays*, still pristine in its 1922 dust jacket, *Lectures In America, Brewsie And Willie*, the 1934 abbreviated edition of *The Making Of Americans*, all for list price or less, a snazzily boxed copy of *Blood On The Dining Room Floor* that had been hand-set and hand-sewn into French marble boards—I'd never seen so beautiful a book—and an autographed copy of *The World Is Round* bound in white vellum.

In 1951, and by that time in the navy, I remembered that the Banyan Press, which had produced *Blood On The Dining Room Floor*, had printed a limited edition of *Things As They Are*, Gertrude Stein's unpublished first book. It cost ten dollars—about one-third of a month's salary for me—but it was difficult to think of the colorful military scrip in which we were paid overseas as having any real value because it looked so much like *Monopoly* money. When my copy of the book arrived, a letter accompanied it, untidily typed, from Carl Van Vechten:

Dear Mr Kellner, . . . the . . . Banyan Press has handed me your letter as I am the literary executor of Miss Stein. . . . Much of her past work is out of print, but if you will tell me what you have I may be able to supply some of your lacks. Miss Stein would be happy to hear this voice out of Korea, but she would not be surprised as the army and navy and most young people have been for her for a long time.

That letter initiated a long correspondence and an intimate friendship embracing the last thirteen years of his life. "The Banyan Tots," as Carl Van Vechten called Claude Fredericks and Milton Saul, the young owners of the Banyan Press, had thought he'd be amused by a sailor reading Gertrude Stein. So he was, following that first letter with books, magazines, clippings, programs, phonograph records, an occasional package of exotic foods from Bloomingdale's, and an astonishing number of letters and postcards of celebrated people he had photographed, all to get me through an otherwise stultifying enlistment.

And now, having given Gertrude Stein her due—here as well as in a hefty reference work called *A Gertrude Stein Companion: Content With The Example* (Greenwood Press, 1988), and in a sixteen-volume edition of her major works for publication in Japan (Hon-no-tomosha, 1995), and having done so first—I can turn to Alice Toklas second, in the order of which she would have not only approved but demanded.

"Tell me anything you like," Carl Van Vechten wrote in his second letter to me which was filled with questions, concluding, "I'm sure, in any case, you'll omit something that Alice wants to know." His third letter contained this:

Incidentally, in writing to Alice, I copied a part of your letter and she wrote to me in return: "And the sailor isn't only intelligent, but delightful. Thanks so much for copying so much. Would you like me to send you a copy of Lucy Church to send him?"

In time, *Lucy Church Amiably* did arrive, and as Carl Van Vechten had requested, suitably inscribed, though I would learn later that the sentiment suggested Gertrude Stein rather than Alice Toklas in its flavor:

> To Bruce Kellner.
>
> In deepest appreciation of his appreciation of the work of Gertrude Stein.
>
> Paris. 24-IX-5 1   Alice Toklas.

I knew nothing about Alice B. Toklas beyond what Gertrude Stein had had her say about herself in *The Autobiography Of Alice B. Toklas*: she'd been born and raised in California, liked to sit with her back turned to the view, and served as housekeeper, gardener, Sunday night cook, needlewoman, secretary, editor, and amateur veterinarian—all for Gertrude Stein who had written her autobiography for her because she didn't have time to write it herself. In those far-off, innocent days, it may have crossed my mind that she was Gertrude Stein's muse and mistress as well, but I did not at twenty-one know exactly what that meant, nor was I perceptive enough to grasp the coded sexuality in so much of Gertrude Stein's work.

In answer to my letter thanking Alice Toklas for *Lucy Church Amiably*, I received a brittle post card, printed some time during the First World War, of Gertrude Stein and Alice Toklas and the car they had converted into an ambulance so they could deliver supplies to the French War Wounded. I recognized that strange, hearse-like tramcar from its description in *The Autobiography Of*

Alice B. Toklas, recalling that Gertrude Stein never learned how to shift into reverse with ease: "She goes forward admirably, she does not go backwards successfully," Alice explains—a cogent observation about Gertrude Stein's progress as a writer, I would learn in time. They named the car Auntie, after Gertrude Stein's Aunt Pauline who "always behaved admirably in emergencies, and behaved fairly well most times if she was properly flattered." "A small souvenir to add to your collection with a kind remembrance from A. B. Toklas," the card read, again in a spidery script.

I did not write again for over a year, and then only with the excuse of acknowledging the death of Basket II, the white poodle she and Gertrude Stein had bought in 1938. She answered almost immediately, saying I would "understand that the flat is even more lonesome now than before." Was there any suggestion in her remark that I continue to write? I didn't, and only learned long after her death how important correspondence had been to her. Another year passed. I longed to correspond on a weekly basis, as I did with Carl Van Vechten—for certainly those letters had altered my life—but probably I feared I had little to say that would interest her. Then, when Donald Gallup's edition of letters written to Gertrude Stein, *The Flowers Of Friendship*, came out in 1953, I took a chance on writing again. I was back in California by that time after a tour of duty in Japan, which prompted some interest:

> You must indeed be happy to be back in California but are you
> never going to be liberated, be through with your service, return
> to civilian life, enfin to a life of your own. But I must not refer to it,
> only to make you more impatient. If you ever get to Santa Barbara
> or Monterey give them my love and devotion, for they were happy
> stomping grounds of my youth.

Although Gertrude Stein had allowed her friend's early life scant attention in *The Autobiography Of Alice B. Toklas*, those first years were not barren of interest. Alice Toklas had studied to be a concert pianist and even gave public recitals. She traveled rather more widely than most young women of her generation, to Germany, Austria, and England. She smoked a lot. She read widely, learned how to garden from her mother and how to cook from the family domestics—chores that would serve her well in later years during her marriage to Gertrude Stein. After her mother's death she kept house for her father and brothers, escaping for holidays along the California coastline. She lived through the San Francisco earthquake—her father observed that it would "give them a black eye in the East"—picnicking on the sidewalk and burying the family silver in the garden in case the fire spread.

Gertrude Stein's brother Michael and his wife Sarah hastily returned from Paris because of the earthquake, to inspect their San Francisco properties for damage, and bringing with them some paintings by Henri Matisse, the first to come to America. In her own memoir, *What Is Remembered*, dictated in her old age when her memory was perhaps not entirely reliable, Alice Toklas uses her response to the paintings as part of her impetus for accompanying the Steins back to Paris. She met Gertrude Stein the day she arrived. It was love at first sight.

Their life together has been often told: the long years of obscurity alternating with ridicule; then financial success for a book that had little to do with Gertrude Stein's work; a successful American lecture tour; surviving the German Occupation by hiding out in the South of France where they had a summer home. It was not always serene—what marriage is?—but they were indispensable to each other, and when Gertrude Stein died, just four months before I first discovered her work in *Selected Writings of Gertrude Stein* in 1946, Alice Toklas was devastated. Over the remaining twenty years of her life she gradually discovered her own voice, not only in her books but in her remarkable letters.

I didn't reply immediately to her inquiry about my release from the navy, and a few months later Alice Toklas wrote again, a long and chatty letter, full of information and sufficiently friendly to urge me on to more frequent communications. We became occasional if not regular correspondents. A month later she wrote to thank me for some photographs that Carl Van Vechten had taken of me, "though they are very different one from the other, almost as if they were of two young men." Apparently I had sent some information concerning Gertrude Stein, doubtless something several others had already told her about:

> And thanks a lot for all the news of Gertrude Stein's works. You
> will understand that if it is already known to me it is the kind that
> gives me the greatest pleasure to hear again.

The Alice B. Toklas Cook Book came out that year, with its line drawings by Sir Francis Rose about which she wrote, "You see how fortunate a mere little cook can be." I thought they were not very good, but Sir Francis Rose had been one of Gertrude Stein's last protégés—I believe she owned thirty of his paintings at the time of her death—so I kept my mouth shut. Most of the recipes came from "the archives of French families," but she no longer had the time or strength or money—"particularly the latter," she added in parentheses, "for it would make the other reasons less serious"—to perform in the kitchen as she had so often done for Gertrude Stein and their guests, especially in Bilignin, the tiny hamlet near Belley, in the French Alps, where she and Gertrude Stein had spent half the year in a rented manor house. She doubted the book would sell in America, since the recipes were probably "not made for American palettes or kitchens," but I assured her that some of them were when, the following year, as a graduate student I began to cook for myself. Then, as the "disagreeable necessity" of which she once spoke became more and more a preoccupation and fascination, I discovered that Alice Toklas and I had something else in common to write about.

The following fall, when I had a new job, teaching in Cedar Rapids, Alice Toklas wrote to congratulate me, remembering that Gertrude Stein "used to say that Iowans all had a distinction." Some time later, when I groaned about the grim landscape there—intellectual as well as geographical—she chided me gently. It must have been about this time that I asked her if she would not address me as Bruce; I got my comeuppance with the salutation that followed: "My dear Kellner."

> Your complaint about Carl [Van Vechten]'s native town reminds me of the answer a woman in Belley gave me when I told her I had discovered a fantastic baker in a small dull little town not far away. Ah then she said it cant be a dull little town if it has a fantastic bakery. And she was right. If Grand Rapids [sic] produced Carl and Coe College it has great distinction.

She was furious about a new biography of Gertrude Stein. Carl Van Vechten said that was no surprise. Except for Donald Sutherland's obliquely scholarly study, *Gertrude Stein: A Biography of Her Work*—a masterpiece of the so-called new criticism in its final decadence, in which Alice Toklas is never mentioned—anything written about Gertrude Stein could only encourage Alice Toklas's wrath, especially if it dared to tread on the private life they had shared for nearly forty years:

> If you havent heard of an odious book, Gertrude Stein Her Work and Life [sic] by a Mrs Sprigge I hope you havent and will desist from looking at it. It quite upset me when I first saw it. The American edition is just out. Now I am quite callous to its vulgarity. But let me warn you. Not of course that either Gertrude Stein or her work need any defence.

A few months later, Alice Toklas's temper had sweetened somewhat when she wrote again:

> This is the day nearest to spring and so I am celebrating by writing to Iowa where you may still be.

The heating system at 5 rue Christine, she wrote, had been improved and the plumbing in the bathroom had been repaired. That was "a comfort, at a ruinous price but I refuse to consider this." She was about to depart with Anita Loos—an old friend from the Twenties—for northern Italy to take the mud baths at Aqui to ease the arthritis which plagued her annually. It was in this letter that she sent me the first of several recipes, some of which did not appear in either of her cook books. Some I never attempted, but one for a ratatouille of extremely complex flavors was perfection. It is well worth substituting now and again for the more familiar, robust version, and like many of Alice Toklas's recipes, bears following closely:

> Heat 1 tablespoon olive oil, 1 oignons cut in thin slices, 1 pulped tomato from which the seeds have been removed, 1 sliced unpeeled

zucchini, 1 peeled sliced egg plant, 2 sliced peppers seeds removed, 1 crushed garlic bead, 1 sprig thyme, 1/3 bay leaf, 1 cubed piece of Hubbard squash. Simmer 1 hour covered. Stir occasionally so that it does not scorch, add another tablespoon oil if necessary. Enough for 2 or 3 persons. Serve hot or cold. Delicious.

Once, in describing a meal she had prepared for friends, she sent along a recipe from an new Indian cook book, with which I would "have great success." She had made this fish dish "followed by a baron of mutton with 8 (!) cloves of garlic." The dessert sounded more extravagant than anything her own cook books contained: wood strawberries with cream and "disguised" strawberries and chestnuts:

Disguised strawberries are fresh ones dipped in strawberry fondant (icing). Disguised chestnuts are made with concentrated puree of chestnuts dipped in an icing of syrup boiled until it is coffee colored. The lunch was easy to cook, the fish was the only complicated dish and there was all morning to prepare it, set the table and cook the rissoles potatoes (butter "rendered" clarified) the day before.

Sometimes, a whole letter consisted of cooking hints, no salutation, no signature:

If your lettuce is getting old soak it root down in 1 inch water. The Indian way to blanch almonds. Soak almonds overnight. Next morning peel them. The skins will slip off easily. The almonds will be somewhat tender. Almonds blanched in boiling water are hard and quite tasteless.

A couple of years later, Alice Toklas wrote to ask about a small payment she had received from Hartwick College in New

York, where I was teaching at the time. With her permission I had staged some pieces from *The Gertrude Stein First Reader*, but my budget had allowed me to offer her only a pittance for royalties.

> About the cheque, I am confused, how can there be royalties if there is no admittance charged? I shall not cash it until you let me know the answer. I cannot accept it if it was part of your shoe string.

She was in Rome at that time, taking a lava bath cure for her arthritis. "Roman ruins and renaissance palaces bore me," she wrote, "but the markets and cooking are wonderful. . . . Have you a garden," she queried, "can you grow artichokes?"

In the summer of 1962 my wife and I took an extended holiday in Europe. I had written to Alice Toklas before our departure, saying I hoped to be able to see her and offering an approximate date. From Austria, Margaret and I side-tripped to stop in Aix-les-Bains and ferret out Bilignin where Gertrude Stein and Alice Toklas had spent fourteen happy summers. We spent three enchanted days discovering their *manoir*, the church at Lucey from which came Gertrude Stein's novel, *Lucy Church Amiably*, Culoz where they sat out the Second World War, and the beautiful Rhône Valley. Then we stopped in Paris only long enough to locate a hotel, drop off our extra luggage, and post a note to Alice Toklas before driving up to Le Havre to deliver our car for shipment back to the United States.

But Alice Toklas had already written to us, in care of American Express. She had just returned from Italy where she and Donald Sutherland had been taking the lava baths, she wrote, and "now I am here from which I do not budge. But please let me know as far in advance as possible when you would propose coming to see me for I have several boring engagements (dates uncertain) that I must keep." And her invariable and familiar "Always Cordially" had given way to "Appreciatively." I sent her the name of our hotel—the Hotel "At Home," with arguably the narrowest *grand lit* in all of Paris, just a few blocks from 5 rue Christine—and proposed several alternative dates. There was a letter at the hotel when we returned from Le Havre, inviting us for tea on the fifth.

Margaret and I sight-saw on August second, third, and fourth, ferreting out the Bateau Lavoir, 27 rue de Fleurus, and other locations so memorable in *The Autobiography Of Alice B. Toklas.* On the fifth, we were called to the lobby of our hotel to discover Alice Toklas's Spanish servant in volatile conversation with the manager. Had we forgotten our appointment on the fourth, yesterday afternoon? In halting French and forgotten high school Spanish, I translated the confusion for her, and she departed wreathed in smiles, having assured us we were still expected. I had already wondered if, at eighty-five, Alice Toklas's memory would have suffered any deterioration. Who would have thought that five years later, wasted and infirm, she would tap her forehead with her fingers and say, "*This* will be the last to go!"

We arrived on the stroke of four, to be admitted by the Spanish maid into the high-ceilinged hallway at 5 rue Christine and led from there to the large drawing room, its stark-white walls revealing the larger and smaller squares and rectangles where paintings had hung before their removal by the French authorities—at the insistence of Gertrude Stein's greedy heirs—to the vault of the Chase Manhattan Bank in Paris. There they would sit, thirty Picassos among them, until Alice Toklas's death, thereby denying her the right to sell any of them—or all of them, for that matter—for her maintenance, in accordance with Gertrude Stein's will.

It was a large, comfortable drawing room, with tall windows and an ornate fireplace with a crowded mantel, over which a cloudy, crazed mirror hung, facing a brown satin horsehair sofa. There was a large double-door cabinet, in which had lurked, I supposed, those thousands of pages of Gertrude Stein's manuscripts before they'd been shipped off to Yale some years before, a small pie-crust table with a collection of silver gewgaws, faience jars, a doll made of shells, a silver pedestal ashtray with a cherub handle, and under everything worn, oriental carpets.

Alice Toklas sat in an enormous armchair, nearly hidden in its recesses, in a corner of the room against the tall windows that gave a gray afternoon light through the drizzle of rain. I remembered her remark about landscapes: she liked a view but she liked to sit with her back turned to it.

"Will you forgive me? Will you forgive me for confusing the days?" the bass voice croaked, rich from years of cigarettes.

The tables on either side of her chair had ashtrays overflowing with Pall Mall butts, and she added to the debris, chain-smoking as the afternoon progressed. A rosary lay on one table, a reminder of her recent conversion to Roman Catholicism, and from time to time during our visit she held it or wound it around her wrist. Her black hair, only lightly streaked with gray, was combed forward over her forehead to just above her eyes, and she wore glasses with lenses as thick as coasters for a davenport. A large, beautiful brooch of some dull stone rested at the neckline of her loose dress, and she had old sandals on her feet. Her nose was beaked, her eyes bright, her skin tissue-papery, and she had a quite definite, quite dark and downy moustache.

Alice Toklas's vision was severely impaired by that time—I read a couple of letters aloud for her—but a magnifying glass helped her for really important matters, she said. Her hearing was weak as well, but she was less bothered by that than by her failing sight. When I asked about the paintings—their loss or theft—she saw them in her memory sufficiently, she said, tapping her forehead. I commiserated by telling her about the hearing problems that Carl Van Vechten and his wife had been having. Did I overstate it? For the rest of the afternoon she referred off and on the Van Vechtens' deafness, "poor old Carl" and "poor old Fania." By the end of our visit she'd persuaded herself that their hearing was far worse than hers.

But we spoke primarily of Bilignin and Aix-les Bains and described as best we could our visit there: the back roads in search of that particular view across the Rhône Valley that had first urged Gertrude Stein and Alice Toklas to negotiate renting the *manoir* at Bilignin; our circuitous drive to Lucey to see the church, by that time fallen to disrepair; the good food; the climate; and, in Bilignin itself, the rich and heady odor of fresh manure. She had never had the courage to return, she said, since they'd been forced to leave there during the war.

We talked about cigarettes too. Both Margaret and I smoked at that time, but we could not have kept up with our hostess. She sometimes lit a fresh one from the butt of another; she seemed, too, to enjoy having a match struck for her, bending toward it, inhaling deeply, then holding her cigarette between her fingers in a modestly outstretched hand while she exhaled. Had Gertrude Stein smoked, I wanted to know. Only in the early days,

Alice Toklas said. At some point around 1915, when they were sitting out part of the First World War in Majorca, they'd run out of cigarettes, and Gertrude Stein smoked something local. Apparently it was not tobacco but a form of *cannabis sativa* or other drug. It disoriented her thinking, and that frightened her. She never smoked again. Also, she drank alcohol only sparingly for much the same reason. Nothing mattered to Gertrude Stein but that her head be clear for her writing. She would have wanted no part of Baudelaire's "artificial paradises" that poet Brion Gysin had promised in his recipe for hashish fudge, included in *The Alice B. Toklas Cook Book*. Alice Toklas herself had never tried it, so the stories that grew up after her death about her marijuana brownies that inspired Gertrude Stein's literary flights had no foundation at all.

At some point the Spanish servant gave us a sweet sherry and two pastries that Alice Toklas had not made, her time in the kitchen by then long behind her, and she apologized because she could not offer us something memorable for the occasion of our meeting.

What do I remember most clearly? Her vivacity despite her infirmities, her sense of fun and malice, the croak of her voice and the deadpan economy of her wit, her warmth to two virtual strangers, her moustache.

When we prepared to depart after about two hours, she seemed in no hurry to terminate the visit and pressed on for answers to questions that, I continue to believe, she asked out of genuine interest: How did my students respond to Gertrude Stein's writing? Did I teach *The Making Of Americans*, since Gertrude Stein considered it her *magnum opus*? What of my own writing? My biography of Carl Van Vechten, then making the rounds of publishers? Would I not call a friend of hers about it? Surely he would help me if she asked him to. Did Fania Marinoff still wear beautiful hats? When would we return to France? Could we come by again before our departure?

It did not occur to me for several years—and then only in reading accounts of her last, lonely days, or in seeing Fania Marinoff abandoned by nearly all of Carl Van Vechten's friends after his death—that Alice Toklas might have desperately wanted us to stay on.

I wrote a few more times after that, but she did not reply beyond an immediate letter of thanks for our visit, until *What Is Remembered* was published. I had written to tell her how much I had enjoyed her memoir of her years with Gertrude Stein, although it was a tired book, suffering from inconsistencies and factual errors. My enthusiasm was only a slight exaggeration, only a white lie. When next I did hear from her, an amanuensis had taken over. In answering, I insisted that she no longer feel compelled to acknowledge my notes, although I said I would write now and then to say hello, and I did that.

My last direct knowledge of Alice Toklas came to me through Robert Lescher—earlier her editor and later briefly my agent—who had visited her not long before her death in 1967. She had been evicted from 5 rue Christine by that time, and her new surroundings were grim. But she was as quick as in the past. Bedridden and impatient to join Gertrude Stein in some immortal garden where roses always grew in circles, she held her usual court, elegant and economical, under a beautiful patchwork quilt, her rosary in one hand and her Pall Mall in the other.

Ten years later, to observe Alice Toklas's one hundredth birthday, Margaret and I gave a dinner party and prepared everything from recipes in the Toklas cook books and my letters from her: Savoury Biscuits, Purée of Artichoke Soup; Bass for Picasso, decorated in designs that he'd said should have been made in honor of Matisse instead of him; Covered Cock in Cumin, which included among other oddities in the stuffing some poached calf brains; Extravagant Mashed Potatoes, made with a half a cup of butter per potato; Green Peas à la Goodwife; and Bavarian Cream Perfect Love. Inevitably, I suppose, we concluded with Hashish Fudge, thanks to the enterprising efforts of one of my students who got some good Colombian for me. As *The Alice B. Toklas Cook Book* rightly observes, ". . . it should be eaten with care. Two pieces are quite sufficient." Our hangovers were monumental, intermittent gales of hilarity from my wife all day long, a friend who had to crawl on hands and knees from bed to bathroom, my own inability to read more than three consecutive lines in the morning paper.

Three years earlier, in 1974, at the time of Gertrude Stein's centennial, I prepared a fairly extensive observation at Millersville University, where I was teaching: an exhibition of my own collection of books, dozens of photographs, a rotating slide show of paintings that had hung at 27 rue de Fleurus and 5 rue Christine, a Stein manuscript loaned by the Beinecke Library at Yale University, and three gallery lectures, as well as a program of readings, with some texts set to music. There were, of course, several references to Alice Toklas throughout, including one section of a display case in which I arranged her books, some letters and recipes in her remarkable, spidery holograph, Carl Van Vechten's touching portrait of her with Basket II, made in her lonely old age after Gertrude Stein's death, and the recently published volume of her correspondence, *Staying On Alone*, edited by

Edward Burns. The centennial belonged to Gertrude Stein, but Alice Toklas had spent her life ensuring its observation, so she deserved her widow's mite. After all, she was for over twenty years a bereft widow, so unobtrusively I put in a rosary and a Pall Mall.

Nearly a quarter of a century later, I brought her briefly back to life in *Staying On Alone: The Autobiography Of Alice B. Toklas by Alice B. Toklas*, a monologue based on her letters, cook books, and memoirs. Designed and directed by Ted Vitale, it was produced as a staged reading, 21 and 22 May 1998, to benefit the Theater of the Performing Arts on Cape Cod, with Julie Harris (yet another noble dame).

The Autobiography of Alice B. Toklas
by Alice B. Toklas

The setting should not be traditionally realistic, just a simple but effective space to approximate 5 rue Christine against black draperies: a free-standing doorframe stage right, a free-hanging window stage left, a free-standing fireplace stage center; a Renaissance table and chair, appropriate knickknacks; a large oriental carpet, and a great many empty, free-hanging, gold picture frames of various sizes and styles that silently rise into space and out of sight on cue. Ideally, there should be at least a dozen frames, preferably more, as there were thirty paintings by Pablo Picasso in the collection and thirteen by Juan Gris in addition to others. Isolated downstage right almost to the apron, facing the audience head-on, a small, plain, unobtrusive wooden chair with a large, pale blue shawl thrown over its back. These go unacknowledged until the Epilogue. There is no curtain.

When the audience arrives the room is empty, but through the open windows, or rather from off-stage, drift the faint sounds of a busy Paris street: intermittent taxi-horns, laughter, children squabbling, an accordion perhaps; someone practicing scales on a piano in an adjacent apartment, interrupted once or twice to play snatches of "Sicilienne," "Valse Lente," or "Pastorale in A" by Germaine Tailleferre, or "Canciones y Danses 3, 7, and 8" by Frederico Mompou. These pieces are employed from time to time during the action of the play; so, indeed, are the scales employed. The musical elements should intrude only subtly, to underscore, and while the scales might produce a smile, the pieces should never be designed to wring tears; their use should be minimal.

Alice B. Toklas is sixty-nine years old at the beginning of the play and through Act I; in Act II, she ages from sixty-nine to eighty-nine. Deprivations during the German Occupation of France have aged her early, and she is frail. She looks ancient and at the same time ageless, tiny, spider-like, with a large hooked nose and a noticeable moustache—actually a heavy, dark down. She is black-haired with long bangs, heavy earrings, thick lisle stockings, and open leather sandals. In Act I she wears a loose cotton dress made out of a faded but colorful India print bedspread, with white collar and cuffs; in Act II she wears a not too strictly tailored suit designed for her by Pierre Balmain but with the same stockings and sandals. Throughout the play she moves about from time to time, sitting, standing, walking, smoking a great deal, filing and buffing her nails as she speaks. Her voice is a cultivated baritone croak born of a two-pack-a-day habit. Her chain-smoking can be affected rather than effected, but cigarettes are a significant part of her emotional makeup. Ideally, Basket II, a large, white poodle— eight at the beginning of the play and fourteen when he dies—appears from time to time. The presence of a dog is not obligatory but a nice touch, despite W. C. Fields's admonition about the dangers of children and dogs upstaging on stage.

    The stage directions are sometimes explicit to establish the time frame. The director and actor may find better solutions. There are any number of possibilities for movement; however, it is important that the audience register the dates when they occur in the text, in order to follow the lapses in time. Paragraphing in the text is only suggestive of subject breaks. The erratic punctuation in the script is Alice B. Toklas's and Gertrude Stein's; I have altered it or added to it when necessary for clarity.

ACT ONE

5 rue Christine, July 1946–September 1946

The lights lower; when they come up Alice B. Toklas is sitting at the table, a telephone to her ear with one hand, a piece of stationery clutched in the other; she is frustrated, impatient, anguished, but the whole passage should go quickly. Basket, her white poodle, lies or sits next to her, with his leash around her wrist. There should be brief pauses at the actor's discretion to

indicate responses from the telegram operator on the other end of the line.
Initially, the audience may laugh a bit at her distress, but it should be
quickly sobered up at the end.

Oui, Madame, oui. Il y en a deux de plus, deux de plus. Oui, la
même télégramme, le même message. Oui. Carl Van Vechten.
Non, non, non, Madame. Vous n'ecoutez pas. Ecoutez-moi, s'il
vous plaît. Le nom est Van Vechten—Oui, c'est ça. New York
City. Carl Van Vechten—Van—v-a-n—Oui. C'est une adresse
câblogramme: c-a-r-l-v-e-c-h-t. Câblogramme. Oui, c'est ça. Et
la même télégramme à Donald Gallup   *(she searches her address*
book for the address).   Gallup, Non, non, pas de Galop, g-a-l-l-
u-p, Gallup. Oh, attendez un moment, juste un moment. C'est
—c'est—Ah   *(in desperation),*   envoyez-la-lui à Yale University at—comment? L'Université de Yale à New Haven, Connecticut—c-o-n-n-e-c-t-i-c-u-t. Oui. Ah, non! Haven! Pas
"heaven"! Pas *"paradis"*! New Haven. Oui, c'est ça   *(she weeps),*
c'est tout. Mais, maintenant, Madame, repétez-moi le message
en français.   *(pause)*   Oui, oui, c'est juste: "Gertrude Stein est
morte cet après-midi. J'écris. Je t'embrasse affectueusement,
Alice." Oui, c'est ça, "Alice."   *(pause)*   En Anglais? Oui, "Gertrude Stein died this afternoon. I am writing. Dearest love,
Alice." Oui, merci bien, Madame. Aussitôt que possible, s'il
vous plait.   *(She hangs up the telephone. She sighs again.)*

For us who loved her so completely it should be easy to say it
all—but the emptiness is so very very great.   *(She strokes and*
nuzzles Basket II who puts his head in her lap.)   Just before Christmas Gertrude complained of being tired and said we'd see fewer
people—it had been too exhausting—the German Occupation
of France and then seeing nearly the whole American army.

(She is proud of that.)   But in April the doctor said she needed an
operation and we went to the American Hospital in Neuilly—
both of us full of hope.   *(She rises here, another cigarette.)*   But
then last Friday morning they refused to undertake it. The—
cancer was too far advanced and the pain was great. Tired, suffering Baby dismissed them all and said she never wanted to see
any of them again. She was   *(proudly)*   furious and frighten-
ing and impressive—   *(her eyes flash with excitement and she nearly
laughs)*   like she was thirty years and more ago when her work
was attacked.   *(Proudly again)*   But amongst the surgeons was
one who said, "You don't give your word of honor to a woman
of her character and not keep it. So I shall operate."   *(She sighs,
picks up the vase of flowers to take them and Basket II offstage right but
pauses to look out the window, then turns back to the audience.)*   That
last afternoon Gertrude said—"What is the question," and
before I could speak she went on—"If there is no question then
there is no answer."

And they took her away and I never saw her again.   *(She starts
offstage, pauses at the doorway.)*   Were they not a summing up of
her life and perhaps a vision of the future? Often they mean that
to me and then they are a comfort.   *(She exits to deposit the vase and
Basket II and returns to the stage immediately.)*   And now Basket and
I are in the flat alone where we are definitely staying on alone.

*(A specific break here: she huddles down in the overstuffed chair; the light
has grown dimmer, and now in semi-darkness she stares ahead into a void
no one can see or share, and she does this long enough to make the audience
uncomfortable. Did the actor forget her lines? Is the dog supposed to do something here? There is no music. Then the light brightens again, rather
quickly, and there is a marked change of pace because time has passed;
resignation and resolution take over, perhaps a shuffle around the flat,
perhaps she peers at the Picasso portrait.)*

O could such perfection, such happiness and such beauty have been here and now be gone away? I'd better take Basket out for a walk before it pours—the weather is horrible—the sun never shines. It has been terribly cold, and already I long for spring, six long months from tomorrow officially, and one knows what spring in Paris is. Do you remember how you suddenly can see everything way down the street—that's the first week in May—and the buds on the chestnuts are out. Thirty-eight times we saw it together. Together.

(Another break, another cigarette perhaps. Slow piano scales or exercises drift in from the next apartment. Then a conversational tone takes over, intimate and gossipy, except when the text suggests sharp introspection.)

Gertrude was born in Allegheny, Pennsylvania. As I am an ardent Californian and as she spent her youth there I often begged her to be born in California but she always remained firmly born in Allegheny, Pennsylvania. I was born and raised in San Francisco, California. I have in consequence always preferred living in a temperate climate but it is difficult, on the continent of Europe or even in America, to find a temperate climate and live in it. I like a view but I like to sit with my back turned to it.   *(Music out)*   In San Francisco life went on calmly until one morning we and our home were violently shaken by an earthquake. Gas was escaping. I hurried to my father's bedroom, pulled up the shades, pulled back the curtains and opened the windows. "Do get up," I said to him. "The city is on fire." "That," he said with his usual calm, "will give us a black eye in the East," turning and going to sleep again.

The Michael Steins—Gertrude's elder brother and his wife—had hurried over to San Francisco from Paris to see what repairs would be necessary to their property. They brought with them the portrait of Madame Matisse with a green line down her face. It and the other paintings they brought were the first by Matisse to cross the Atlantic. I met Michael and Sarah Stein through a friend, and the portrait impressed me immensely. Gradually I told my father that perhaps I would leave San Francisco. He was not disturbed by this, after all there was at that time a great deal of going and coming and there were many friends of mine going and so I fled to freedom.

After my arrival in Paris—1907—it was Gertrude Stein who held my complete attention. I met her at her brother Michael's house for tea. She was a golden brown presence, burned by the Tuscan sun and with a golden glint in her warm brown hair. She wore a large round coral brooch and when she talked I thought her voice came from this brooch. It was unlike anyone else's voice—deep, full, velvety like a great contralto's, like two voices. And she had an exceptionally rare laugh. It was very hearty, fairly loud, but oh, it was music. She was large and heavy with delicate small hands and a beautifully modeled and unique head. It was often compared to a Roman emperor's, but her eyes made her a primitive Greek.

Gertrude asked me to come to 27 rue de Fleurus, where she lived with her brother Leo, the next afternoon, when she would take me for a walk. I was late by half an hour, and Gertrude had not her smiling countenance of the day before. She was a vengeful goddess: "I am not accustomed to wait!" After she had paced for some time, she stood in front of me and a smile had broken through the gloom and she laughed again from her brooch. Then Gertrude and I took our first walk in the nearby Luxembourg Gardens, and then she said I should dine with her and her brother Leo on Saturday and meet the painters who would come later in the evening.

When I arrived—on time—Leo opened the door, not that I would have recognized him by his resemblance to Gertrude. He had a beautiful springing step and carried his tall body with incomparable grace. He at this time *(an ominous qualifier)* was amiable. Then there was a violent knock on the studio door and, "dinner is ready," from Hélène. She was one of those admirable cooks thoroughly occupied with the welfare of their employers and of themselves, firmly convinced that everything purchasable was far too dear. I was taken to the small dining room lined with books, on the only free space, the doors, were tacked up a few drawings by Picasso and Matisse. "It's funny the Picassos have not come," said they all, "however we won't wait, at least Hélène won't wait." We had just finished the first course when Pablo and Fernande as everybody called them walked in. He, very dark with black hair, a lock hanging over one of his marvelous all-seeing eyes, small, quick moving but not restless, his eyes having that strange faculty of opening wide and drinking in what he wished to see. He had the isolation and movement of a bull-fighter at the head of their procession. "I am very upset," said Pablo, "you know how as a Spaniard I would want to be on time, how I am never late." "Well here you are anyway," said Gertrude, "since it's you Hélène won't mind." I was next to Picasso who was silent and then gradually became peaceful. After a little while I murmured to Picasso that I liked his portrait of Gertrude Stein. "Yes," he said, "everybody says that she does not look like it but that does not make any difference, she will."

27 rue de Fleurus consisted of a tiny house of two stories, and a very large atelier adjoining. One rang the bell of the house or knocked at the door of the atelier, and a great many people did

both, but more knocked at the atelier on Saturday evening
when everybody came, and indeed everybody did come. And
on all the white-washed walls right up to the very high ceiling
were pictures so strange that one quite instinctively looked at
anything rather than at them just at first. It is very difficult now
that everybody is accustomed to everything to give some idea of
the kind of uneasiness one felt when one first looked at all these
pictures. In those days there was a great deal of Renoir, there
were two Gauguins, there were Manguin, there was a Toulouse-
Lautrec. Once about this time Picasso looking at this and
greatly daring said, "but all the same I do paint better than he
did." Toulouse-Lautrec had been the most important of his early
influences. There was a portrait of Gertrude Stein by Valloton
that might have been a David but was not, there was a Maurice
Denis, a little Daumier, there was in short everything, there was
even a little Delacroix and a moderate sized El Greco. There
were enormous Picassos of the harlequin period, there were
two rows of Matisses, there was a big portrait of a woman by
Cézanne and some little Cézannes. Now I was confused and
I looked and I looked and I was confused. Gertrude and her
brother Leo were so accustomed to this state of mind in a guest
that they paid no attention to it. From time to time one heard
the high Spanish whinnying laugh of Picasso, the gay contralto
outbreak of Gertrude Stein, people came and went, in and out.

Gertrude called me and said she wanted to have me meet
Matisse. He had a very alert although slightly heavy presence
and he seemed to be full of hidden meanings. Hélène did not
like Matisse. She said a Frenchman should not stay unexpectedly to a meal particularly if he asked the servant beforehand
what there was for dinner. She would say, "I will not make an

omelette but fry the eggs. It takes the same number of eggs and the same amount of butter but it shows less respect, and he will understand." "We were talking," Gertrude said, "of a lunch party we had in here last year. We had just hung all the pictures and we asked all the painters. You know how painters are, I wanted to make them happy so I placed each one opposite his own picture, and they were happy so happy that we had to send out twice for more bread. Matisse says it is a proof that I am very wicked." Later I was near Picasso, he was standing meditatively. "Do you think," he said, "that I really do look like your President Lincoln?" I had thought a good many things that evening but I had not thought that. The winter commenced gaily, and in this way my new full life began.

Gertrude was correcting the last proofs of *Three Lives* and working on her monumental book, *The Making Of Americans*. It was very exciting, more exciting than anything else had ever been. Even, I said to her laughing, more exciting than Picasso's pictures promise to be. Picasso had finished his portrait of her which nobody at that time liked except the painter and the painted and which is now so famous, and he had just begun his strange complicated picture of *Three Women*. Matisse had just finished his *Bonheur de Vivre*. It was the moment Max Jacob called the heroic age of cubism. I remember Picasso and Gertrude talking about various things that had happened at that time, and one of them said, "but all that could not have happened in that one year." "Oh," said the other, "my dear you forget we were young then and we did a great deal in a year."

Gertrude during this winter diagnosed me as an old maid mermaid which I resented, the old maid was bad enough but the mermaid was quite unbearable. *(The next sentence, and some of what follows in this paragraph ought to be as hilariously apologetic as it is coyly metaphoric, and then as climactic emotionally as it is geographic—to act, first, as a kind of comic relief and, second, as a prelude to the succeeding love scene.)* But by the time the buttercups were in bloom, the old maid mermaid had gone into oblivion and I had been gathering wild violets. When winter passed, it grew hot, then sultry. Gertrude and her brothers had rented the large Villa Ricci at Fiesole, and we went down by train to Florence. Because of the intense heat I got rid of my cherry-colored corset in the dressing room of the train, throwing it out the window. From Florence Gertrude and I had some unforgettable walks to the mountain tops. One blistering hot day the climb commenced gradually but grew rough, and we slipped on the dry earth. Gertrude took off her sandals, advising me to do the same, and we walked and walked for hours. I gradually undressed, in those days one wore many more clothes than one does now. The sun was giving a torrid heat, so under some bushes I discarded my silk combination and stockings, but even so I dropped a few tears before we arrived. And we did arrive. The higher we climbed the finer the view of the valley below became. On the top we were in clouds.

(She pauses here, remembering. There is piano music from the adjacent flat under this scene. She picks up one of the Italian leather folders and half-recites, half-reads fragments of their conversation from the manuscript, dramatizing them without embarrassment and being deeply moved by the memory, interspersing comments. Gertrude Stein speaks first.)

"I have been very happy to-day. I inhabit a warm country."

I said, And so do I.

"And I inhabit a country in which the heat is so great that probably you would not care to walk about in the heat of the day."

That is quite true.

"As for me, I prefer such heat. And where do we permit ourselves to declare our fond affection."

I said, Here.

And Gertrude said, "Care for me.   *(Ideally, the audience will not know which of the two women speaks the next five sentences.)*   I care for you in every possible way. When all is said one is wedded to bed. Pet me tenderly and save me from alarm. I hear you praise me and I say thanks for yesterday and to-day. And tomorrow we do not doubt. She came and saw and seeing cried I am your bride. And I said, I understand the language. My darling wife may all that's good in life be yours to-day and lasting happiness be yours that shall not pass away. And as the years roll around all gladness may you find and every hour be brighter than the one you leave behind."

(Tenderly, with the whisper of a laugh)   We were so wifely. *(She starts to close the folder, then decides to share a little more of it.)* Gertrude said, "I see you and you see me I reflect you and you reflect me when this you see repeat for me what I repeat when I repeat pleasantly. I am a husband who is very good I have a character that covers me like a hood and must be understood which it is by my wife whom I love with all my life and who makes it understood that she isn't made of wood and that my character which covers me like a hood is very well understood by my wife."   *(Another pause, folder back down on the table, music ceases, a change from reverie to business, efficiently pleasant)*

Our future would be for ourselves alone, and returning to Paris I commenced to teach myself to become an efficient typist and gradually achieved a professional accuracy and speed. *(A joke)*   I got a Gertrude Stein technique, like playing Bach.

My fingers were adapted only to Gertrude's work, and with that I moved over to the rue de Fleurus and then I began to type-write *The Making Of Americans.* Doing the typing was a very happy time for me. I always say that you cannot tell what a picture really is or what an object really is until you dust it every day and you cannot tell what a book is until you type it or proof-read it. It then does something to you that only reading never does.

(Modestly proud)   I am a pretty good secretary and a pretty good editor   *(an afterthought)*   and an extremely good five minute cook. Before coming to Paris I was interested in food but not in doing any cooking. Gertrude said we would have American food for Sunday evening supper; the servant would be out and I should have the kitchen to myself. So I commenced to cook the simple dishes I had eaten in California and gradually my repertoire expanded as I grew experimental and adventurous.

One day when Picasso was to lunch with us I decorated a striped bass in a way that I thought would amuse him and cooked it according to a theory of my grandmother who had no experience in cooking and who rarely saw her kitchen but who contended that a fish having lived its life in water, once caught, should have no further contact with the element in which it had been born and raised. So I made a *court-bouillon* and the fish poached for twenty minutes, then using a pastry tube I deco-rated it with a red mayonnaise, not colored with catsup—hor-ror of horrors—but tomato paste. Then I made a design with sieved hard-boiled eggs, the whites and yolks apart, with truf-fles and with finely chopped *fines herbs.* I was proud of my chef d'oeuvre when it was served and Picasso exclaimed at its beauty.

But, said he, should it not rather have been made in honor of Matisse than of me?

One Sunday evening Gertrude *(she picks up a book)* came in much excited and would not sit down. "Here I want to show you something," she said. I can still see the little tiny pages of the notebook written forward and back. It was the portrait called "Ada"—about me: "She came to be happier than anybody else who was living then. She was telling some one, who was loving every story that was charming. Some one who was living was almost always listening. Some one who was loving was almost always listening. That one who was loving was almost always listening. That one who was loving was telling about being one then listening. Ada was then one and all her living then one completely telling stories that were charming, completely listening to stories having a beginning and a middle and an ending. Trembling was all living, living was all loving *(the crux of the passage)*, some one was then the other one. Certainly this one was loving this Ada then. And certainly Ada all her living then was happier in living than any one else who ever could, who was, who is, who ever will be living." This was the beginning of the long series of Gertrude's word portraits.

One evening Leo took Picasso into his studio. *(Furious but faint scales from the piano here)* When he released him Picasso came in furious, saying, "It was he who said my drawings were more important than Raphael's. Why can he not leave me alone then with what I am doing now?" Leo was quite as disturbed as Picasso and slammed the door between the two rooms. This was the beginning of the trouble between Leo and Gertrude concerning Picasso's painting and her writing. When Leo came in to explain further, she dropped books on the floor to interrupt him. Gertrude said, "Brother brother go away and stay." He had become unreasonable and unbearable. The following summer, Leo decided to move to Italy. She put him and the deep unhappiness he had caused her so completely out of her mind that finally he and it no longer existed. She had purged him and the whole miserable time he had given her. *(Scales out here)* But it is too easy to dispose of Leo. He was as timely as a street vendor, a liberal leader by nature. If he had been English he would have been on the *Manchester Guardian*. "Gertrude hungers and thirsts for glory," he said. "I cannot abide her stuff and think it abominable." He was amongst the majority—the commonplace majority as Gertrude called him—of the sad and mistaken. *(She picks up a file folder, shakes her head wistfully, puts it down and picks up another, removes some letters and reads them, one after the other.)*

"Dear Miss Stein, we hardly see our way clear to making you any offer of publication. The book is too unconventional."

"Dear Madam, I have only read through a portion of the manuscript, because I found it perfectly useless to read further, as I did not understand any of it. I have to confess to being as stupid and as ignorant as all the other readers to whom the book has been submitted."

"Dear Madam, I am only one, only one, only one. Only one being, one at the same time. Not two, not three, only one. Only one life to live, only sixty minutes in one hour. Only one pair of eyes. Only one brain. Only one being. Being only one, having only one pair of eyes, having only one time, having only one life, I cannot read your manuscript three or four times. Not even one time. Only one look only one look is enough. Hardly one copy would sell here. Hardly one. Hardly one. Many thanks. I am returning the manuscript by registered post. Only one manuscript by one post."

(When the audience laughs at this, she looks up, hurt, and speaks sharply.)   The letters are amusing now. They weren't in a bit when they were written. The refusals from editors prevented those days from being joyous. It was a long and bitter time. From 1907 until 1933 it was a constant torment.

We had been advised to go to London and see publishers about Gertrude's work. One night we met Alfred North Whitehead. He had a most benign sweet smile and a simplicity that comes only in geniuses. He was my third genius for whom the bell rang. I may say that only three times in my life have I met a genius and each time a bell within me rang and I was not mistaken, and I may say in each case it was before there was any general recognition of the quality of genius in them. The three geniuses are Gertrude Stein, Pablo Picasso, and Alfred Whitehead. He and Mrs. Whitehead asked us to visit them at their country home the next weekend. Little did we know that the weekend would extend well into the next month. War was declared. When the Germans were finally stopped at the Marne the future was not as terrifying as it had been. At last we went up to London to get our papers to cross the Channel. A secretary at the embassy said, "Will you stand up please and swear loyalty to your country." I said enthusiastically, Oh, I would love to.

We came back to an entirely different Paris and decided to get into some war work. One day there was a Ford car being backed up the street by an American girl and on the car it said, American Fund for French Wounded. There, said I, that is what we are going to do. At least, said I to Gertrude, you will drive the car and I will do the rest. Gertrude wrote to her cousin in Baltimore and in a few months a Ford car came, transformed into something that resembled a second-class hearse, and called

Auntie after Gertrude's Aunt Pauline who always behaved admirably in emergencies and behaved fairly well most times if she was properly flattered. At the headquarters of the American Fund for French Wounded they sent us off to deliver supplies—all over France.

One time, I was sure that we were on the wrong road and wanted to turn back. "Wrong or right," said Gertrude Stein, "we are going on." She could not back the car very successfully and indeed I may say even to this day when she can drive any kind of a car anywhere she still does not back a car very well. She goes forward admirably, she does not go backwards successfully. *(She catches herself suddenly over the verbs and tears blind her briefly.)* Went. *Went* forward. *Did* not go—backwards.

Soon the American army came, and then came the armistice. Very shortly after, Auntie went her honorable way to old age and was succeeded by another little Ford, called Godiva because she had come naked into the world. There was nothing on her dashboard, neither clock nor ashbox nor cigarette lighter, until friends gave us something with which to bedeck her.

Paris, like us, was sadder than when we left it. The old crowd had disappeared. Matisse was now permanently in Nice and in any case although Gertrude and he were perfectly good friends when they met, they practically never met. This was the time when Gertrude and Picasso were not seeing each other. They always talked with the tenderest friendship about each other to any one who had known them both but they did not see each other. It was a period that Gertrude called "Of Having For A Long time Not Continued To Be Friends." But then the writers came.

Gertrude Stein in those days was a little bitter, all her unpublished manuscripts, and no hope of publication or serious recognition. Henry McBride was an art critic in those tormented years. "Laugh if you like," he said to her detractors, "but laugh with her and not at her." Henry McBride did not believe in worldly success. "It ruins you, it ruins you," he used to say. "But Henry," Gertrude used to answer dolefully, "don't you think I will ever have any success, I would like to have a little you know."

Sherwood Anderson came and quite simply and directly as is his way told her what he thought of her work and what it had meant to him in his development and he told it in print immediately after. Sherwood Anderson had a winning brusquerie, a mordant wit and an all-inclusive heart—the combination was irresistible.

In those days you met anybody anywhere.   *(A happy recollection)*   Man Ray, who looked like an Indian potentate in miniature. Jean Cocteau, who prided himself on being eternally thirty. Tristan Tzara. Marcel Duchamp. Glenway Wescott *(a pause, followed by a baleful assessment)*.   But Glenway Wescott at no time interested Gertrude Stein. He has a certain syrup, but it does not pour.

Carl Van Vechten of course we had known since before the war. It was on all sides love at first sight and the beginning of a long rare friendship, indescribable loyalty on his side, complete dependence on Gertrude's side. In season and out he kept her name and her work before the public. We called him   *(a nostalgic joke)*   Papa Woojums. He had a delightful habit of giving letters of introduction to people who he thought would amuse Gertrude. He sent us Paul Robeson. We gave them a party, and Robeson sang several spirituals. A little Southern American woman asked Robeson, "You are from the South, are you not?" "Oh no," said Robeson, "I was born and raised in New Jersey." "What a pity," said she. "Not for me," said Robeson.

Later, when Gertrude went to tea, Sylvia Beach asked her if she would come across the room and speak to James Joyce—his eyes were very bad—which of course she did. They said how do you do to each other and she said to him, "After all these years." He said, "Yes, and our names are always linked together." She said, "We live in the same neighborhood." And he said nothing. And that was all they had to say to each other, they could not think of anything more to say.

When Ernest Hemingway came to Paris, Sherwood Anderson gave him letters of introduction. He was an extraordinarily good-looking young man, twenty-three years old, rather foreign-looking, with passionately interested, rather than interesting eyes. He sat in front of Gertrude and listened and looked. "Begin over again and concentrate," she said. One day I heard her say, "Hemingway, after all you are ninety per cent Rotarian."

"Can't you," he said, "make it eighty percent." "No," said she regretfully, "I can't." The next time Sherwood Anderson was in Paris they often talked about him. Hemingway had been formed by the two of them and they were both a little proud and a little ashamed of the work of their minds. And then they both agreed that they had a weakness for Hemingway because he was such a good pupil. He is a rotten pupil, I protested. "You don't understand," they both said, "he takes training and anybody who takes training is a favorite pupil." And that is Hemingway, he looks like a modern and he smells of the museums.

Scott Fitzgerald, the first of the lost generation as Gertrude called them, was brought to us in Paris by Hemingway, and Sylvia Beach from time to time brought groups of young writers. It was at that time we met Ezra Pound, he talked about Japanese prints among other things. Gertrude said he was a village explainer, excellent if you were a village but if not, not. Ezra also talked about T. S. Eliot. Gertrude was not particularly anxious to meet T. S. Eliot, but we all insisted she should and she gave a doubtful yes. Eliot and Gertrude had a solemn conversation. He said, "Can you tell me, Miss Stein, what authority you have for so frequently using the split infinitive?" "Henry James," said Gertrude. Eliot said he would very much like to have an article by Gertrude for his literary journal. "Yes?" said Gertrude. "But," said Eliot, "it must be your very latest thing." That evening Gertrude wrote a portrait of T. S. Eliot which she called "The Fifteenth of November," that being this day so there could be no doubt but that it was her latest thing.

But to come back to Ezra. He met Gertrude one day near the Luxembourg Gardens and said, "But I do want to come to see you." "I am so sorry," answered Gertrude, "but Miss Toklas has a bad tooth and we are gathering wild flowers." All of which was literally true, but it upset Ezra, and we never saw him again.

Edith Sitwell came to see Gertrude and said that she should come to England to lecture at Cambridge. Then came an invitation from Oxford as well. Gertrude was very upset at the prospect, peace, she said, had greater terrors than war. She was somewhat disturbed about reading her lecture and asked various people what she should do. A very charming professor said, "Read as quickly as you can, never look up, use a low voice." Another acquaintance said, "Speak as slowly as you can, as loudly as you can, and never look down." At Cambridge Ger-

trude had a quiet and intense audience. After the lecture the
men asked a great many questions. The women said nothing.
Gertrude wondered whether they were supposed not to or just
did not. Oxford was very exciting. The attentive audience
became lively and amused after the lecture. Up jumped one
man to ask a question. Then another man, next to him, jumped
up and asked something else. Then the first man jumped up and
said, "You say that everything being the same, everything is
always different, how can that be so?" "Consider," she replied,
"the two of you, you jump up one after the other, that is the
same thing and surely you admit that the two of you are always
different." "Touché," he said. The Sitwells wanted us to extend
our English stay but Gertrude felt that she had had enough of
glory and excitement. Not that she could ever have enough of
glory.   *(Smugly)*   After all, as she always contends, no artist
needs criticism, he only needs appreciation. If he needs criticism, he is no artist.   *(Another sharp pause over the verb tense,
despair, perhaps tears)*   Contended. As she always *contended.*

   *(Another deliberate change of subject. She lights yet another cigarette;
indeed, she should almost chain smoke, lighting a fresh one with the butt
of another now and then.)*

   Godiva, our two-seated runabout, had been taking us successfully to places in the neighborhood of Paris. It was time to give
her a wider field. In early spring she would lead us down the
Rhône Valley to a small town on a hillside with varied landscapes on all sides. Belley is its name and Belley is its nature.
We took a walk around the outside of the town and were
enchanted. The next morning we drove in Godiva in all directions. The country was beautiful and diversified. It was too
good to be true. Before the end of the summer we realized that

we must either buy or rent a house somewhere in the country near Belley. But there were no houses that we would have moved into. We were miserable until one afternoon we glimpsed the perfect house in the village of Bilignin— from across the valley.

Gertrude said, "I will drive you up there and you can go and tell them that we will take their house."

I said, But it may not be for rent.

She said, "The curtains are floating out the windows."

Well, I said, I think that proves someone is living there. It was let to an officer in the garrison at Belley. How did one dislodge a tenant without a legal reason? The owner of the house considered us quite mad, but he told us that his tenant was only a captain because there were already too many majors in the battalion. That was enough to inspire us. We would get two influential friends in Paris to have him promoted, he would be ordered to another garrison, and the house would be free for us. Soon we were ecstatically tenants of a house which we had never seen nearer than two miles away. In spring we drove down to Bilignin with a white poodle pup—Basket—to find the house better than our dreams of it.

For fourteen successive years the gardens at Bilignin were my joy, working in them during the summers and planning and dreaming of them during the winters. The summers frequently commenced early in April with the planting, and ended late in October with the last gathering of the winter vegetables. It took me several years to know the climate and quite as many more to know the weather. Experience is never at a bargain price. In a corner a snake's nest had been found, but so were raspberries and strawberries. The work in the vegetables—Gertrude was undertaking for the moment the care of the flowers and box hedges—was a full-time job and more. Later it became a joke. Gertrude asked me what I saw when I closed my eyes and I answered, Weeds. The first gathering of the garden in May of salads, radishes and herbs made me feel like a mother about her baby—how could anything so beautiful be mine. There is nothing that is comparable to it, as satisfactory or as thrilling.

When we came to Bilignin there was a fine old laurel tree. The laurel was a constant delight. A bouquet of laurel leaves was always in the bedroom of our young guests, writers and painters and occasionally musicians, as a symbol of a future wreath. None of them remarked the leaves. We received numerous visitors in the country, amongst them Carl Van Vechten and Henry McBride and Bernard Faÿ—"always stimulating and comforting," Gertrude said of him—and Picasso and Virgil Thomson, who had put a number of Gertrude's things to music. He used to dream at night that there was something there that he did not understand, but on the whole he was very well content with that which he did understand.

But those years were a nightmare—Gertrude so desperately wanted the endless manuscripts published. And so I now myself began to think about publishing the work of Gertrude Stein. I asked her to invent a name for my edition and she laughed and said *(as if to say, "plain old edition," with the accent on "edition")*, "Call it Plain Edition." And Plain Edition it was. She sold the beautiful Picasso painting of the girl with a fan held in the air, which quite broke my heart. And then when she told Picasso it made me cry. But it made it possible to publish the Plain Edition. Our first volume was badly printed and I complained bitterly, saying, Look how badly the pages fit together. The printer said to me, "What can you expect, madame? It is machine made, it is not done by hand." But I did not want these books expensive. After all, Gertrude Stein's readers were writers, university students, librarians, and young people who had very little money. Gertrude wants readers not collectors, she wants her books read not owned. *(Another break over the verbs, another cigarette to ward off despair)* *Wanted* readers, *wanted* her books read.

Many people had been asking Gertrude to write her autobiography and she had always replied, "Not possibly." She began to tease me and say that I should write my autobiography. "Just think," she would say, "what a lot of money you would make." She then began to invent titles for my autobiography. "My Life With The Great." "Wives Of Geniuses I Have Sat With." "My Twenty-five Years With Gertrude Stein." I am a pretty good housekeeper and a pretty good gardener and a pretty good needlewoman and *(for the next two categories she makes clear to the audience that she knows she is repeating something she has already said)* a pretty good secretary and a pretty good editor and a pretty good vet for dogs and I had to do them all at once and I found it difficult to add being a pretty good author. Gertrude said, "It does not look to me as if you were ever going to write that autobiography. You know what I am going to do. I am going to write it for you. I am going to write it as simply as Defoe did the autobiography of Robinson Crusoe." And she did *(holding up a book from the stack on the table)*: *The Autobiography of Alice B. Toklas*—by Gertrude Stein: a best seller in 1933.

In 1934 it was suggested by a lecture bureau that Gertrude should go to America. Bernard Faÿ said to me, "Won't the persistence of the population in wanting to speak to Gertrude Stein annoy her?" *(Dismissively, but as a joke)* No, I said, to her it will be exactly like the country neighbors at Bilignin.

Crossing on the S.S. Champlain we landed in the bay of New

York, quickly recognizing the skyscrapers and gradually finding ourselves next to friends on the dock. At Times Square I saw electric lights revolving. They said, "Gertrude Stein has arrived in New York, Gertrude Stein has arrived in New York." As if we didn't know.

Long before, Virgil Thomson had asked Gertrude to write an opera for him, and it was to be in Chicago that Gertrude and I would see for the first time *Four Saints In Three Acts* *(then, as a delighted afterthought)* —about Saint Theresa, with, uh, twenty-seven saints and four acts. We were enchanted. Virgil Thomson's music and the stage settings were so beautiful. After a perfect performance, Bobsie Goodspeed gave a supper party and had us meet the people who were in charge of the lectures. She was interested not only in painting but in music and in the ballet, an interest her husband did not share, so that one evening when a party was lasting quite late he suddenly appeared in his pajamas and said, "It's time for you all to go home."

Back in New York we picked up Carl Van Vechten who was going to Richmond with us on the lecture tour. At an epicurean dinner I was paralysed to find myself next to the novelist James Branch Cabell who asked me, "Is Gertrude Stein serious?" Desperately, I replied. "That puts a different light on it," he said. For you, I said, not for me.

And then— *(a hasty list)* lectures in Virginia, Ohio, Nebraska, Minnesota, Connecticut, Christmas with the Fitzgeralds in Baltimore, tea with Mrs. Roosevelt at the White House, a seminar back in Chicago with Thornton Wilder who for so many years retained a place in our hearts, dinner with Charlie Chaplin and Dashiell Hammett, North Carolina, South Carolina, Louisiana, Texas, all by air. *(An afterthought)* Has food on American planes improved? It has not in Europe, it is incredibly bad, even worse than on trains. Do they cook these meals in the locomotive and in the fuselage?

And then we were off to California—God's country. It was even more so than I remembered it. A great part of the United States that we had seen had been new to me, it was a revelation of the beauty of our country, but California was unequaled. It was abundantly satisfying. Coming back to San Francisco was exciting and disturbing. It was all so different, and still quite like it had been. In the lecture hall, an endless number of familiar faces bowed and waved their hands to me. After the lecture, one of them said to me, "You know we were tremendously fond of your father, your mother was an angel, and you are very dear to us." I noted the descending order.

This was the beginning of the end of our American visit. It was not until we were on the Champlain again that I realized that the seven months we had spent in the United States had been an experience and adventure which nothing that might follow would ever equal.

After returning to Paris we discovered we would have to move from the rue de Fleurus. The landlord was giving our flat as a present to his son, who was marrying. We thought it would be difficult to leave but it was not and when we found this apartment we were thrilled. Gertrude blew her fuse at least once a day and I completely lost my temper and succeeded in getting what we must have from recalcitrant gas companies and from gentle but obstinate carpenters. So we moved into 5 rue Christine and continued to alternate between Paris and Bilignin with rumors of war, of course, flying.

When war was declared Gertrude wheedled a military pass to

come up to Paris so that we might protect the pictures against concussion and get some papers and our passports. We soon found that wall space was four times larger than floor space, so the idea of putting the pictures on the floor was abandoned. The passports were so safely put away that they were not to be found, but in hunting for them our poodle's pedigree turned up and I put it in my bag. Later the authorities gave a ration to pedigree dogs and Basket was not too badly nourished during the years of restriction. *(An afterthought)* Oh, it's Basket the Second. Poor old Basket died in 1938 and in 1939 a new baby Basket came to us. Basket? Basket! *(She leaves the stage briefly and returns with Basket II.)* We took Cézanne's portrait of Madame Cézanne and Picasso's portrait of Gertrude Stein and returned immediately to Bilignin. As—Jews, and, later, as—enemy nationals, there was always a possible danger one refused to face, but Bernard Faÿ said he persuaded Marshall Petain to direct the Prefet and Sous-Prefet in Belley to help us, watch over us. Bernard was a friend of Petain, not of Vichy or heaven forbid of the Germans, but later he was imprisoned as a collaborator. *(A sad pause and reflection)*

In the beginning, like camels, we lived on our past. We had been well nourished and we didn't feel hungry until some weeks after strict rationing had been enforced. The meat allowance of a quarter of a pound a week per person was not altogether satisfying, but the Rhône River nearby supplied us with salmon trout. From the gardens we had quantities of all kinds of vegetables and fruits of an excellent quality, in the wine cellars a delicious dry white wine. We were really very well off. What was lacking was milk, butter and eggs. There was an infinitesimal amount of these on our ration cards, but by the time the Ger-

mans had collected their requisitioning there was nothing left
to distribute. Friends would come out to have a cup of real
China tea with us. Hospitality consisted in two cups of tea
without sugar, milk or lemon, and one cigarette. Gertrude had
bought for me all the American cigarettes she could find. If they
weren't nourishing, they certainly acted as a stimulant at this
time. Six months were to pass before the blessed black market
was organized. It is not with money that one buys on the black
market but with one's personality. Gertrude when no one else
did would return from a walk with an egg, a pound of white
flour, a bit of butter.

Then the Americans came into the war, and we were ejected
from our home in Bilignin. The French army had been dissolved, and the landlord—a military man—had no other place
to put his family. The Sous-Prefet told our lawyer, "Tell these
ladies that they must leave at once for Switzerland, tomorrow if
possible, otherwise they will be put in a concentration camp."

Gertrude said, "But how can we go, as the frontier is closed."

"That," he said, "could be arranged."

"You mean pass by fraud," she said.

"Yes," he said, "it could be arranged."

"No," Gertrude said, "I am not going, we are not going, it
is better to go regularly wherever we are sent than to go irregu-
larly where nobody can help us if we are in trouble. Here we are
and here we stay."

Friends found us another house, near Culoz, farther up the
Rhône. And—a German regulation requiring our names to be
registered in the village files was winked at by friendly French
officials.

With the house went a very fine cook who announced at once

that she could not cook with the scanty materials the coupons allowed. She was too discouraged to pay attention when I tried to show her how to make a restricted meat loaf with one cup chopped veal, three cups of breadcrumbs soaked in dry white wine (glory be for the inexhaustible provision of it), pepper, basil, tarragon, chervil, parsley, bay leaf, onions, shallots, and one treasured egg. In the village two of the shopkeepers said it was their patriotic duty to sell what the Germans forbade. In which case was it not mine to purchase what they offered? The country boys went down to the Rhône and fished clandestinely. They not only brought us fish but flour, lard, nuts in small quantities and an occasional hare or rabbit. But late in 1943, feeling we could no longer impose on friends, we made a dangerous journey to the Swiss frontier where we met a Swiss art dealer and sold him the Cézanne portrait. Thus were we able to survive the last year of the Occupation and the first year of the Liberation. At dinner one day a visitor remarked the absence of Madame Cézanne from the wall. We are eating her, I confessed.

Suddenly we had Germans billeted upon us. Two officers and two soldiers. One day an orderly gave the cook a tin of their substitute for bread and potatoes. She in turn gave it to our most treasured possessions, four hens. They ran eagerly toward it, pecked at it and walked away. When the Germans left, then came some Italians, two officers and thirty soldiers were billeted upon us. Presently the soldiers were selling me on the black market such cigarettes as they could spare, a most welcome relief. I had been smoking something called garden tobacco. We smoked anything we could roll except fig leaves, which had poisoned a friend. The Italian tobacco was agreeable, convenient and plentiful; our young maid found the soldiers equally so. Then, when news reached the Italians that their country had surrendered, they tore up their military papers. There were about six hundred Italian soldiers in the neighbourhood and the frontier was only 125 kilometers away. We hoped they would cross it safely. Later we heard that they have all been killed by the Germans.

Events were precipitating themselves in the happiest confusion. The northern landing had taken place. The Germans knew we knew. Discretion was thrown to the winds. We thought we heard someone singing *Le Marseillaise*. That afternoon over a hundred Germans were billeted upon us. The officers' dogs were roving about the house as their nags and donkeys were roaming in the flower beds. The next morning they killed a calf on the terrace nearest the house and cooked it on an improvised spit. In the afternoon they left, helping themselves to our small supplies and souvenirs.

But within six weeks the southern landing had taken place. We were jubilant. *(In relating the rest of this paragraph she is markedly ambivalent, hesitant, alternately delighted and appalled, and in the end deeply disturbed by her own words.)* The Resistance had not only disrupted the railroad tracks but had blown up the main highway in several places. When we heard over the radio that Paris was liberated we were wild with excitement. The end was near. So the boys of the Resistance came down quietly from their mountain top one morning, drove the seven hundred Germans from Culoz and the neighborhood into the marshes, surrounded them, and wiped them out. It was glorious, classic, almost Biblical. *(A long embarrassed pause)*

Life after the Liberation became busier than it had ever been. *(Now chatty and amused)* Gertrude and I toured Germany for several days in an American bomber. We also went to Belgium where Gertrude spoke to the American soldiers stationed there. Our home again became a salon. There were almost constant visits from American G.I.s who had come up to Paris "to see the Eiffel Tower and Gertrude Stein," Thornton Wilder said. Once a soldier said to Gertrude, "It is all very well for you to sit comfortably in your nice flat and advise us to go home and pioneer in some new field. Advice from an armchair isn't convincing." *(Kindly but proudly)* "I think," she answered him, "I have given proof of having accepted the pioneer's hardships." *(Now a pause. She starts to speak, stops herself. She picks up from the table the piece of stationery—the text of her telegram—with which she first entered. This will be difficult to say.)*

Suddenly, in April, Gertrude was *(how can she say "ill" without saying "ill"?)* no longer well, and the doctor thought her illness might become grave. But she went on as usual. She even bought herself a little car, but on the road she was taken ill. At an inn they gave us a room and sent for a doctor who said, "Your friend will have to be cared for by a specialist, and at once. An operation." *(She glances at the telegram message, then away, then starts to read it and gets no farther than the date.)* 27 July 1946.

At the hospital Gertrude was in a sad state of indecision and worry. *(She is haunted.)* She said, "What is the question," and I didn't answer thinking she was not completely awakened. Then she said it again. "What is the question" and before I could speak she went on, "If there is no question then there is no answer." *(She stares ahead into a void as the stage darkens.)*

A C T   T W O

5 rue Christine, September 1946–May 1963

The set has not been markedly altered, although a small gray file box is now on the table, and a flowered slipcover has been put over the overstuffed brown satin chair. When the lights come up, the room is as it was. She is standing by the tall windows, looking out. She has just come in from shopping and holds a furled umbrella, a handbag and a market basket filled with fresh vegetables. Basket is on a leash, held in her other hand. In addition to her loosely cut gray suit, she is wearing a fantastic black hat, widebrimmed, with several ostrich plumes rising out of its band. It might be at home on a seventeenth-century cavalier. She shuffles offstage right, stopping just before she gets to the door to address the audience with a sly smile and almost a wink.

But we do love clothes, don't we? *(She exits slowly — it is a heavy load she totes — to leave her hat, bag basket, umbrella, and the dog, and then returns to sit at the table. She dates a letter she has started before going out on errands. Through most of Act Two, despair is replaced by irony, more humor, and — when Gertrude Stein is mentioned — nostalgia. The prevailing tone, however, should be intimate, gossipy from time to time, with frequent deadpan humor if appropriate, and always conversational, never didactic.)*

   September 1946. *(She scans the letter agreeably, wearing glasses as she does whenever she reads anything; then, as if to reinforce it, she begins to read it aloud to the audience. Soon, however, she stops reading and simply talks the letter, minus her glasses. Throughout the act she does this frequently, turning her letters to friends into speech.)* Dearest Papa Woojums, no, Gertrude certainly wanted *everything* published — neither she nor I seemed to think that there was much of the early work unpublished — Baby always concentrated on the present—the continuous present—but she certainly meant everything.

She said it in her will, she said it to me twice—you are to edit the unpublished manuscripts   *(she retrieves a copy of the will from a file folder and reads from it)*:   "I desire my executors"—Gertrude's nephew Allan Stein and me—"to pay Carl Van Vechten such sum of money as is necessary for the publication of my unpublished manuscripts." She told me she had asked you to do it—our Papa Woojums—because she had all confidence in you and in no one else. And the Picasso portrait   *(she looks at it above the mantel a long moment)*   goes to the Metropolitan Museum. And I am to stay on here.

I've just packed up Gertrude's library—it goes to Yale University. It's a deep regret that the rest won't stay together after me. Sometimes I think the objects on the table, the chairs on the rugs, the pictures, will refuse to be separated and will perish when one forces them. Ah, they're after all the things Gertrude touched. But it's a satisfaction to know that books and manuscripts and letters are going to be together at Yale.   *(She whistles for Basket II who does not come, so she goes offstage long enough get him and bring him onstage. He lopes on, then sniffs around or lies down or comes to be petted or whatever occurs to him.)*

Tomorrow an ex-G.I. is calling for me in an ex-jeep to take Basket to the vet's. He has to have something done to what if he were a chicken would go over the fence last. He's such an original dog—who but he would have thought of contracting such an inconvenient malady, happily it is nothing. He will spend the day there and in the evening (the jeep willing) we'll call for him. O, a strange thing happened the other morning, marketing is such a hectic experience—lines for everything from geese to parsley—the street is so filled with us that we hold up private cars by numerical strength. One of the streets we invade leads directly from the Seine to the Senate where the peace conference is going on, so frequently smart limousines try to push their way through. All the market streets and there are four of them know Basket—that is the shopkeepers and stall keepers. New customers discover him joyously—a sheep, a cub! Well, one day I was struggling along when I suddenly realized someone was speaking English. "That's Basket, surely that's Basket." It came from inside a car as it forced its way through—and then very loud, "Is that Basket?" I nodded my head. Once, after the Liberation, we were visiting a hospital for American wounded. I heard a soldier say to the man in the bed next to him, "Do you see that dog, that is Basket. I wish I was as famous as famous as he is."

(The first transition: She simply stops talking to the audience and starts to write another letter, speaking it as she does so, and after the first part of the long first sentence she picks it up as if to read what she has not yet written and sooner or later puts it back down on the desk again and continues, not writing it but speaking it.)

October 1946. It is very sweet of you to order food for me but you really mustn't as we who weathered the Occupation know how to make a little go very far and can therefore with care afford the necessary amount for health through the black market.   *(By this time she is free of the letter and speaks the rest of it to the audience.)*   It has been decided that prayers will be said for Baby in the crypt of the church, where she has rested since her death, with only a few friends present next Tuesday morning at 10 o'clock. Then they will take Baby to Père Lachaise. It is a new separation—it seemed that perhaps in time it would be alright for Baby to be there near the Seine she loved so much. This new separation—this going away again—is very hard, it makes a new pain.

I wish to God we had gone together as I always so fatuously thought we would—a bomb, a shipwreck, just anything but this.

February 1947. Dear Kiddies, I'm always forgetting to tell you that I don't in the least mind typewritten letters. It doesn't happen to be one of my tests of good manners. Once I wrote to another friend, Can it be said with all possible appreciation of the distinction of your handwriting that it is illegible more frequently than not? Does no one say this cruel thing to you? And do you forgive me for doing so? *(Then to the audience)* The old Baronne Pierlot covered pages and pages, she was a great letter writer with a marvelous calligraphy that absolutely no one could decipher. Gertrude once said to her, "Its beauty and its illegibility are quite independent, one upon the other," which made our old friend cackle, but it was too late to be effective. *(The telephone rings. She answers it, pausing at the actor's discretion for responses from the caller.)*

Allo? Oui? Oh, hello, dear. No, the portrait of Gertrude is still here. The president of the bank and the lawyer came over to arrange to take it early next week. So much chichi, and now they want Pablo to sign a paper guaranteeing it to have been painted by him and I just said I wouldn't insult him by asking him and the banker shook his head and said of course anyone can testify to the authenticity of the signature. No answer from me—it isn't signed. Good God, don't they know it's Gertrude by Picasso? I can't bear to think of its not being here. Gertrude always sat on the sofa and the picture hung over the fireplace opposite and I used to say in the old happy days that they looked at each other and that possibly when they were alone they talked to each other. Yes, yes, well, thank you for asking, my dear, thank you. Do come to see me soon. Goodbye, goodbye, my dear.

(She stares at the portrait as it is drawn up out of sight; She has not moved and is still staring, now at the space where the portrait hung.)

Picasso came early and stayed a long time with me alone. He was very sweet, at his very best, and then when he got up to go he said, "Eh bien, neither you nor I will ever see it again." And then he stood in front of it quite a few minutes drinking it in as only his eyes can. And then he saluted it quite seriously, quite simply, and he kissed my hand and said "Au revoir, chéri." After all, the portrait is of their youth, its intensity and theirs are all one. And I missed its going very much.

(She picks up a small stack of mail, riffles through it, selects a letter in some consternation about its likely content, opens it and reads it standing, steadying herself against the table as she fumes silently, then sits again to fire off a hasty reply. Is it possible to convey — simultaneously — her defensiveness, her fear of disclosure, and her anger? She reads the whole letter as she writes it, deliberately and icily.)

June 1947. To Julian Sawyer: as one of Gertrude Stein's defenders, you will understand I hope my objections to your repeated references to the subject of sexuality as an approach to the understanding of Gertrude's work. It should not lead you to other errors. She considered it the least characteristic of all expressions of character.   *(Directly to the audience as she crams the letter into an envelope)*   Gertrude always said she did not like private judgments.   *(She addresses it and stamps it in a fury. Then she selects another letter which puts her in a greater anger, and she tosses the still-sealed envelope aside to pace about the room.)*

The horrid administrator in Baltimore—his name is Edgar

Allan Poe!—is doing everything he can to retard work on the unpublished manuscripts. It's unbearable, unthinkable that what Gertrude wanted is not being done. My efforts become more risky, more hazardous and less successful.

(She calls off stage for her femme de ménage.) Gabrielle! Qu'est-ce qu'il y a? Apportez-le moi le caffe tout de suite! Aussi vit qui possible, s'il vous plaît! Gabrielle! Si'il vous plaît! Gabrielle? Gabrielle! Everybody says it is going to be a cold winter but Gabrielle says "No, not when the onions peel as they do this year." And how do they peel this year, I asked. And she said, "Easily!" In New York you can't predict winter weather by peeling onions because your onions are peeled when you first see them. Since I heard that eggs with two yolks are bought by the dozen there, why shouldn't onions grow peeled? *(Now a revelation)* Which brings me to the question of my cook book. Suddenly it came to me, why not gather my recipes, make a cook book, and get a job? I am a passionate collector of recipes. Perhaps they are not made for American palates or kitchens. To cook as the French do one must respect the quality and flavor of the ingredients. Exaggeration is not admissable. Flavors are not all amalgamative. What is sauce for the goose may be sauce for the gander, but is not necessarily sauce for the chicken, the duck, the turkey, or the guinea hen.

Austerity has gone so far that the population has become submissive through lack of physical resistance. The strikes in the mines have already cut two days electricity a week—which is a bore—but if that is all, one can manage. The only thing that is a temptation is heat. As the winter has been unusually mild and the electrical company mysteriously lenient to me, the room here has been comfortable except for the two days the current is cut. I'm better off than many and am properly grateful, though

a friend from New York, for whom I preheated this room ruin-
ously, wrote to another friend in New York, "What will she do
when it gets cold?"

April 1949. My dears, there isn't much news. It is warm, the
chestnuts are green, and the peach trees in blossom. The rue
Christine indulged in a small excitement the other afternoon
late. Some students—mostly from the Beaux Arts—wanted to
force their way into no. 7, next door—an empty building—
because they could no longer afford the continuously rising
prices in even the little hotels and Gabrielle who is a great gossip rushed to the front door when she first heard the noise and
thereafter naturally every quarter of an hour with more regularity than she bastes a roast. So later the police took a half dozen of
the loudest students to the police station for the night. Gabrielle has been in one continuous state of temper ever since and
Basket and I avoid her as much as we can contrive to. If she
would only retire to the country but no, having achieved Paris
she clings to it.

*(A necessary stroll here, to take in the room and the view from the tall
windows; Basket gets a nuzzle and some petting; she opens or closes a window, as a time transition.)*

The rents are being raised according to a new law which
requires an expert to convince even my most amiable of landla-
dies that the stairs are not carpeted, that seven windows never
see the sun, so that the rent cannot be increased to what she
hopes for. Gabrielle who had been unusually calm and reasonable for two weeks had a rather serious outbreak last night. Gertrude always treated drunken people as if they were sober—so I
use that technique on the unbalanced. However, I do think
Gabrielle is a little overdoing it.

In January 1951, Allan Stein suddenly but not unexpectedly

died. So many of my past anxieties were useless, so many futile efforts to be provident and forethoughtful. I had told my lawyer—after asking him to take a last precaution—that it wasn't really necessary as I intended to outlive Allan. To which he answered me like a stage lawyer, "I hope so, Miss Toklas, I sincerely hope so!"

March 1951. Dearest Papa Woojums, Now about the Yale Fund—let us call it that—for Gertrude's unpublished writings, I have a plan to sell the pictures, but I am waiting for Allan's wife to take the chestnuts out of the fire with their children. As soon as I hear that she has come to terms with them, I will open the subject with my lawyer, then with her as guardian, then with Mr. Poe—et vous voilà—it will then only remain for me to put through my long cherished little dream of selling them en bloc to a museum so that Baby's collection will not be dispersed over the landscape. This is the only thing that Allan's death will have facilitated.

(She riffles through some manuscript pages with a sigh, starts to read a little, picks up a pen to make a correction, grows impatient, shoves them aside. She is frustrated, angry with herself.)

My long projected cook book *has* to materialize. *(She flips the pages impatiently again.)* Years ago when I spoke of it to Thornton Wilder he only said, "But Alice, have you ever tried to write?" Not since I was ten or eleven years old, so perhaps one has to have some experience of writing for even a cook book. But can't one count and build upon conviction, prejudice and passion—my inadequate equipment? *(Diffidently)* I have *sold* a cooking thing that I scrambled together to a magazine. It has been accepted but not paid for yet. I hope they won't forget. Once when I was terribly hard up—after my mother died—I sold a joke for five dollars to a magazine and as our family was witty and amusing I made my plans when I cashed the check to provide the magazine with six per month, far above the average of the one they had accepted. But they never cared for any others. Will cook books be no more enduring than witticisms? Besides, one hasn't at over seventy the same aplomb one has at seventeen.

My best news is that the Yale University Press has accepted —to publish all the unpublished work of Gertrude Stein since it will be underwritten by the Stein Estate, and with enthusiasm. It was more than I had dreamed of. The news came a week ago and has left me limp and overwhelmed—bathed in the light of having beheld a vision. And as a nun said to us on the day of the armistice of 1918, "And to think it was done by human means." *(Basket exits at this point or at any convenient time before the Garbo passage below.)*

It is now ten days since Gabrielle has gone and the second liberation is gradually becoming a convincing fact. The end was so quiet, it made one nervous. There will be extra work for me but I can manage that easily and it will be an economy.

Well, to change to something gay and lively for the cook book. *(She stands to move about; she is no longer writing to a friend but giving directions quickly, even breathlessly, to the audience.)* Pound to a paste as many cloves of garlic as you can stand—in the midi they count two per person or four per yolk of egg—add salt to taste, no pepper or mustard. Pound and stir until it becomes an emulsion, then add olive oil drop by drop. When it begins to become firm add lemon juice. When it is once more firm add a dessert spoon of tepid water, *(dictatorially)* I repeat *tepid* water. *(Conversationally again)* Very few people are indifferent to either the aroma or flavor of garlic. One is affected favorably or unfavorably. It may have been the odor of garlic with which Henry James was greeted when he went to call upon George Eliot for the first time and which he later described as the right odor in the wrong place. Though I had not tasted garlic as a young girl when I read this, it had the alluring *mysterious* quality of the *unknown* for some years after.

Which reminds me that a few nights ago Cecil Beaton and Greta Garbo came in. Cecil very tousled, exhausted and worshipful, Garbo a bit shy, quite Vassarish, unpretentious but very criminal. She asked me with simplicity and frankness, "Did you know Monsieur Vollard, was he a fascinating person, a great charmeur, was he seductive?" She was disappointed like a young girl who dreams of an assignation. Do explain her to me. She was not mysterious but I hadn't the answer. The French papers say Cecil and Garbo are to marry, but she doesn't look as if she would do anything as crassly innocent as that. Expliquez moi, as Picasso used to say to Gertrude.

(She sits again; the next letters are written/spoken in sequence without protracted breaks between.)

January 1952. The winter has been too much for Basket's and my resistance. For two months we huddle and cling to the radiator and each other. You know that he is more to me than a faithful companion and it's all wrong that he should have to go on.

October 1952. Poor sweet old Basket who is blind and deaf now fell off the roof to the roof some twelve feet below and besides the shaking up he got off fortunately. But with the misadventure he lost the little confidence he had, so that he needs someone to stroke him frequently. Isn't it too sad that this is the way he is to end his days?

December 1952. Basket is no more. He ate his lunch, wagged his tail, and collapsed. The flat is emptier than before without him. It is hard to become accustomed to his not being here.

(She looks around the empty room, sighs. After a pause, doubtless another cigarette, an announcement, more or less, to the audience with some enthusiasm.)

The cook book is started and very soon bending over an imaginary stove will keep the temperature a-mounting and a-mounting. As cook to cook I must confide that this book with its mingling of recipe and reminiscence was put together as an escape, and I daresay nostalgia for old days and old ways and for remembered health and enjoyment lent special luster to dishes and menus. *(She begins examining cards from a gray recipe box, selecting or discarding as she proceeds, for what might be included in her cookbook.)* Alice's Cookies; Bavarian Cream Perfect Love; Roast Beef for a Rainy Day; Bird's Nest Pudding; Omelette in an Overcoat; Mutton Chops in Dressing Gowns; Giant Squab in Pajamas; Chicken in Half-Mourning; Truffle Turnovers; Extravagant Mashed Potatoes. *(She is overcome by this one and has to share it, first cheerfully, then defensively, then urgently.)* For four people bake four large potatoes, peel and put through the food mill. While the potatoes are still hot add two cups of butter and one teaspoon salt. Undoubtedly one pound of butter is extravagant but try it once. *(Back to sorting recipes)* Veal with Sauce as Green as a Field; Hare Simmered in Champagne; Cabbage Pancakes; Green Peas à la Goodwife; Gateau Gavotte; The Ribbons of Sarah Bernhardt.

Cook books have always intrigued and seduced me. When I was still a dilettante in the kitchen they held my attention, even the dull ones, from cover to cover, the way crime and murder

stories did Gertrude. When we first began reading Dashiell
Hammett, Gertrude remarked that it was his modern note to
have disposed of his victims before the story commenced. Goodness knows how many were required to follow as a result of the
first crime. And so it is in the kitchen. Murder and sudden
death seem as unnatural there as they should be anywhere else.
They can't, they can never become acceptable facts. Food is far
too pleasant to combine with horror. All the same, facts, even
distasteful facts, must be accepted and we shall see how, before
any story of cooking begins, crime is inevitable. That is why
cooking is not an entirely agreeable pastime.

My first victim was a lively carp brought to the kitchen in a
covered basket from which nothing could escape. The fish man
who sold me the carp said he had no time to kill, scale or clean
it, nor would he tell me with which of these horrible necessities
one began. It wasn't difficult to know which was the most repel-
lent. A heavy sharp knife came to my mind as the classic, the
perfect choice, so grasping, with my left hand well covered with
dishcloth, for the teeth might be sharp, the lower jaw of the
carp, and the knife in my right, I carefully, deliberately found
the base of its vertebral column and plunged the knife in. I let
go my grasp and looked to see what had happened. Horror of
horrors. The carp was dead, killed, assassinated, murdered in
the first, second and third degree. Limp, I fell into a chair, with
my hands still unwashed reached for a cigarette, lighted it, and
waited for the police to come and take me into custody. After a
second cigarette my courage returned and I went to prepare
poor Mr. Carp for the table.

Later, a crate of six white pigeons was left us with a note from
a friend saying she had nothing better to offer us from her home

in the country, ending with, "But as Alice is clever she will make something delicious of them." It is certainly a mistake to allow a reputation for cleverness to be born and spread by loving friends. It is so cheaply acquired and so dearly paid for. Six white pigeons to be smothered, to be plucked, to be cleaned and all this to be accomplished before Gertrude returned, for she didn't like to see work being done. A large cup of strong black coffee made me lively and courageous. I carefully found the spot on the poor innocent dove's throat where I was to press and pressed. The realization had never come to me before that one saw with one's fingertips as well as one's eyes. It was a most unpleasant experience, though as I laid out one by one the sweet young corpses there was no denying one could become accustomed to murdering. Many times I held the thought to kill a stupid or obstinate cook, but as long as the thought was held, murder was not committed.

(At this point, three small frames, ostensibly holding Picasso sketches, rise out of sight, while she busies herself at the table writing letters. She takes no notice of this. Again, three letters in sequence but with no breaks between)

Dearest Louise, About the cook book. You won't think too badly if I throw myself upon you with a thud, will you? The publishers are willing to give me an advance and a contract when 30,000 words are in their hands, and they want 40,000 more. So one chapter will be devoted to recipes from friends. Carl Van Vechten (garlic ice cream) and Carl's wife Fania Marinoff (herb butter); Virgil Thomson (shad roe mousse); Mary Oliver (two dozen plucked larks with rashers of bacon and raw Spanish onions); oh, another from Mary Oliver (cut up one small octopus, dip particles in honey, roll in paprika, plunge in garlic batter, boil in olive oil); Natalie Barney (stuffed eggplant with sugar). May I add your Circassian Chicken and with permission to use your name?

Dear Harold, Your recipes are perfect, precise and seducing, and I thank you more so than I can say for so generously giving them to me for the cook book. *(She puts a few pages on top of a pile of manuscript.)*

Dear Brion Gysin . . . *(A beat. Deliberately, with a sly smile, she picks up an envelope and says with feigned surprise.)* From Brion Gysin! *(She slits it open and reads, with considerable interest, to the audience.)*

"Hashish Fudge. This is the food of Paradise—of Baudelaire's Artificial Paradises: it might provide an entertaining refreshment for a Ladies' Bridge Club or a chapter meeting of the DAR. In Morocco it is thought to be good for warding off the common cold in damp winter weather and is, indeed, more effective if taken with large quantities of hot mint tea. Euphoria and brilliant storms of laughter; ecstatic reveries and extensions of one's personality on several simultaneous planes are to be complacently expected. Almost anything Saint Theresa did, you can do better. Take one teaspoon black peppercorns, one whole nutmeg, four average sticks of cinnamon, one teaspoon coriander. These should all be pulverized in a mortar. About a handful each of stoned dates, dried figs, shelled almonds and peanuts. Chop these and mix them together. A bunch of *cannibus sativa* can be pulverized. This along with the spices should be dusted over the mixed fruit and nuts, kneaded together. About a cup of sugar dissolved in a big pat of butter. Rolled into a cake and cut into pieces or made into balls about the size of a walnut, it should be eaten with care. Two pieces are quite sufficient." *(She registers her approval, puts the page with the rest of the manuscript.)*

The recipe was innocently included without my realizing that the hashish was the accented part. And then I was shocked to find that America wouldn't accept it because it was too dangerous. This was an offense to the American eye and the American thought, and so my publisher wired to Washington and asked the administration if it were possible to use such a recipe, and he got us an answer: "You may do anything you please except eat it. That is forbidden by law. You may grow it, you may manufacture it, but you may not sell it and you may not eat it." So that was that. It didn't go into the American edition. The English are braver. We're not courageous about that sort of thing.

But the sale of the cook book permitted a two months' vacation. In Nice we were surrounded by small villas of retired functionaries. But Antibes was in full sun, windows open to the sea day and night, no mistral, almonds, peaches, and mimosa blossoms, a lovely long day with Picasso, a day in Provence to revisit old cities and alas to revive old memories. Picasso is very sad. Françoise when she left him took their two young children and permits him to see them once a month. He loves children and adores his and it's a very feminine revenge Françoise is taking. He has a new lady. She is a well bred, well educated bourgeoise of about twenty-six with fine eyes but no particular looks. She is in full possession but is it lasting? Is she sampling life with Picasso? Olga is slowly dying in a clinic at Cannes. She says Pablo has been very good to her in every way. Do you remember Picasso's Fernande? She has grown enormous, like several bags of potatoes piled one on top of another, but still retaining vestiges of her old beauty and grand manner.

March 1955.   *(Another letter)*   Thanks for the very original story of Gertrude and Picasso being lovers. If that had been true one could have added incest to the scandal for she really felt herself as an older sister to him—taking him by his lapel and gently shaking him once, I remember, when she was displeased with him to which he responded by kissing her on either cheek. They understood each other in spite of saying dreadful things when they were irritated. Gertrude thought nothing of the poetry he wrote. One evening Salvador Dali came to see Gertrude and after considerable palavering he asked what she thought of Picasso's poetry. And she told him and all the reasons in detail were included. After Dali left she said to me, "Pablo sent him to find out what I did think." Well, when we saw Pablo the next time he pounced on her and said, " Why did you tell Dali what you hadn't told me?" To which Gertrude replied, "You know very well that it is not necessary to explain to an intelligent person, one only explains to a stupid one." Isn't it a deliciously characteristic story of each of them?

(She sorts through some more mail.)   Oh, Knoedler again!   *(She slits open a new piece of mail as she speaks.)*   The Knoedler Gallery in New York wanted—quote—"to borrow a selection from the paintings at 5 rue Christine"—unquote. They wanted all the Picassos and all the Gris. Nor would I accept their invitation to be their guest and—quote—"be at the gallery as often as you can"—unquote. Ça n'est pas dans mes moeurs. So I answered that honoring Baby is one thing and advertising Knoedler another. They are as much an honor to Baby here as chez Knoedler. Then they wrote a letter saying it was getting time to arrange for the autumn show of the pictures. Sly, that. I answered that they had evidently forgotten my last letter. *(Now she reads the new letter aloud in indignation.)*   "Under what

conditions would you consider it?" *(She tears the letter in half, deliberately.)* Do they think the pictures are vegetables and I am a market woman?

(A marked change in the following five letters, preceded by a stroll in lone-liness about the room. Piano music in the next apartment begins and contin-ues under the letters. First, she deliberately runs her hand over the blank spaces on the wall where the three small frames hung and smiles in satisfac-tion. When she returns to the table, she writes/speaks her five letters with a growing serenity.)

April 1956. Dearest Isabel, Thank you for your Easter greet-ings. At the Benedictine monastery at Solesmes, Holy Thursday through Easter morning, the changing of the service was ineffa-bly beautiful and elevating, particularly the midnight mass for the resurrection.

October 1956. My very dear William, Surely what you say moves me like nothing has these last solitary years and in the direction I want you to lead me. Will Saint Anthony find a ray to show me the way to God? Yes, I was baptized a Catholic as a small child with my mother's knowledge. Then I wandered— only the saints remained. *(She picks up a rosary and winds it about one wrist, holding it in her hand for the rest of the play, even when she lights cigarettes.)*

Christmas Day 1957. Dearests, What there is to tell you on this blessed happy day will perhaps surprise you. On the fête of the Immaculate Conception I was admitted to the Catholic Church, confessed and was given Holy Communion. There is everything to learn but with a catechism and a missal I shall make up for lost time, and that is what is such a comfort to me now—the peopled heaven, not only God and Jesus but the angels and *(a great pause that somehow includes Gertrude Stein)* saints. Gertrude had no faith in a future life but reconciled this with her faith in miracles and saints. Her faith in her work and her love for humanity, were they not her religion?

January 1958. Sam dear, When I first went back into the Church I lost Gertrude and then suddenly it was clear. She had been with God all her life, and that brought her back with a radiance I had never known. No, dear, the past is not gone. Nor is Gertrude. Life is everlasting—my confessor has made that clear. It left me in a dither when suddenly it came to me— where was Gertrude. She is there, waiting for us. I pray for you, my dear.

(The music stops, an abrupt change, perhaps preceded by another silent stroll, a cigarette in one hand, a rosary in the other, and now she leans lightly on a cane when she walks about. Indignation is followed by smug complacency in the first paragraph, then chatty gossip to the audience in the next.)

5 rue Christine has been sold to speculators who will sell the flats. The tenants all bought their flats except me. The French law protects aged ladies so I can stay on for the rest of my days. When the owner came to look at it, she said, "You have a great many pictures," and I said, They don't go with the apartment. In the meantime everyone has come to Paris—some amusing, others less so. So many people write or telephone to know more about Gertrude—serious students (good), not so serious and not students at all, undesirables whom I once was fond of who now want sympathy, advice, or just the address of a good hotel in Istanbul, or the address of a school mate, or an autograph of Gertrude's youth. It keeps me busy.

(The telephone rings, she answers it, pausing at the actor's discretion for responses from the caller.) Allo? Oh, it's you! How lovely to— what? Oh, I shan't be able to come. I am going again next week to Aqui in Italy to take the cure. Arthritis is bad. Ten baths in

three groups, one day between three baths (not mud, more like powdered soapy volcanic earth, put on in great slabs, wrapped up in sheets of rubber plastic, very hot and soothing, then bathed to remove the application). The baths will be just as effective as last year and nearly as dull and the weather can be called more suitable for truffles than for humans.   *(A pause while the caller speaks)*   Oh, no, I haven't had time for that. Life is hectic, real and earnest, at least every other day! I had lunch at another restaurant, exhausting, fatiguing, and unhealthy. I burn holes in everything. When I have settled in my convent in Rome— peace and quiet having descended on me—I shall be O.K. *(Another pause)*   Oh, no, they were wonderful at the embassy about the passport. They gave me a fistful of papers to fill out which took all my spare time for three days ("Where are your divorced husbands and nieces and their children by previous marriages"), then I got there with the papers filled and the photographs and the old passport and a man came and asked me to swear allegiance and fidelity (which I haven't had to do since 1914).

(A frame, ostensibly holding Picasso's "Green Still Life," hanging so prominently that its disappearance cannot be missed by the audience, rises out of sight, even as she continues to speak.)

I shall be a paying guest with the nuns of the Adoration of the Sacred Blood, very comfortable and very happy—mass mornings at half after six, benedictions Sundays and holidays. Gertrude said nuns were like birds—they are happy in their faith—and to a certain degree we share it with them. If I were sixty years younger I would want to enter their order. Well— I must fly. Thank you, my dear, for thinking of me. I shall ring you when I return. Yes, I promise. Goodbye.

(It is important that she come down very hard on the next date. She then

walks forward toward the front of the stage and stays there to speak this let-
ter and the succeeding one.)

June 1960. Dear Bernard, At once let me apologize for illegibility. Writing is done by feeling not by sight. *(She turns*
around to look at the paintings as she speaks; by the end of the passage she is
facing front again and does not look back.) Mrs. Allan Stein is threatening to appoint a legal guardian for the pictures and to avoid
insurance to lend them to a museum. It is a nuisance but my
nice lawyer, Russell Porter, will do what he can.

(She stands perfectly still. All of the remaining frames rise out of sight,
all at the same time. She does not move; she does not look at the bare
walls.)

June 1961. *(Again coming down hard on the date and still facing*
front) You must know the shocking news that greeted my
entrance to the flat after my long winter in Rome. The walls
were bare—not one Picasso left. The children of Allan Stein
want the pictures adequately insured which of course I could
not do. And now they are in the vault of the Chase Manhattan
Bank here in Paris, until my death. *(She returns to the table, rif-*
fling some papers.) From Rome I had written to my lawyer six
months ago, in January *(retrieving a copy to read):* It is unfortu-
nate for me that Mr. Edgar Allan Poe should have left so long a
time to lapse before acting upon the will of Gertrude Stein.
(She fumbles about the desk in search of the will, finds it, and reads from
it.) "My Estate I give and bequeath to my friend Alice B.
Toklas to her use for life and, in so far as it may become necessary for her proper maintenance and support, I authorize my
Executors to reduce to cash any paintings or other personal property belonging to my Estate." *(Back to the Porter letter)* In the
meantime, it is I who am paying the rent of the flat, its upkeep,
the char, doctor's bills.

Then Mr. Edgar Allan Poe *Junior* wrote me to sell a picture to cover my expenses, which I did, the Picasso *Green Still Life*, for sixty thousand dollars. A few days later Mr. Poe wrote me that he was going to consult the Stein children concerning the sale of a picture. I insist on being paid the remittance for the three months he withheld without warning. About my sale of those three drawings in 1954   *(she gestures here to the space where they hung and then rose out of sight)*   there was nothing clandestine about it. I made no secret of it. I asked Picasso's consent. The drawings are not missing; they were sold in aid of seeing through to publication all of Gertrude Stein's unpublished work, which I had the right to do according to Gertrude Stein's will.

   (She waves the letter and the will helplessly, even wildly and in tears, so truly distraught for the first time that she is not in control of herself; then she casts them aside to turn about the barren room, her head moving slowly up and down. She turns back to the audience.)

   But I can see the pictures in my memory. My dim sight could not see them now. It makes no difference. Besides   *(she raps firmly on her forehead with her middle finger)*   I have them all here. This will be the last to go.

   In the fall I slipped and broke my knee and was moved to a nursing home where I was treated by massage and exercise so I could walk again. The nursing home is a fit subject for a novelette. There are ten people on the staff and they all hate each other. In any case they never agree, and they would come bounding into my room as if it were a way station and say, "Is she here?" Then I fell and broke my wrist. At my age falls are natural, aren't they? Don't worry about me. I am eighty-four years old. All old people fall, an aunt skating on the ice, a granduncle jumping off a streetcar.

(A new letter, business-like) Dear Mr. Porter, Six months have passed. I am shocked and surprised at not having received a remittance for so long a time. What has happened to Mr. Poe and his son? I have been living on an advance royalty for a book, but this money I was keeping to pay my expenses for another cure at Aqui, which I sadly need for the arthritis has become painfully acute. What can you do to make Mr. Poe activate? I am down to bedrock. It has not been easy for me to write these things to you. Gertrude Stein—in her generosity to me—did not foresee that such an occasion could arise.

(Another pause for an unsteady stroll. By this time her walk is genuinely halting, and she must feel for furniture to be certain where she is. The effect should let the audience know that some considerable time has passed before she speaks to the audience again.)

In May 1963, the woman who bought the flat when the house was sold several years ago sent a hussar yesterday morning at seven-thirty who said the police would come with an expulsion order. *(Now a little joke.)* My maid thinks that if General De Gaulle is not going to save me, I had better go to a hotel at once. *(She straightens up, as much as she is able to, then defiantly she speaks.)* If I leave this apartment it will be to go to Père Lachaise.

E P I L O G U E
16 rue de la Convention, November 1963–March 1967

The lights do not dim. Music from the next apartment drifts in but only until she speaks again. She looks about the room for a last time, and then she walks slowly but unhaltingly—head up—to the chair downstage right and sits squarely on it, arranging the pale blue shawl over her shoulders, facing

the audience, her hands in her lap, by which time there is no music. All of
her subsequent movements are minimal. Except when otherwise indicated,
her lines are directed not so much to the audience as into space. Her speech is
vague, alternately frustrated and serene, but serenity prevails at the end.
She does not lose her sense of humor, and she does not ask for sympathy.

Having lost a lawsuit I was evicted from the rue Christine.
(She looks slowly right, then slowly left, as if to ask "where am I?" but she
sees nothing. She removes her glasses.)   Well, here I am at my age in
a new home, very modern, but with no right to drive nails into
the walls   *(a laugh)*—in a country of painting! The walls are so
thin one hears everything. A neighbor sneezed the other day
and I heard it distinctly. An earthquake would bring us all into
the court five flights below, and I don't promise to survive.
(She suddenly thinks of something that might amuse the audience.)
Oh, I had a cataract removed! Last time the doctor came he said,
"Look at me now. Can you see me?" To which I replied, Yes, for
the first time. Which he didn't think was funny, but I did.
(Still to amuse the audience, but with absolute conviction)   Virgil
Thomson says I had my cataract removed so that I will see Gertrude clear.   *(She lights up, one last cigarette.)*   And I've taken to
filter-tipped cigarettes as a step to not smoking—I think.
(A shrug of her shoulders)   It isn't getting me anywhere.   *(A long*
pause, time's chronology having begun to wander)   Have you a pretty
garden this year? I shall never have a garden again. I wish I
could have shown you our flower garden at Bilignin—the terrace in front of the house, facing that lovely valley and the tim-
bered mountains opposite. I was happier then than today.
(A long pause)   Gertrude said the eternal truths that nearly every
old woman in a village knew could be counted on your ten fin-

gers. Her last one was "go home and be a martyr—that is what you both need, your country and you." Gertrude never left home in the same way I did. She was always at home through the language, but I was at home only through her.

(A long pause)

"What is the *(a pause)* answer," she said. I was silent. "In that case," she said, "what is the *(another pause because she is not certain of the order, and she says "question" to indicate her uncertainty)* question." *(A long pause)* I don't know *(another pause)* what is to become of me. The Steins' lawyer is trying to make some sort of settlement without selling any of the pictures. But how he's going to manage that I don't know. *(Another pause, then a little joke)* Do come back soon. *(A last drag on the cigarette as the lights begin to fade)* I shan't last forever.

Miss Young, My Darling

I remember, when the grey fog heaved outside the many-windowed nursery, when the fog swept like a heavy skirt outside and the wind sighed, Miss MacIntosh was dressed as for a long voyage, wearing her whaler's hat, her sea boots, there where we said our monotonous factual lessons. It was for self-protection that she dressed thus. We were not going anywhere, she continually reminded me, but that common sense demanded we should be dressed for the gale. Her voice always boomed like a man's above the roar. She stood with her head thrust back, her cheeks rosy in the salt air. But as I was a child and accustomed to her habits, it did not seem strange to me then that my old nursemaid looked as if she could be equipped with a compass, a steering wheel, a map of the stars, charted and uncharted. I fear I took her for granted then and imagined her eccentricity to be as common-place as she imagined it to be. For she was just like other people, she always said, blowing out her cheeks—she was absolutely normal although she was sometimes sorry she was not a whaler or a fisherman.

I first encountered Marguerite Young through that opening paragraph of "The Arctic Explorer at the Stock Exchange," a story I read in *The Tiger's Eye*, an avant-garde literary journal, when I was nineteen years old. The whole of it was bewildering and funny, and the prose was incantatory, laced with extravagant locutions, about a nursemaid recounting a thwarted love affair. But I was then myself embarked on embracing the avant-garde in whatever form it came to me, having fallen under the spell of Gertrude Stein's writing three years before. I never forgot that story by Marguerite Young, or at least I filed it away in a memory that had begun to store selectively. I did not remember the name of the author, and I did not remember a note about her which had indicated that the story was part of a work in progress, to be called *Miss MacIntosh, My Darling.* That was in 1949.

In 1935, Marguerite Young—then a graduate student at the University of Chicago—sat at the feet of Gertrude Stein in a writing seminar; in 1955, I sat at the feet of Marguerite Young in the Writers' Workshop at the University of Iowa. The symmetry of that is mightily pleasing to me. Marguerite's own writing bears no more resemblance to Gertrude Stein's than mine does to Marguerite's, but I believe that I learned from them both what I should not try to do. By some kind of literary osmosis, they were equally powerful influences on me. I knew Gertrude Stein only through her words, but I thought I knew Marguerite Young's words only after I knew her, and subsequently, for some time anyway, only through passages from her work in progress. Her arctic explorer never turned up again, but I can still recall the shock of recognition when I first rediscovered Miss MacIntosh in her work.

Marguerite had been laboring over this monstrous rock of a book for ten years when I met her, and nearly another decade of Sisyphean labor would pass before it finally got published—all twelve hundred pages, printed in small type on oversize leaves, minus a nearly four-hundred-page, self-contained section that had been dropped at the urging of her editors—only to endure the indifference or downright hostility of most readers.

The Writers' Workshop met in two converted Quonset huts on campus at the University of Iowa, left over from World War II. The first contained offices and a reception area where the poetry workshop met, and the second served for the fiction workshop, each during one long afternoon a week; both buildings held other classes at other hours of the day, while students met with their individual writing advisors.

Paul Engle, the poet who had founded the Writers' Workshop long before, could be by turns benevolent and malicious, encouraging and even fomenting feuds—real or imaginary—among the rotating group of professional writers who stayed a year, sometimes two, sometimes longer. Paul shepherded his whole flock of aspiring young poets and novelists, but he farmed them out to his visiting luminaries.

Before my arrival and long after my departure, the Writers' Workshop employed a remarkable number of talented authors to guide students through the rigors of learning, not so much how to write but how to develop the discipline to write, to expose us to literature we had not in all likelihood encountered, to criticize our work. When I arrived there in the fall of 1955, Robert O. Bowen, Calvin Kentfield, and Marguerite Young taught fiction; Paul and his minions Henri Coulette and Donald Justice taught poetry.

We were obliged to choose the writer with whom we wished to work during our tenure in the Workshop; knowing nothing about any of them, I turned to a new friend, Peter Marchant, an English emigrant that year, who urged me to sign on with Marguerite Young. She was then about forty-five, with a face like a friendly basset hound, lank hair chopped off in a long Buster Brown or maybe Prince Valiant bob, wide skirts and crisp blouses and often some eccentric necklace or brooch, a massive handbag over her shoulder always stuffed with food and manuscripts. She was possessed of a kindly, solicitous patience with her sub-flock of young writers. I thought she was crazy. She found things to praise in the worst writing and never criticized anything unless simultaneously she had something positive to say as well; it was a trick I did not catch on to for a long time, but it worked and kept us at it.

I required several weeks to muster the courage to submit something to her, and then at Peter's insistence turned in a revision of a story I had written in the navy two years before, about a Japanese whore who threatened to contact the American wife of a sailor with whom she'd been living. The language was crude, because I'd made a genuine effort to reproduce as faithfully as I could the richly vulgar navy argot to which I'd been exposed. I was convinced that Marguerite would be sufficiently shocked to suggest that I transfer to Robert O. Bowen's roster. He was an ex-Marine with a novel called *Bamboo* behind him, full of sex and violence and self-conscious guilt. Instead, Marguerite went over my manuscript with me as if it had been about children playing hide-the-pebble or spinsters knitting afghans—and before long I was trying to write stories about them instead. It was enough to put the navy behind me and concentrate on language's magic. More significantly, I think, I learned from Marguerite that writing—all writing—was good or bad not so much on the basis of its content but on the basis of its words. Words were seductive for her, and eventually they came to be for me. Long after my time with Marguerite, I began to realize what she had given me.

Never at any point did she make any effort to turn her students' prose into a clone of her own, and more than once she slapped my hand for doing so unwittingly. She was unerringly giving of her time, and I wondered when she wrote herself, for she was always available to us, and frequently with us outside the classroom too, over meals or coffee or beer.

But she did write, regularly and resolutely. During the six-year interim since I'd read that first selection from *Miss MacIntosh, My Darling*, Marguerite's prose, both in manner and in content, had grown increasingly maze-like. She often spoke the way she wrote, or seemed to, in interminable dependent clauses of the dream and the illusion, the reality and the truth, of life reflecting art rather than the other way around. When I first met her, she said she had about two hundred pages to go on the novel; when she left Iowa City a year later, she said she had about four hundred pages to go.

I don't know exactly when she wrote. After the novel was published she claimed, in a *Bookview* interview in September 1965, that she arose at nine, had a cup of coffee, and wrote until five:

> I'm absolutely ruined if my schedule is disrupted. I can lose a couple of weeks if I miss a day. Sometimes I spend a whole day on one sentence. Sometimes I write four pages in a day. I write like a snail. I can feel, almost chemically, the instant the inspiration is waning. I work on each sentence until it is perfect and then I never rewrite it. I'm Scotch and I never throw away an image. I store them in my mind till they fall in place like a piece in a mosaic.

She could not have maintained that schedule when I knew her; too much of her time was taken up with us. She slept late, rewrote in the mornings and wrote at night, drinking endless cups of coffee that collected on every surface in her quarters in Iowa City. Marguerite's apartment had been furnished by her landlord with castoffs. In what should have been her kitchen—a very large room—stacks of typing paper in various stages crowded a trestle table for space with her typewriter; books spilled over shelves into stacks against the walls; in her other room, a remarkable collection of gimcracks and doodads, including a lot of toys and ornaments, decorated every surface, and more books crowded each other for space. It was a little like a second-hand shop. I don't know where she slept. The kitchen was never in use for cooking so far as I know, just two rooms in which she entertained and worked, sometimes simultaneously, because she'd read sections of the book to us—sometimes only a paragraph to illustrate some point or other, sometimes lengthy passages. She was not asking for approval. She was merely sharing a remarkable collection of people with us.

In conversation, Marguerite spoke frequently about her characters, and always as if they were friends: Vera Cartwheel, who was her narrator, the daughter of a drug-addicted heiress in a gloomy mansion on the New England coast; Mr. Spitzer and his twin brother—Joachim and Peron—one an earnest Jamesian lawyer and the other a seductive gambler, although once upon a time they had been physically identical, and now one of them was dead, though the living one didn't know which one he was; Esther Longtree, perpetually pregnant; Cousin Hannah, a fanatical suffragette; the stone-deaf man; and Miss MacIntosh herself, destined for an early disappearance in the novel, a homely bald governess who sometimes dressed in drag and looked like Yul Brynner and behaved like Don Juan.

Marguerite spoke of them fairly straightforwardly, but on the page she snaked their lives out in labrynthine sentences—to challenge Proust or Joyce or Stein at their most maddening, laced with her own unique dependent clauses dripping with high Gothic decor, seemingly endless qualifying adjectives, and phrases that looped back over each other. The sixty-sixth chapter of the novel begins with that relatively direct first paragraph I had read in 1949, but elsewhere in the book one encounters locutions of amazing circuity:

> He knew—for the spirit voice had told him—which player thought he was on a baseball diamond, batting the ball, the glaring midnight sun to the farthest empyrean, beyond the shores of light—batting the earth beyond the moon—rushing from star to star—knew who had knocked himself out of the starry ring—knew what great contention was fought for more than an hour by continual feinting and false attacks, with never a blow from either side, and was declared a draw by the bemused umpire of the fight, who could not decide whether he was dealing with two cowards or two men of exceptional courage. Both were bridegrooms. It was the night before the bridal night. Perhaps there was no bride.

Or this:

> Speak not to my sleeping mother of the soul which was divided into only two parts—or of the reversals of polarities, the meetings of opposites, the imperial organization of chaos—but of that disorder which seemed itself innate, a greater mystery than life or death, the spirit messengers reciting revelations in the darkness, eyes burning like stars in the fog, sea birds with burning feathers drifting before their eyes, dolphins with shining curls upon the long wake of the waves, the swell of the sea which breaks upon the distant shore, the foam of sound caused by the breaking billows.

In private tutorials Marguerite never referred to her work and concentrated instead on ours, with an unerring attention that was exhilarating. It was impossible not to feel like a *writer* after one of those heady sessions. On occasion, however, she would read aloud in the evenings, sometimes formally in Carolyn Morgan's dance studio—where I picked up some loose change as a rehearsal pianist two days a week—and sometimes over coffee in her apartment if we asked her to. In either instance, if the readings went on too long they encouraged the auditors to glaze over or even doze off. I could not have summarized the content of whatever she'd read to us, but the effect of it could be beguiling the way chamber music sometimes is: the mind wanders but hears anyway.

In the weekly Writers' Workshop seminars, Marguerite was defensive, naive, and cerebral enough to alarm nearly everybody. When she was obliged to supply something by one of her students for discussion—every third week, the three teachers' students occurring in regular rotation—Marguerite would defend it in advance of any discussion, to the exasperation of the entire class. Student writers were always anonymous and only declared themselves at the end if they wished to, but Marguerite regularly carried on, riding point for a caravan, as if she feared we would be pilloried.

Once a not very good story of mine—I'd handed it in at the last minute in desperation because it was my turn—was attacked by another student, a Mrs. DeLuna, who was intense, middle-aged, rachitic, humorless, and perpetually angry, especially at men. (Privately we called her Claire.) She saw penises in church steeples and vaginas in all fruit but bananas; she loathed stories about children; she mistrusted long sentences. I knew that much from earlier sessions, when she jabbed away at the air with her king-sized cigarettes in an ivory holder. She insisted that my tree trunk—a little girl playing house under it burned up another girl's doll—was a penis since the story was obviously about child abuse and sexual molestation. The story was overrun with *too* many symbols, and they all contradicted each other, she said, and, as for that, the tree was insulting to women. I hadn't known there were any symbols at all, and I certainly hadn't known about that tree trunk. Marguerite and I had never discussed anything so preposterous. She rose to my defense with an elaborate construction that turned my poor piece into a subtle Freudian dream of incontrovertible symmetry that left me behind in a miasma I could not begin to penetrate even now, but I knew at the end of it that my tree was female and not male and that Mrs. DeLuna had barked up the wrong one.

Through all this, the other faculty writers sat benignly, waiting for the next round. Paul Engle looked amused, as usual, hoping for fireworks, maybe blood; Calvin Kentfield looked bored; Robert O. Bowen looked angry. Ordinarily, Marguerite was at loggerheads with Bob over stories in workshop; he distrusted myth and symbol and went instead for a story's jugular with a combination of military angst and precision. Marguerite was even somewhat afraid of what she saw as a latent violence that might turn against her. But when Mrs. DeLuna protested that she'd been misunderstood, and began rather desperately to talk about policemen's billy clubs and rape and male dominance through force, punctuating the air as usual with her cigarette, Bob spoke up for Marguerite. Mrs. DeLuna should consider, he said, that policemen used the sides of their billy clubs not the ends, and that—guns and rifles notwithstanding—even a pool cue just gently tapped its quarry. Then he suggested that she might want to give up those phallic symbols she was smoking.

Later, over beer at Kenny's, a local bar where we usually ended up after the workshop seminars, Marguerite said she'd been absolutely sincere, even though she hadn't known how fabulous my story was. *Fabulous* was one of Marguerite's favorite words.

"But it's not," I protested. "I wasn't thinking about sex organs and incest."

"Oh, I know you weren't," she smiled beatifically, "that's what makes it so fabulous."

Marguerite took me under her wing, I think, when she discovered that I had been born in Indianapolis, for she had too—"the largest city in the world not on navigable water," she used to crow proudly. Also, to her astonishment, I could quote James Whitcomb Riley's *Little Orphant Annie*, and since she loved his poems, that tied us to each other permanently. Indiana, she claimed, was as fabulous as anywhere on the planet.

She had known a doctor there who delivered imaginary babies, a virtuoso violinist who played without strings on his instrument, a whole community of deaf mutes; once she had seen a sow at the wheel of a Ford with fourteen pigs as passengers, stalled because they were out of gas; the electric chair factory there, where she'd once worked briefly, had gardens in which the flowers wilted every time there was an execution; Indiana apples could fall up as easily as down if you held them the right way. If, on occasion, she saw Edgar Allan Poe hurrying along the street in Greenwich Village, she had certainly seen James Whitcomb Riley back home again in Indiana long after his death. Under every fantasy there was a hard truth; under every illusion there was a reality, though not always the same reality, and nobody else's reality but hers. Nothing whatever in *Miss MacIntosh, My Darling*, Marguerite claimed, had been invented. Everything came from the world around her: news stories, history, gossip, encyclopedias, films although she never went to films, books. Who needed to invent fable, myth, symbol? We breathed them, and our dream life and our real life were identical in their search for utopia, not lost and found but "lost and rediscovered," as she said in her old age. "All my writing is about the recognition that there is no single reality. But the beauty of it is that you nevertheless go on, walking towards utopia which may not exist, on a bridge which might end before you reach the other side."

Marguerite began to write when she was six, joined "The Author's League" when she was eleven, took a bachelor's degree at Butler University and a master's degree at the University of Chicago, read aloud for pay to a wealthy woman too drugged to listen, and published her first book of poems, *Prismatic Ground*, when she was twenty-nine. She'd given up writing poetry by the time I knew her and said it was a part of her "dead life," though writing poetry had taught her how to write prose.

I had begun to collect books by that time and was curious enough to sleuth out a copy of *Prismatic Ground*. I liked the poems: most of them rhymed and had recognizable forms, even if I did not immediately or sometimes ever grasp their density or many of their literary and mythic references; also they were a respite from the seemingly formless free verse about pedestrian matters that so many students were churning out in the Writers' Workshop. Marguerite hadn't seen a copy of *Prismatic Ground* for years, she said. Her inscription gives a nod to another of her protégés, my friend Peter Marchant who was writing a novel about a woman in love with a white horse named Bradshaw:

For Bruce Kellner,
the Resurrectionist,
from
My skull
Marguerite Young
(Gone to join
the
Heavenly Choir
with
Bradshaw)

Marguerite's second book of poems, *Moderate Fable*, was published seven years later, in 1944. It was much different in both form and content, and it was perhaps between these two books that she had put in time working in the electric chair factory and reading to the woman who would become the model for the Opium Lady in *Miss MacIntosh, My Darling*. The later poems gave me equal if different difficulties when I'd tracked down a copy of that book as well. I asked for another inscription and got one rife with inside jokes: this time, in reference to a story I was writing about a woman pope (who Marguerite believed would never have worn a mitre) and a wind-up toy I'd added to her collection, which eventually turned up in *Miss MacIntosh, My Darling*:

Signed for Bruce
Kellner, My Darling!
Marguerite Young
(Pope Joan. But
where's my hat?)
Thanks for the
violinist playing the
silent violin.
Thanks for you!

Between those books of poems, she'd completed her degrees, taught high school in Indianapolis, and written her astonishing history of the religious communities at Father Rapp's Harmony and Robert Owen's New Harmony in Indiana. If I needed any persuasion that documentary language did not have to be pedestrian, that it could indeed be as rich and beautiful and—Marguerite's favorite word again—fabulous as the language in verse and fiction, *Angel in the Forest* gave me the proof. Here was a book of historical fact rich enough in its language to get drunk on, although an isolated passage—as in this one about religious ecstasy expressed through labor—cannot begin to represent the book's full effect:

> Although the cosmos might fluctuate, every day went according to rigorous schedule. Never a deviation from what was here the normal order. Each morning, when the cowsherd blew his ivy-wreathed horn, then out of their stalls in back gardens, the cows came marching toward greener pastures, two by two, their bells clanking. The cowsherd, known as Gabriel, no relation to the angel or a very remote one, drove a wagon on wheels, known as Noah's Ark. An old sailor on the prairy, he could measure his course by shadow and star, tacking due northwest past apple trees, due southeast past a knoll of locusts. Or he might follow the equatorial line, a rail fence at the end of the angelic hop meadow. Gabriel had at least that power of choice. Gabriel blew the trumpet for the Rappites to awaken. On the side of Noah's Ark, they read the community newspaper, which contained no news but news from nowhere—though it was short and sweet. Lo, the Lord was with them, wherever two or three were gathered together, they were informed, day after day. Lo, they should go forth, as assigned, to the loom, hattery, apple picking, distillery, furnace, piggery. Lo they were the heirs of sal-

vation, though the earth should be destroyed and the heavens, also—for they and the Lord should both endure, above time, above space, above accident.

The method in *Miss MacIntosh, My Darling*, that was to follow, was already at work in Marguerite's writing, the languorous qualifying phrases, the use of the catalogs of examples, the odd and the ordinary in immediate proximity. I believe I imitated this prolix style a good deal in the beginning—or tried to until she set me straight—but I learned as well, on my own, what not to do that she did; I think her influence on my writing is still pervasive, if only to make me careful as I proceed, regardless of what form the writing may take, including business letters and notes to friends. Marguerite liked to quote Yeats's "Adam's Curse" about that:

> I said, 'A line will take us hours maybe;
> Yet if it does not seem a moment's thought,
> Our stitching and unstitching has been naught.'

Extracurricularly, I mark my friendship with Marguerite through a number of memorable occasions. She thrived on her work, but she thrived on people too. She was a good listener, and she could remember the most casual remark days later; moreover, she had the habit of picking up a conversation where it had ended and carrying on as if there had been no break at all. That was apparent from the beginning of our acquaintance, and it continued long after we'd both left Iowa.

Marguerite was a great friend of the painter James Lechay, and his wife Rose; Peter and I both knew their daughter Jo, a dancer who went on to found her own company in Canada. We all met around Rose's splendid table for meals from time to time, although Marguerite was largely indifferent to food. I never saw her cook anything herself; I never saw her eat very enthusiastically; she drank little or nothing alcoholic. She smoked a good deal, and I suspect she looked forward to the end of a meal more than to the start of one, whether the fare was Rose's mirific stews and soups and breads, or Peter's scrambled eggs, or a veal paprikasch over which I labored a long time for a dinner party, or a quick sandwich in a local pub.

When Marguerite's old friend Maya Deren came to Iowa City to show her experimental films, we strolled together over to the auditorium where they were to be run. Maya Deren walked ahead of us on somebody's arm—perhaps Peter's—and Marguerite and I fell in step behind them.

"My God," Marguerite whispered in mock dismay, "I've managed to avoid looking at her movies for twenty years and now I'm going to have to watch them."

Bob Karr and Marguerite and I took Maya Deren out for supper afterward. I had been mesmerized by her films; now I was mesmerized by her makeup, her electrified red hair, her brillliant eyes swimming in some drug or other, and her near-monologue, not a word of which I now remember. At about midnight, Marguerite went home, exhausted, she said, and Bob and I sat up with Maya Deren until dawn in some all-night diner—at the bus station, I think—until somebody whisked her away to some other campus in a nearby town.

But Marguerite told time by nobody else's clock, and she telephoned me more than once at about two AM, wide awake and full of ideas. I was living in Cedar Rapids then, about twenty-five miles north, where I taught at Coe College. She'd just finished reading a story I'd turned in to her, about a religious conversion during the 1937 flood in Louisville, Kentucky. Marguerite was excited over it and wanted to talk about Kierkegaard, a name I had never encountered until her call. A day or so later I got a letter from her, sent airmail, although the distance between Iowa City and Cedar Rapids was about half an hour's drive, from "Dame Marguerite Young, 618 Bowery Street in the Gulch, The Sign of the Rose, Iowa City, Iowa," and addressed to "Hon. Bruce Kellner, Keeper of the Jewelled Mace." On the back of the envelope she wrote: "Brought by messenger pigeons across several seas." It was a page of manuscript, numbered 910, but in reading *Miss MacIntosh, My Darling* more than once in later years, I never discovered it in print. That is no assurance it is not there, of course, buried in that dense forest of words that encourages enchantment and somnolence in just about equal measure.

At the bottom and on the back of the page, she wrote: "Bruce, My Darling, Perhaps from this casually selected page—it happens to be the one I'm working on at the moment—you can glimpse what I mean by the Kierkregaard (sp?) sort of theme. If not, then not. Are you an elegant mourner? Or are you, as I suspect, Peron who wears the red rose and is quite gay about the whole thing, being not dead as so many suppose, and even he supposes at times? Lovingly yours, Marguerite." Here is the page she sent:

> woman might be man, and sun might be moon, and dog might be owl, and turrets spoke with human voices, and men were sea-shells, and hands flew through clouded, opalescent heavens stretching endlessly like the memory of alien thought. Perhaps he had asked too much of life, too much of death, even though the very fact that he had made no demands, no unusual demands of any kind, that he had been passive and receptive, asking noth-

ing, it seemed to him. He had been content to follow his usual routines which had been protective, setting his watch where there was no time. Or perhaps the haunted questions were the only answers as the autumn leaves fell, fell with long whirling and sighing, fell through him, fell where there was no one. Perhaps he fell, clutching at a rope of song sparrows like some mad bell-ringer forever ringing himself. Perhaps there was no creator but the temporal creation forever changing, that which was this chaos rolling like the dark flood, and he was part of it even as his dead brother was, his brother being that faceless face upon the darkening flood, and every man was every other man, and mortal was immortal. And immortal was mortal, mortal like the white rose Mr. Spitzer wore, mortal like his hand wearing its mother-of-pearl, its veined jewel like a carbuncle sticking to him. How could he be both mortal and immortal? Could he be, at one time, both the living and the dead? Perhaps there was no other creator but the dream dreaming him, dreaming this body filled with its sad reverberations and ready whispers and premonitions of an impossible future life—and there was only Mr. Spitzer drifting down the winter wind, singing as he drifted—for when there was no song or sound, yet his pale lips moved as he whispered to himself, hearing nothing, not even the crackle of burning tree branches or ripple of leaves, trying to find courage to go on when all was lost, when the snow particles drove into his moth-white face. Surely, he had been wrong in imagining boundaries, in imagining separate worlds, perhaps divided by worlds, perhaps divided from each

And then it simply broke off in the middle of the sentence. Who knows what followed?

At a big party in the apartment Hugh Wass and I shared in Iowa City, Candace Hilligoss—a Marilyn Monroe blonde in the theater department but nobody's fool and later the star of what was to become a cult horror movie, *Carnival of Souls*—had the collective attention of all the men, while Marguerite, representing everything that Candace was not and wouldn't have cared to be anyway, sat in a corner, not neglected but at the same time without her full coterie of acolytes at her feet. "Swans are mute until they die, and when they die, utter a single cry," she announced to nobody in particular but in a voice guaranteed to turn heads and reorganize the seating arrangements.

Another party might have ended in mayhem but didn't. Calvin Kentfield invited the entire Writers' Workshop over one evening to the house he and his wife were sub-renting. That covered the rest of the faculty, including both Marguerite Young and Robert O. Bowen. Bob distrusted Marguerite, all that her writing represented, all of her influence over her students, and he had no use whatever for the protracted sections of *Miss MacIntosh, My Darling* that had been published in posh and influential journals and magazines. His own novel, *Bamboo*, a sincere but turgid war story reflecting his subsequent guilt over his apparent involvement, not only in battle but with an Asian woman, had drawn little attention, critical or commercial.

Bob's latent violence—just what Marguerite had earlier identified and feared—proved all too true that night. He roamed through the house, very drunk, pausing to stare at her, smile maliciously, look fierce, and in every likelihood playing a game to unnerve her. While she sat in the living room holding forth with one or another of her fabulous stories—and interrupting herself with half-serious asides now and then that Bob was going to kill her—he was out in the kitchen, whittling cheese with a large butcher knife. Once or twice he wandered into the other room, not brandishing the knife exactly, but looking hard at Marguerite and having a good time. Kentfield tried to get him to put down the knife, but Bob snarled and went back to the cheese. Suddenly he turned to me with an idiotic grin on his face and laughed and said, "Goddam Bruce Kellner!" Then, hacking away at the cheese, he echoed himself: "Goddam! Goddam! Goddam Bruce Kellner!" And then accidentally he cut himself very badly and bled all over the countertop, the floor, himself. He'd inflicted a severe wound on the palm of his hand, and he got carted off to the emergency room at the hospital.

I was not entirely certain what it all had meant, except that Bob had made no bones about his distaste for Marguerite's writing and must have seen my involvement with her as tantamount to treason in "Form and Theory," his course in which I was enrolled. I liked Bob, rather; he was always forthright with me, he had never directly mentioned Marguerite in my presence, although I knew how he felt about her work, and I had learned a lot from him that year about how to read closely. Also, he set me on the right track when in response to the papers I had done for his course, as well as to the stories I had turned in for discussion during the Writers' Workshop seminars, he told me he did not believe I had much talent for writing fiction, based on what he had seen produced under Marguerite's tutelage. The analytical quality of my head, he contended, pointed in another direction if I wanted to write professionally. He was right, although I was not ready to admit that for another decade. Bob Bowen left at the end of the school calendar that year, or perhaps he was not invited to back. Marguerite returned for another semester and then moved to New York permanently.

A third party at the end of her tenure in the Writers' Workshop is a somewhat sweeter memory than the Kentfield disaster.

At the close of spring semester, Paul Engle invited everybody to
his summer home—a farm out in the country from Iowa City—
for a celebratory picnic. Coincidentally, my parents had driven
up from Kansas City for a visit, so I took them along since Paul
had urged us to feel free to bring friends. People played ball outside, and in Mary Engle's big kitchen others were singing old
songs, like *Pony Boy* and *Red Wing*. Marguerite and my mother—
who could scarcely have been more different one from the other
in intellect, in appearance, in interests—discovered that they
both knew *You're the Kind of a Girl That Men Forget* and har-
monized it, in absolute sincerity, Marguerite in a quavering soprano, my mother in a husky baritone:

> You're the kind of a girl that men forget,
> Just a toy to enjoy for a while,
> For when men settle down they always find
> An old fashioned girl with an old fashioned smile.
> And you'll soon realize you're not so wise
> When the years bring you tears of regret.
> When they play, "Here comes the bride,"
> You'll stand outside—
> Just a girl that men forget.

Everybody listened in silence and then lustily applauded the curious pair: sisters under the skin, with nothing else in common
but their affectionate, unrehearsed performance.

Subsequently, I clock my meetings with Marguerite by decades: chance or planned encounters, at first circa 1960 in her
Greenwich Village apartment, crammed with angels and paintings, a carousel horse, books beyond reckoning, the collections of
a lifetime; or in a variety of coffee shops or restaurants; or on the
street. And then, circa 1970, 1980, 1990, while her career pro-

ceeded to take her to Fairleigh Dickinson, Fordham, and the New School of Social Research, where she continued to teach writing for over three decades.

She weathered the attacks when she finally laid her egg, a giant turkey clocking in at three and a half pounds, *Miss MacIntosh, My Darling*. It appeared in 1965 to a largely negative press, mostly male, mostly bewildered, mostly angry. William Goyen in the *New York Times Book Review* praised it, but *Time* made cruel fun of it, and so did plenty of others. She survived that to immerse herself in a biography of, first, James Whitcomb Riley, a long ago promise to herself to resurrect the reputation of our fellow Hoosier, and then, instead, Eugene V. Debs, whose life would occupy the rest of hers and result in a manuscript of about twenty-five hundred pages. In Marguerite Young's obituary in the *New York Times*, an editor at Alfred A. Knopf was quoted as saying that the book needed "just a little more pruning"; Knopf had accepted it three years before, with 1995 as a projected date of publication. It finally appeared in 1999 as *Harp Song For a Radical*, severely truncated to about one fourth its length. Who knows if it would have been more coherent and less a collection of fragmentary biographies had it appeared as Marguerite intended it?

Sometimes I would let her know when I was going to be in town; sometimes I would simply spot her in the Pennyfeather and go in for a cup of coffee. Once my wife and daughter and I encountered her at the Sheridan Square subway entrance. She came sailing toward us, scarves and poncho and long full skirt billowing out behind her, and stopped for a chat.

Along the way, she invited me to parties where I met her friend Ruth Stephan, that strangely beautiful novelist who wrote strangely beautiful books I could never finish, and her husband John, who'd published *The Tiger's Eye*, the notable first post-war avant-garde magazine. Marguerite took me over to meet Mari Sandoz, elegantly dressed and fastidiously spoken in her spartan apartment who wrote books about her native Nebraska and Indians and collected the lost lore of the Midwest. The contrast between the two could not have been more apparent, but their affection for each other was just as apparent while they talked—and I mostly listened—through a marathon evening that lasted nearly until dawn.

Long afterward, Marguerite met me at some restaurant in Greenwich Village to introduce me to "the greatest new novelist in America"—I have forgotten his name, and I dare say he has forgotten mine—and to whom she introduced me as "the greatest authority on the Harlem Renaissance in the world." We were both sufficiently embarrassed by this to let Marguerite tell us about Eugene V. Debs for four hours.

I think I saw her last in the fall of 1990—and that time by chance—in a coffee shop on Bleecker Street. I just happened to pass the window and see her at a table by herself and went in to say hello. We spoke as if we'd picked up a conversation we'd interrupted for one reason or another a couple of days earlier. She showed no surprise at seeing me after such a long time, but she did show a good deal of delight, and I listened—as one usually did with Marguerite—while she told me about the book of her collected poems being edited on the West Coast, about the first volume of Eugene V. Debs, "Prelude in the Golden Key," probably coming in at over two thousand pages, ready for her agent, about the second volume all but done, about her plans to revive her interrupted biography of James Whitcomb Riley. Together we recited a few lines of his *Little Orphant Annie*, that earliest bond between us.

She seemed much the same to me, still dressed like a bag lady but one who had done her rummaging in the best thrift shops in town: a voluminous skirt of many colors, a shawl and a serape, a battered, oversize leather catch-all, thick stockings and baby-doll shoes with straps. Her hair, no longer in its Prince Valiant cut, was streaked with gray and fell thinly to her shoulders. She seemed to me terribly frail, and she had grown to look rather like W. H. Auden when his face had turned into a complicated road map. She wanted to know, too, what I was working on and as always was full of advice about agents and publishers. She hoped I'd send her a copy of *The Last Dandy*, my biography of Ralph Barton then scheduled for publication the following year, but she said I mustn't be cross if she didn't acknowledge it until she saw me the next time, because at eighty-two she had begun to write poems again and after her daily bout with that she was unprepared to write anything else.

Not too long afterward, I learned that she had at last given up her Greenwich Village apartment and returned to Indiana to live with her niece, although her obituaries indicated that she left no immediate heirs. She died there in November 1995, at eighty-seven. She had already sold her papers to the Beinecke Rare Book and Manuscript Library at Yale, and in time I will send along my brief Marguerite Young shelf to join them, including the page of manuscript for *Miss MacIntosh, My Darling* that seems never to have made it into the published version, several literary journals and magazines with her work, including that copy of *The Tiger's Eye* where I had first encountered her remarkable prose, and of course her books. When *Miss MacIntosh, My Darling* first appeared, it was Marguerite's habit to go into bookshops and sign copies, "Marguerite Young, author." I have one of those, but I also have a first edition of *Angel in the Forest*—a book from which I learned more, perhaps, than from any other about the extraordinary landscape that language can embrace in critical prose and other non-fiction forms—with an inscription that I treasure:

> For my darling Bruce
> Kellner, fellow Hoosier,
> star of Indianapolis,
> from Marguerite Young

CARLO'S WIFE

$\mathcal{C}$arl Van Vechten was photographing me, on 5 May 1953, when Fania Marinoff came whirling into the studio in their Central Park West apartment. "I'm taking the path to New Jersey!" she cried, exchanging kisses with her husband, and pausing long enough to be introduced and to fire half a dozen fast questions at me. Her lips were painted bright red and her eyes flashed under extraordinary eyebrows, like sloping Spanish tildes which gave her a wistful expression that her voluble chatter belied. In New York for the first time, I pictured her path as some bucolic route into the New Jersey countryside, although she was hardly dressed for hiking: a black bonnet perched atop her dizzy grey curls, dark red flowers at its peak and a black veil front and back, a dark red suit with a flared skirt, a heavy silver necklace, and black high-heeled shoes with a lot of straps. Later I learned about the PATH from Manhattan to Hoboken, as everybody called that leg of the New Jersey Transit system, and that Fania Marinoff went there regularly to record books for the Blind Association.

That first afternoon, following her hasty grilling—what plays had I seen? *Oh, not that!* Which of the dancers did I prefer? *Her?* Where was I reared? *Where?* She stared hard at my cufflinks, tiny bronze scorpions from a Japanese sword which I'd had made when I was overseas in the navy. Carlo had been posing me to show them off to advantage. "Oh, I don't like those at all!" she announced as she spun on her heel and vanished. I was crest-fallen.

"Pay no attention to Miss Marinoff," Carlo said. "She liked you; otherwise she wouldn't have asked you anything. Probably she's jealous and would like to have those cufflinks for earrings."

The next day, she joined us for lunch at the Sherry Netherland, and her costume once more impressed me: lavender taffeta, again with a full skirt and strappy shoes, and her hat was a beautiful helmet of artificial white and lavender flowers, tied under her chin in a satin bow. When I complimented it, she promptly took it off to show me the underside: a complex network of safety pins, straight pins, and criss-crossed stitches; she'd made the hat herself. Later I learned she made a lot of her own clothes, recycling them from one era to another, still wearing parts of dresses she'd had for twenty or thirty years. During the time I knew her, she did not ever follow current fashion, but she had a style that was right for her, exotic fabrics and patterns, bright stoles, many bangles, often a girlish hair ribbon in her grey curls; the effect was slightly eccentric but with a certain chic.

I knew little about Fania Marinoff at that point, except that she had been an actress—"a very good actress, perhaps a great one. She was born in Russia but she has always proudly defined herself as a Jewess," Carl Van Vechten had written to me. We had begun corresponding in 1951, mostly about Gertrude Stein because he was her literary executor. Two years later, when my ship returned from overseas, I flew from California to New York to meet my curious pen pal and his wife.

He always addressed her as "Miss Marinoff" in my presence and she always addressed him as "Carlo" and "Lamby," but he referred to her as "Fania" or "FM" in letters, and she referred to him as "Carl" or "Carlo." The list of their private nicknames and terms of endearment in letters to each other was as long as it was ridiculous. At the beginning of an acquaintance, everybody called her "Miss Marinoff" because she insisted on her own identity—and indeed during her popular heyday, circa 1915, Carlo was identified regularly as Mr. Marinoff—but eventually, because she asked me to, I called her "Fania" and sometimes "Fanny." That was her real name, although curiously she did not tolerate anybody else calling her "Fanny," but in the beginning I was a little afraid of her, and "Miss Marinoff" was just fine with me.

She was actressy much of the time, like a hammy *grande dame* overdoing it onstage maybe, but I learned eventually that she was only shy, and her melodramatic outbursts, flaring temper tantrums, and haughty pronouncements were more often than not masquerades. I think they were defense mechanisms too, to compete with Carlo, for he was a formidable act to follow, and in temperament he was Fania's antithesis. He was born in Iowa, she was born in Russia; he was an atheist from a Unitarian family; she was a romantically religious Jew; he held a bachelor of philosophy degree from the University of Chicago, she did not complete the fifth grade; he was tall and fair, she was tiny and dark; he was bisexual, she was not. In his interviews for the Columbia University Oral History Project, Carlo said that Fania was "more frequently governed by her heart, I by my head." Nobody would ever refer to the Marinoff-Van Vechten alliance as serene. They quarreled almost incessantly, and violent discussions could erupt into volcanic arguments—in their apartment, in theater lobbies, in restaurants, at large parties or intimate dinners, even in elevators. Carlo could be adamant, imperious, and loud; Fania could be hysterical, shrieking, and louder. Was it all an act? It was always exciting. "Fania's native intelligence is great . . . but her volatile temperament and her really considerable charm provide her in the end with a mellow background," Carlo concluded.

He hadn't fallen in love until he was thirty-four when, he wrote me, "love hit me hard, but I'm more in love now than I was then." That was on the eve of their fortieth wedding anniversary, in 1954. A few years later, when Fania had just excused herself after dinner one evening—she liked to retire early—Carlo said to me in a more measured voice than he ordinarily employed: "I . . . simply . . . cannot . . . imagine my life . . . without her."

She was born in Odessa, in 1887, a date she denied for most of her life. I incurred her anger when I gave her actual birth date in the manuscript of my Van Vechten biography. Carlo had been my source of information, and she was furious about that because *Who's Who in the American Theatre* listed 1890. Why did everybody have to know when she was born anyway? Why couldn't I just say, for instance, that she was born "at the turn of the century"? She was about seventy-five at the time.

Fanny, as she was called, was the thirteenth child of ageing Russian Jews, in Sinok, who had first produced six girls in a row and then six boys in a row. When Fanny was an infant, her mother died and her father remarried almost immediately. He was loyal to the memory of his wife, but he was strong in his religious conviction that a Jew should be married. The whole family emigrated to America, Fanny hiding under the voluminous skirts of her stepmother to avoid paying a transportation fare. They settled in Boston's Salem Street ghetto, where Fanny's father worked as a tailor, taught school and, until his death, sat in the dark of a honeycomb tenement poring over the Talmud, while her stepmother attempted to keep a kosher house and observe the high holy days. But Fanny went to gentile sewing parties on Shabbat, and ate bread on Pesach, and anything she could beg on Yom Kippur. She ran wild through the streets of Boston, stealing from peddlers' carts, selling matches for pennies, wailing and shrieking at funerals of strangers if that meant a tip afterward. She went from one house to another, inventing different names for herself and asking for handouts. The actress in her was born early on, and early on that histrionic ability had to find an outlet. By the time she was six, she could cajole like a professional hawker, mimicking for attention, flashing the expressive dark eyes that were to become an asset on the stage. The following year, when her brother Jacob—next in age but several years her senior—went to Denver to join their older brother Michael and his childless wife, he took Fanny with him. Younger guardians were thought best to raise the uncontrollable little girl. Michael's wife turned her into a kitchen slavey, and often left her alone in their flat without even a candle. Fanny grew up terrified of the dark, largely because of the rats, and in her old age she still slept with a light on next to her bed.

When Jacob married an aspiring singer who could not sing, Fanny got passed on to them, only to be sent out to work in another household in exchange for room and board. Soon she was hiring herself out to houses where the owners allowed her to attend school, however sporadically, and she always announced in advance, "I want it understood that I am to go on the stage and shall leave you." At eight, she did that for the first time, playing a boy in *Cyrano de Bergerac* at Elitch Gardens, the city's resident theater. At nine she got free lessons at the Robert E. Bell School of Oratory, the only professional training she ever had. At ten she was able to recite extensively from *Hamlet*, and she could still do that at eighty. One evening in the middle of a meal Fania held my wife and me under her steadfast gaze and delivered with a good deal of fervor Hamlet's speech to Horatio about loyalty. When I expressed my astonishment, she offered us a lengthy exchange between Hamlet and Ophelia, taking both parts. How many years had it been since she had said those lines? She had never appeared in the play.

When Fanny was twelve, she joined the Camilla Martinson-St. George Company. It was a kind of travelling whore house, she later realized, when it wasn't performing melodramas in small midwestern towns. The Ogalallah, Nebraska, newspaper called Fanny "a bright little soubrette" who "possesses 'the divine spark' of real dramatic talent, and all who have seen her perform predict a great future for her." But the company folded right there in Nebraska, and Fanny went to work washing dishes to earn her way back to Denver. Then she got a job with Blanche Walsh—an actress of some reputation—to act in *A Broken Heart*, and when the star took the play to New York in 1903, the other actors chipped in enough to send Fanny along too.

Blanche Walsh attempted to arrange an alliance for a wealthy friend of hers in New York, Stephen Wood Roach, when he requested that she send over one of the actresses from her troupe. At sixteen, Fanny was still a virgin; further, despite the gypsy life she had led in the Camilla Martinson-St. George Company, she was fairly innocent. She reported to Roach's family brownstone palace as scheduled, to find a setting out of a world she had only known in stage fantasies: an opulently furnished museum. Her would-be seducer took one look at her and burst out laughing.

Stephen Roach, then about fifty years old, was the son of John Morgan Roach, who had made a vast fortune building ships. He was an idle, genial founder of the Lamb's Club, he served as an officer for the Morgan Ironworks, and he enjoyed spending his father's money. He became Fanny's protector, sponsor, and patron, as well as her first lover. She remained faithful to his friendship until his death in 1917—and he to hers, supporting her until she had independently established her reputation on the New York stage, photographing her in several of her roles, and "giving her away" in marriage to Carl Van Vechten in 1914.

Almost immediately upon her arrival in New York, Fanny found small parts in several plays, and on tour, somewhere between Los Angeles and Seattle in 1909, Fanny changed her name to Fania.

Long afterward, she told me she regretted that she had known nothing about Russian patronymics at the time; otherwise, she would have changed Marinoff to Marinova. "Fania Marinova! My God! Who knows what I might have done? Luybov in *The Cherry Orchard*! All three of *The Three Sisters*! I never played Chekhov! Or *Resurrection*!" We were washing dishes at the time, and she was up to her elbows in soapsuds, with an apron and a blue grosgrain hair-ribbon, and she didn't look very Russian. Carlo was in the drawing room trying to calm a bereft Armina Marshall, the recent widow of the Theatre Guild's Lawrence Langner, who had recently died. During dinner together around the kitchen table, Fania had said something that set Armina off, something thoughtless, something to the effect that, after all, Lawrence had been dead for several weeks and Armina ought to get on with her life; Fania was given to sudden outbursts that she regretted almost immediately. I too on occasion felt the sting of her hair-trigger wrath.

One Thanksgiving, two elderly actress-friends of Fania's were flirting with me over coffee after dinner around the kitchen table. "Stop that!" Fania cried out to them, "You're not going to whore in here and, besides, he's too young for you!" Regina Wallace laughed gaily and decided it was time to go home, but Virginia Hammond collapsed into hysterics and Carlo had to take her off to the drawing room. That was the night—again while we did up the dishes—that Fania told me, more than half-seriously, she rather believed she had been a birch tree in Russia in an earlier life, since its calm existence compensated for her current incarnation.

Back in New York in the fall of 1910, after her West Coast tour, she drifted into vaudeville for a few weeks and then, during the following season, her career got a boost when she was cast in a small part in *The Rainbow*, a play designed as a starring vehicle for the popular actor Henry Miller. "They're going to cut this part," Fania confided in Regina Wallace. "It's too good to leave in." Most of the theatrical pages of the city's newspapers explained that she herself had "been too good"—that is, Fania had stolen the play from Miller—and he himself admitted as much in an interview, desiring "that it be known to the profession generally." Moreover, he paid her the salary he would have paid had she remained in the play until it closed.

By the time Fania first met Carlo, her name was fairly well established in theatrical circles, and parts came her way with regularity. Her picture had appeared on the cover of *Redbook* in 1910, and she was frequently interviewed in other popular magazines. For Carlo, it was love at first sight, for he was staggered by her magnetism, vivacity, sexuality, odd beauty. He had heard of her, of course, but Fania had never heard of him—a tall, prematurely gray, dandily dressed, wobbly, buck-toothed assistant music critic on the staff of the *New York Times*. The photographer Paul Thompson introduced them in a restaurant where he was having dinner with Fania. It was August 1912, just one month after Carlo's divorce from Anna Snyder had become final.

Carlo and Fania met for the second time after a performance of *Within the Law* by his friend Bayard Viellier. He'd gone by chance to see the play a second time, without knowing that Fania had taken over a role in the cast. He hastened backstage to say now that he had found her again he had no intention of losing her. Fania did not want to believe what she knew to be true, that she too had fallen in love at first sight, or at least at second sight. He courted her properly and wooed her gently—for three days, and then they slept together and were afterwards inseparable, at least for about seven years.

Their initial passion was mutual, and, for Carlo, his first experience with a woman's full sexuality. He rarely spoke to her about his first wife, but Fania assumed that Anna Snyder's frigidity had been as much a part of the trouble as Carlo's homosexual dalliances. Mabel Dodge Luhan, in her 1936 memoir, *Movers and Shakers*, believed that the Marinoff-Van Vechten alliance was "rooted in eternity, odd and everlasting." Although "he was full of dead sweet affectionateness," as she termed it, demonstrated throughout his life "in warm friendships with men, it was Fania he loved then and ever after."

Soon they were an item for gossip columnists: "Clever Carl Van Vechten remains constant in his devotion to the fascinating Miss Marinoff," *Town Topics* reported in the spring of 1913, "a darksome and delightful slip of a girl. Play-going, table d'hoting and turkey-trotting, they are quite inseparable." Even living in the same city, Carlo wooed her by letter as often as in person, and when he left for a European holiday in the spring of 1913, he arranged for his sister to post daily letters to Fania while she was appearing for the summer season in New Haven.

In the fall, she went into rehearsals for *A Thousand Years Ago*, Percy MacKaye's adaptation of the play by Carlo Gozzi, later lifted in part as the libretto for Puccini's *Turandot*. Carlo went to work as drama critic for the *New York Press*, and through the season their romance ripened. In the spring, when Fania was between plays and Carlo had been fired from his job, they went abroad together, first to London, then to Paris and Venice—a leisurely holiday until Fania had to return to begin rehearsals for *Consequences*. As soon as she left, Carlo realized how deeply in love he was and wished he'd returned with her. He proceeded instead to Florence to visit Mabel Dodge at the Villa Curonia, got caught by the outbreak of the war, returned on a cattle boat in October, and promptly proposed.

They were married in Connecticut—divorced people could not marry in New York at the time—on 21 October 1914, attended by Regina Wallace and Stephen Roach. Fania and Carlo each had a tiny apartment under lease, so during the first few months of their marriage they lived apart. In a subsequent newspaper interview, Fania said, "He'd go over to see me or I'd go over to see him and sometimes we visited each other for a day or so. . . . The tradesmen were horrified. . . . As for me, I was having an affair with my husband. Living in sin, you know." They were constant correspondents when Fania was out of town in tryouts, and their plentiful letters surely indicate that the marriage was equally romantic and erotic, even embarrassing to the eyes of subsequent readers. Still, Carlo carefully preserved almost all of their letters for posterity, knowing they would be eventually read by strangers.

Fania made her first movie that fall, a picture starring Hazel Dawn, best remembered as the eponymous *Pink Lady* from the recent popular operetta. *One of Our Girls*—a nitrate movie now lost or disintegrated—led to a dozen others during the winter and into the new year, with a break in the spring when Fania played Louka, the sexy servant girl in George Bernard Shaw's *Arms and the Man* on Broadway. Most of the movies she made were forgettable, even embarrassing. She swam in a Florida river full of alligators, got shipwrecked off Long Island, picked roses in New Jersey on a freezing day in December, drove through a small town as a bride in an open Victoria and down Fifth Avenue in a grass skirt. Fania did not regret that none had survived.

In April 1915, Carlo's ex-wife sued him for back alimony when she learned that he had remarried. Rather than pay, he went to jail for a month; she settled for a flat $1,000 payoff. Finally free of her, Carlo went off to join Fania in the Bahamas where she was making another shipwreck movie. He even had a small role in it himself, as a riverboat captain. *Nedra*, based on George Barr McCutcheon's popular novel, was one of the first films ever made on location.

When Fania and Carlo returned to Manhattan, they took a top floor flat on East Nineteenth Street, known at the time as "the street of little hotels." Carlo had no job and was seriously in debt.

He couldn't get work on any of the local newspapers, not even freelancing, and so he wrote his first book instead.

Fania made some more movies, but she only took pride in one of them: *Life's Whirlpool*, based on Frank Norris's relentlessly grim novel, *McTeague*, in which she played Trina. It failed at the box office, but ten years later, Erich von Stroheim remade *McTeague* as *Greed*, with Zasu Pitts playing Fania's role. When Fania met him at a Hollywood party in 1930, he clicked his heels smartly and brushed her hand with his humorless lips and murmured, "I regret, Madame, that you were not my Trina. I have seen *Life's Whirlpool*, and I regret that you were not my Trina." Then he backed away, slowly and formally, and vanished into the crowd.

In the spring of 1916, Fania had a great success as Ariel in *The Tempest*, in an opulent tercentenary production, photographs of which are often included in theater books designed to hold down coffee tables. Usually the photographs—made by Stephen Roach—are of Fania, up a tree or casting spells, in a *Bride of Frankenstein* fright wig and a sprite's outfit with gossamer balloon sleeves and a hemline sufficiently abbreviated to show off her sturdy legs.

A year later Fania nearly went to jail when she appeared as the fourteen-year-old Wendla in the first American production of Frank Wedekind's *Spring's Awakening*. This 1891 German play, about repressed adults racked with puritanism and their sexually precocious adolescent children, includes rape, masturbation, homosexuality, and suicide—all candidly on stage—and is withal a highly moral work that suffers not at all from prurience. Shortly before the curtain was scheduled to rise on the play's debut, the city commissioner of licenses arrived to prevent its doing so; but a last-minute injunction allowed the performance to go on. According to the *New York Times*,

> With many sniggers, rollings of the eye, and gestures indicating intellectual freedom, a large and strangely compounded audience assembled yesterday afternoon . . . to witness "Frühlingserwachen" at its first performance in what you might call English. . . . Present were Emma Goldman, Geraldine Farrar, and Elisabeth Marbury, who withdrew as soon as possible. . . . There was an elderly gentleman who whiled away the intervals between acts reading "The Birth Control Review."

The audience witnessed the solo matinee performance before the police stepped in to close the controversial curtains. Nor did a partial second performance in the courtroom—of scenes designed to demonstrate the play's serious intentions and lack of sensationalism—persuade the judge to allow the production to continue. Fania always considered Trina in *Life's Whirlpool* and Ariel in *The Tempest* and Wendla in *Spring's Awakening* her best parts, her best performances.

At this time—the spring of 1917—Fania may have been pregnant. If so, she may have had an abortion or given the child up for adoption. All three possibilities seem improbable, despite clues pointing in their direction. The evidence is circumstantial, based largely on extant correspondence, the coincidence of dates, the length of time it took mail to travel halfway across the country, and the memories of descendants, but also on the fact that Carlo may not have preserved all correspondence and family documents, despite his claims that he did.

In June, Carlo and Fania made the two-day train trip to his home town, Cedar Rapids, Iowa, to visit "Father," as they both called Charles Duane Van Vechten. They left there on the seven-

teenth according to a note from the elder Van Vechten. A week
later, one of Fania's nieces wrote to her: "I suppose you received
my letters, addressed to Iowa." No envelope has survived to determine where the letter was sent. Although Fania and Carlo corresponded incessantly whenever they were separated because of
rehearsals, tours, and location movies, no letters from her to him
have survived from August 1917 until the following June, after
which they resumed their regular pattern. Similarly, although
Carlo corresponded frequently with his father and his brother
Ralph, there is a gap in their letters to him from August 1917
until February 1919.

During the 1917–1918 theater season, while Fania was in rehearsals in New York and then performances there in *The Walkoffs*, Carlo sent her various cards and greetings and some pseud-
onymous fan letters signed "Hector Burnside" and "Stanford
Hennisy." Three months later, in June, he wrote again when
Fania was visiting a friend in Tompkins Corners, New York, and
she replied:

> I hope you are enjoying my absence as much as you should and are
> taking advantage of the knowledge that I cannot possibly "butt
> in" on you.
> . . . Be as good as you feel BUT remember you have a loving
> faithful charming little wife.

Fania's next letter is dated 12 September 1918, but there is no
indication of where she was when she wrote it, and no envelope
has survived. The content makes clear that she was again visiting a friend, somewhere familiar and comfortable, but her maddeningly elliptical postscript can only encourage re-examina-
tion of the previous year's calendar:

I shall be thinking particularly
of you to-morrow
Baby Van Vechten
I wish I could say more
but I can't
anyway
I don't feel like Father
all love always
your Fan
7 p.m.
Wednesday

Both Fania and Carlo regularly observed every date of any significance between them with cards, small tokens, flowers, little
gifts, the day they first met, the second time they met, the first
time they slept together, their wedding day, their birthdays. To
the best of my knowledge, September thirteenth carried no such
significance. Carlo and Fania sometimes addressed each other as
baby, but "Baby Van Vechten" gives me pause in its context. Did
she have a child and give it up for adoption? Did plans for that
eventuality occasion their trip to Cedar Rapids? Was it fear of
another pregnancy that took Fania out of town or off on European holidays and cruises during the years that followed, thereby
allowing Carlo some sexual latitude? If so, she had to have considered what direction that would take.

At some time between 1918 and 1920, Carlo's childhood
friend, Leah Maynard Storm—the younger sister of his brother
Ralph's wife—took in a young child, from the Cedar Rapids Orphanage for foster care. The child's name was Evelyn, but Leah
and her husband Henry renamed her Marilyn at some later date.
All records of the transaction, subsequent adoption, and even the

date of the child's birth, held by the Cedar Rapids Guaranty Bank and Trust—the Van Vechten family bank for three generations—were apparently destroyed. Several years after Marilyn had gone to live with the Storms, Ralph Van Vechten's wife wrote to her sister Leah that "everything has been arranged to take care of Evelyn's adoption." The five- or six-year delay before adoption would not have been unusual; Duane Van Vechten, the "adopted" daughter of Ralph and his wife, was never legally adopted.

Carlo had always corresponded with Leah Maynard Storm and continued to do so until her death, although he never mentioned Marilyn in any of his extant letters to her. Leah herself refused to discuss Marilyn's origins, and when she died most of her papers were destroyed in accordance with her wishes. In early photographs, Marilyn Storm bears no marked resemblance to Fania other than their similar cupid's bow mouths, nor does Marilyn carry the distinctive Van Vechten dished profile and Dutch chin. However, in 1980, another member of the Van Vechten clan confided in Marilyn but without explanation, "You are on our family tree, you know." Marilyn had suspected this all her life but had no evidence.

In the fall of 1917, when Marilyn Storm may have been born, Carlo aspired to be a successful writer, although three published books had not produced a living wage. Fania aspired to be a serious actress, and moreover she was already under contract to appear in *The Walkoffs* on Broadway, even though it was just the sort of commercial vehicle she tried to avoid. A child would have been emotionally as well as financially impractical, and that inevitably raises questions about adoption and abortion.

Was history only repeating itself? Some years later, Carlo's first wife, Anna Snyder, confided in Leah Maynard Storm that she had been pregnant by Carlo when they were married in the spring of 1907. In the fall of 1906—although dates can easily enough add or subtract a year long after the fact because of faulty memory or by deliberate design—Charles Duane Van Vechten "found" a male infant on his front porch. The Van Vechtens' recently retired cook and their milkman married well into middle age and took in the child to adopt. I am now obliged to quote myself in repeating what I wrote above about Marilyn Storm Cory's adoption: "All records of the transaction, subsequent adoption, and even of the child's date of birth, held by the Cedar Rapids Guaranty Bank and Trust—the Van Vechten family bank for three generations—were apparently destroyed." Charles Duane Van Vechten then paid for Richard Henecke's piano lessons and for his education at Coe College, in Cedar Rapids, and then offered him a job in the family bank. The "foundling" refused, determined to make his own way. Photographs made in early middle age of Don Henecke, the son of Richard the "foundling," would be identified by anyone who ever saw Carl Van Vechten as Carl Van Vechten himself. The resemblance is uncanny. Of course both Richard Henecke and Marilyn Storm Cory might be the result of Ralph's indiscretions.

Back in New York, together again in the fall of 1918, Carlo and Fania found life less than calm. Sexual tension may have hung in the air if my speculations are accurate; certainly money, or rather the lack of it, threatened time and again to tear them apart. Beginning in early 1917, Carlo's brother—by that time a wealthy Chicago banker—had begun sending Fania $25 a week to see them through. Otherwise, they survived by taking things to pawn shops and getting loans and small payments from Carlo's occasional magazine articles. Books of musical and literary criticism brought in very little return, and the kind of theater that Fania aspired to was unlikely to produce much income. She had signed for a season's engagement with the Greenwich Village Players in a series of decidedly non-commercial pieces: a religious cycle from the middle ages, a commedia dell'arte play, impressionistic mythology in verse, and naturalistic drama by Arthur Schnitzler. When she was interviewed for *Puck* magazine at the end of the season, she made her case:

> I have never been so happy in my life. This is what I have dreamed of—what I have scarcely dared to hope for. It is the ambition of my life realized. It is my emancipation from the commercial theatre. . . . Broadway! . . . What does Broadway mean? It means that every night the actor is miserable as he asks himself, "I wonder if we close Saturday"; that perhaps there isn't "money" in the house; that he never knows from one minute to the other what will happen to him and his play. Broadway! One has to be a "type" rather than an actor to succeed on Broadway— and I hate being a type. . . . I have been on the stage since I was eight years old . . . and I know its bitter side thoroughly. My rôles were always limited to my looks, as I have just said. I was small, and dark, and peculiar. The idea of being engaged by the yard does not appeal to me. . . . I don't want to go through my stage life acting rôles that I *look*. You see, I look so few. . . .
>
> I am tremendously fond of the stage, . . . and not at all in a stage-struck way, you know. I like the work. I enjoy congenial rôles—rôles that mean something. I am not particularly interested in Broadway parts—and by that I mean the sort of thing that "goes" on Broadway. I want a part that I can study, one that has subtlety and significance. Then I am happy.

Meanwhile, Carlo's books did not sell for another four years, and in 1919 he was obliged to start cashing in some of the principal on the investments Carlo's father had made for him years before. By that time, prohibition had begun to spawn hundreds of speakeasies all over the city, and drinking, which had not been so resolute a pastime, became a major preoccupation for many people, at private parties as well in the illegal joints. The daybooks that Carlo kept from 1922 through 1930 offer more than ample evidence of just how much of their lives was taken up with and wasted by the social milieu of what he later called "The Splendid Drunken Twenties." Toward the end of the decade he wrote, "If I don't stop drinking, I'm going to blow up."

Carlo was out of control a good deal of the time when he'd had too much to drink, insulting guests at other people's parties as well as at his own, staging monumental rows with Fania, threatening to bite somebody and crying, "Woof! Woof!" A morning hangover only portended another night's bender. He could be abusive too, when he was drunk, physically as well as verbally. More than once he noted in his daybooks, "I get rough with Marinoff." Often, Fania spent the night with Regina Wallace, sometimes in anticipation of late rows, sometimes leaving the apartment in the middle of one; four times in two weeks she had to spend the night there, "as I am soused," Carlo wrote, and he was always contrite. But after four bouts in two weeks, Fania left him after the last of these altercations—permanently, she insisted, moving out to New Jersey with her brother Jacob.

Carlo was beside himself, distracted, grief-stricken, contrite, and his daybook entries are hysterical and uncontrolled, at first because he did not know where she had gone, later because she refused to see him: "I shall go out of my mind." "I shall go mad." "She says she is through forever. If she is what is there in life for me?" The next day they reconciled, and he never touched her again except in affection.

Their sexual marriage resumed sporadically and continued for several years, although at the time Carlo was having an intermittent affair with Donald Angus, a nineteen-year-old boy whose interest in opera and music had first drawn them together. Angus was Carlo's most constant companion through the twenties, long after their affair had ended, especially on late night forays into Harlem. Fania adored Angus, just as she adored Avery Hopwood, the popular playwright who had been one of Carlo's liaisons before he met Fania, and she knew he had been involved with other men as well. In her very old age, she said that she had never understood her marriage: it was a sexual marriage, yes, for a long time, but more importantly it was a spiritual marriage, and she resented—as strongly as she regretted—that she had outlived Carlo because she had no desire to live without him.

"It is completely unnatural, darling," she once averred, "to live with another person all the time, and it is just as unnatural to live alone all the time. Carlo could drive me mad when we were together, but I could be just as mad when we were apart. Who can explain that?"

When Carlo's career as a writer began to pay off in 1922 —with four best-selling novels in four years—their financial worries were well behind them. He was a celebrity. Newspapers chronicled their social life, and Fania gradually withdrew from the stage. There were a few more engagements, but by the mid-Twenties she had more or less retired from the theatre to the speakeasy. By that time, she and Carlo had taken a large apartment on West 55th Street and begun to entertain lavishly, in a still largely segregated New York. They counted among their closest friends James Weldon and Grace Johnson, Paul and Essie Robeson, Walter and Gladys White, Nella Larsen and Elmer

Imes, and many single people as well, like Ethel Waters, Nora Holt, Dorothy Peterson, Zora Neale Hurston, and Langston Hughes. Their apartment was called in more than one black newspaper "the midtown office of the N.A.A.C.P.," and their parties were written up as a matter of course in black gossip columns.

Away from home, Fania went to the theater with one or another of a battery of male escorts, visited women friends and her vast army of Marinoff relatives, or took European holidays. Carlo, at the same time, was regularly slumming in cabarets and at rent parties and buffet flats, attending late night entertainments at the Lafayette Theatre in Harlem, dancing with drag queens, and, when Fania was out of town or abroad, having an occasional black call boy up for an evening or an overnight. Carlo spent far more time in Harlem pursuits than Fania did, but her commitment to social and aesthetic equality was no less passionate than his.

Revisionist critics easily dismiss the white patronage of the Twenties that attempted to integrate black artists and writers during the Harlem Renaissance into mainstream culture. Sometimes they do so by rewriting history. Such was the case on the night that black pianist Porter Grainger brought Bessie Smith up to sing at a Van Vechten party. Carlo refers to it in his daybook as a "party for Bessie Smith who came (soused). . . ." She sang three songs eloquently for a group that included, among others, Walter White and James Weldon Johnson of the N.A.A.C.P., the actresses Constance Collier, Cathleen Nesbitt, Regina Wallace, Harry Block, the caricaturist Miguel Covarrubias, Blanche Knopf, Donald Angus, and the Peruvian contralto Marguerite d'Alvarez, who also sang that evening. Then, when Bessie Smith prepared to leave, Fania attempted to kiss her in gratitude and got knocked to the floor by a wide swing from the singer's substantial arm. "What is this shit?" she muttered as Grainger hustled her out the door in a hurry. Most of the guests were unaware of the occurrence.

With the passing of fifty years or so, the story got revised. Carlo forced liquor on a "cold sober" Bessie Smith to keep her singing, "with the eagerness of a man kindling at last a long-awaited fire." Then, when she and Grainger prepared to leave, according to the singer's biographer, Chris Albertson, "an effusive woman stopped them at the front door":

> "Miss Smith," she said, throwing her arms around Bessie's massive neck and pulling it forward, " you're not leaving without giving me a kiss goodbye!"
>
> That was all Bessie needed.
>
> "Get the fuck away from me," she roared, thrusting her arms forward and knocking the woman to the floor. "'I ain't never *heard* of such shit.'"
>
> In the silence that followed Bessie stood in the middle of the foyer, now looking as if she were ready to take on the whole crowd. . . .
>
> Under the horrified stares of the guests, [Grainger] . . . escorted the Empress out the door and down the richly carpeted hall to the elevator.

Carlo's published account does not mention any of this, nor do his daybooks account for the incident. In their old age, Carlo, Fania, Donald Angus, and others remembered the evening less melodramatically.

During the heyday of such high bohemia, Fania turned down a number of roles, including—ironically, since she had longed to

play it a few years before—the lead in the Theatre Guild's production of *Caesar and Cleopatra* by George Bernard Shaw. Many
years later, I asked Armina Marshall Langner why she thought
Fania's career had ended early. She put it down to Fania's refusal
to do that particular part. It could have insured her permanent
ranking as a star, but Fania was thirty-seven years old then, and
the Serpent of the Nile was a teenager. The role went to Helen
Hayes. Aside from some radio broadcasts, playing Ariel in *The
Tempest* and Viola in *Twelfth Night*, Fania did not act again for
several years. Instead, she made half a dozen voyages to Europe,
three with Carlo. During a trip to London in 1926 she tried,
at Avery Hopwood's urging, for work on the British stage, but
whatever failed efforts she may have made went unrecorded.

In 1928, Hopwood died, leaving Fania and Carlo each the
equivalent of about a fifth of a million dollars, no small sum at
the time, for a million now carries about ten times its value during the Twenties. Hopwood had considered the Van Vechtens his
closest friends. They staggered with him through his drinking
bouts; his incredible financial success on Broadway; and his abusive relationship with his longtime lover John Floyd, offering
them alternating solace after particularly bloody bouts. Hopwood died of a heart attack soon after an altercation with Floyd
in Juan les Pins.

As a result of Hopkins's largesse—to say nothing of just over
a million dollars in trust that Carlo inherited from his brother
at almost the same time—neither of them needed to work any
longer. Still, Carlo went on to write two more novels, and Fania
was involved is some serious talk about a production of *Othello*,
with Paul Robeson, but nothing came of it. In 1930, Fania went
out to Hollywood to make a test, since the movies were all talk-

ing by that time, and many of the actors simply could not, not in public anyway. Fania always had a richly resonant contralto when I knew her, affected but very beautiful too, and the few people I knew who had seen her on stage all spoke of its quality. She liked her screen test: it wasn't "bad," she noted in one of the few diaries she ever kept, "voice wonderful, eyes interesting. Photography might have been better. Show enormous power and decision, good possibilities." But no offers came her way. She was then forty-three years old, and despite her diminutive size she looked her age.

Fania returned to New York and sailed with Carlo on the Mauretania for a long summer in Europe, stopping first in London to see George Moore, the Robesons, and Jacob Epstein; then visiting Carlotta Monterey and Eugene O'Neill at their chateau, and Gertrude Stein and Alice Toklas at their manor house in Bilignin, both in France; then they went to Berlin. It was "like Rome under Caligula," Carlo later said after several nights hanging out in homosexual bars.

On their return from Europe, Fania acted for two seasons with the Westport Playhouse, being run then by their friends Lawrence Langner and Armina Marshall of the Theatre Guild, and in 1934 she returned to Broadway for a personal success in Elmer Rice's *Judgment Day,* although the play failed after a brief run. Three years later she appeared as Charmian with Tallulah Bankhead in *Antony and Cleopatra,* a major catastrophe for everybody involved, backstage as well as onstage. It sent her into more or less permanent retirement except for a Broadway flop with Fritzi Scheff and a revival of Thornton Wilder's *The Skin of Our Teeth* a few years later. Meanwhile, Carlo had fallen in love with photography and spent the rest of his life making portraits of just about anybody of note he could get to sit for him. Simultaneously, he fell in love with Mark Lutz, a Richmond, Virginia, writer twenty years his junior who, like Donald Angus before him, remained an intimate friend afterward, even following Carlo's death.

In between, the Van Vechtens moved again. A garage had opened on West 54th Street, right under Fania's windows and she couldn't stand the noise. They took an apartment at 101 Central Park West, with a large foyer featuring a black and white marble floor and floor to ceiling bookcases, a mammoth drawing room with a fireplace, a formal dining room, bedroom suites, a studio for Carlo's photography, and plenty of wall space for their art collection.

Also, in between, Fania took a new role, playing an actress—playing herself—when the Stage Door Canteen opened during the Second World War. She had been one of the first members of the Theatre Guild to sign on for regular shifts in the basement of the Forty-Fourth Street Theatre where, in early March 1942, the first flank of thousands of servicemen began the invasion. For three years, Fania and Carlo never missed their Monday and Tuesday shifts. She danced with the boys, served up food, washed dishes. As a Captain of the American Theatre Wing, Carlo was responsible for his own regiment of busboys, all of whom were homosexual and on the make. Patriotism was not the only incentive for volunteering to clear tables, wash dishes, take out the trash, and sometimes the clientele.

Fania had let her hair go gray by then, and Saul Mauriber—a self-described dress-designer and decorator who had joined Carlo's stable of young men—gave her home permanents to keep it curly. Soon enough, he had become the Van Vechtens' unpaid factotum, and for some years he and Carlo were lovers. His loyalty to both Carlo and Fania is unquestionable; he shopped, hung pictures, served as bartender at parties, acted as escort for one or the other or both of them. More importantly, he acted as lighting assistant during photographic sessions and brought all of the photographs and color slides into order by indexing and cross-referencing them. There were over thirteen hundred subjects and eventually over fifteen thousand photographs since many subjects were photographed many times. Mauriber then dry-mounted many of them, catalogued, wrapped and shipped them off to various collections Carlo established over the years in university and museum libraries. When I first met the Van Vechtens, in 1953, he was around so much of the time that I thought he lived with them but was forcibly set straight on that issue by both Fania and Carlo.

For several years after our initial encounter, I saw Fania fairly regularly, although she travelled a good deal during the Fifties, long cruises of the Mediterranean and the Baltic, weekends with the Langners and other old friends, so she was often out of town when I called. But I remember her at a succession of large gatherings at 146 Central Park West, another large apartment, to which they'd moved shortly after we first met. In a whoosh of baubles, bangles, and beads, she'd play the room like an old-time stage star, although on other occasions she'd simply disappear early on and go to bed. She could also spin up to somebody, just like a little top—as she did one evening to a friend of mine, there for the first time—say, "Hello, who are you? I don't know you," and spin away again. A line like that didn't get delivered *sotto voce* either. Both she and Carlo were hard of hearing; one was obliged to speak up, even after they acquired hearing aids. They both always spoke up themselves, and Fania was not above shouting if she felt especially enthusiastic or angry or delighted or just wanting a little attention.

At one party, after Alvin Ailey and Carmen de Lavallade had kicked off their shoes for a deliriously sexy dance in the foyer, the singer William Warfield told raunchy stories. Fania pretended to be indignant that so many "intellectuals," as she collectively identified us, couldn't have "an intelligent conversation instead of turning my house into a brothel!"

Everybody laughed but Carlo. "Miss Marinoff speaks from experience, having been reared in one," he intoned in a dead-pan bark.

On another occasion, Peter David Marchant, a young academic who had just completed his master's degree with a thesis about Carlo's writings, complimented Fania on her perfume. She dashed from the room, thrusting guests aside en route, returned with the bottle, and insisted that he take it home with him. That was the evening she looked up at Beverly Sills—then very young and very pretty, with cascades of bright red hair, towering above her hostess on steel high heels—and announced loudly enough for everybody to hear, "You're going to be a great star, darling!" Fania had not yet heard her sing, but a few nights later at Lewisohn Stadium she screamed out her enthusiasm and Carlo barked forcibly, "Woof! Woof!" when Beverly Sills made her debut there.

In theaters, their vocal outbursts could vex less indulgent audiences. They always sat in the first row if they could, got hushed and hissed at by adjacent members of the audience, and rarely heard the complaints. They hooted too loudly at Leontyne Price's bloomers in *La Fanciulla del West*, and barked out something to everybody sitting around them about Julie Harris wearing the same dress two acts in succession in *A Shot in the Dark*. But Fania could be circumspect too. We first went to the theater together in 1953 to see *Wonderful Town*, in which a boy spilled a glass of red punch all over his white suit. It got a huge laugh from the audience, but Fania murmured, "Rather expensive joke."

Once, returning to their apartment building, she threatened to burst into hysterics when the elevator stuck momentarily between floors, screaming at Carlo to do something. He stunned her into temporary silence with a roar to shut up, and then they both began yelling until it started up again and didn't cease until we reached their floor. As soon as we entered the apartment, Fania stormed down the hall to her bedroom suite. Half an hour later, she joined us for dinner at a card table in Carlo's library, wreathed in smiles and sweet talk.

That was not the first nor the last instance when I witnessed one of their public performances. Dining with Carlo and Fania a few years later at the Women's Exchange, her favorite restaurant at the time, I made the mistake of asking where they had met. Carlo claimed that the initial encounter had occurred in Claridge's, a popular restaurant of the period where singers and actors frequently gathered. Fania insisted that they met first at Rector's, another place popular for the same reasons. A huge fight ensued. But they'd had so many screaming arguments there—Fania always did nearly all of the screaming—that the management took no notice.

Carlo was adamant and sullen, and he kept repeating in a loud, flat voice, "You don't know what you're talking about. You don't know what you're talking about."

Fania's internal thermometer soared higher, and inarticulate gasps punctuated derisive barks and cries of disagreement. She sounded as if she were going to hyperventilate, although Carlo continued to eat his dinner placidly, telling her between mouthfuls like a broken record that she didn't know what she was talking about. Finally she shouted, "I was never in Claridge's in my life!"

"Miss Marinoff, we had our first wedding anniversary dinner at Claridge's. You don't know what you're talking about."

There was a long pause. "Oh, lamby, wasn't it lovely?" she cooed.

I think I did not feel entirely comfortable with Fania for a long time, but the wrath I'd witnessed against others never really came my way with any serious force; I think she liked me. She liked the first draft of my projected Van Vechten biography until she got to the fourth chapter—about herself. She had reacted "quite violently," Carlo said, although I had included only what he had told me, or what she had told me, or what I'd read in her own scrapbooks, so I was quite prepared to defend myself. In the end she was only disturbed by the fact that I'd given her correct date of birth. After that, my relationship with her was quite different, easier, more intimate. She asked me to call her Fanny. She liked my fiancee a lot, and said so, when I took Margaret around to meet the Van Vechtens several months before we were married.

Carlo said he'd never put much stock in my earlier romances and liaisons—some of whom he had met—but he heartily approved of Margaret, and announced that he was going to be my best man, which prompted Fania to announce that she would be matron of honor. Margaret and I didn't have much to say about that, but that was okay, even a sweet idea, since we had planned on a wedding in New York City anyway.

We converged at the chapel of the Little Church Around the Corner just off Fifth Avenue on 29th Street, on a rainy, late December afternoon: Carlo and Fania and me in one cab; Margaret, Margaret's mother, and my best friend Richard Rutledge in another. Richard was the congregation, and Margaret's mother gave away the bride. The Van Vechtens were on their best behavior, Fania in quiet lavender and Carlo in a white shirt and pale blue tie and black jacket. I was a little disappointed that Margaret's mother didn't get a good look at the eccentric garb we'd warned her to expect, especially Carlo's garish silk shirts and ties, deliberately assembled to clash, I always thought. Fania wore a beatific smile until Carlo had to be prompted more than once to come up with the rings, but she kept her mouth shut, at least until the brief ceremony was over.

"Is that all?" Fania cried, raising her voice in indignation when I kissed the bride. There were exclamation points as well as a question mark hanging in the air. Then we repaired to 146 Central Park West for dinner—served in the photography studio—and champagne.

Two days later, Fania was too ill to attend a party being given for us by a mutual friend, and from that time on it seemed to me that she was always ailing. Minor illnesses had plagued her for at least twenty years. She was exhausted after a Mediterranean cruise; she was operated on for diverticulitis; her sight began to deteriorate; her hearing further diminished. She'd go to Atlantic City for the fresh air and return complaining of the crowds; she'd take long recuperative weekends at spas in the Catskills, only to feel worse afterward. About three weeks before their fiftieth wedding anniversary, Carlo wrote, "FM has every kind of nerves there is and she has had a grand time to exploit them." Then, in the middle of December, he wrote that "Fania is better, and I am in the pink." She was then seventy-seven, and he was eighty-four.

On December twentieth, Carlo went to bed right after dinner; that was unusual, and Fania went in to check on him. He had changed into his pajamas. Was he asleep? "Carlo!" she cried, for he never went to bed so early.

He was immediately alert. "I tried to sleep," he said, "and you woke me."

"Goodnight, Lamby," Fania said, and leaned down to kiss him.

The following morning the customary smell of coffee did not awaken her. She walked down the strangely silent hall to Carlo's bedroom and entered. His eyes and mouth were open. She knew he was dead. Later, she said she was unaware of her actions, as if she were watching someone else perform them. She closed his eyes. She carried his chamber pot into the bathroom and emptied it. Then she went into the kitchen and made herself some coffee. It was a cold morning, with a gray sky like a shroud over the city, but she opened the windows in the pantry and breathed deeply. Then she summoned the elevator operator and asked him to find the house physician. Then she called Saul Mauriber.

By late afternoon, telegrams had gone out to several friends: "=CARL VAN VECHTEN PASSED AWAY THIS MORNING IN HIS SLEEP=FANIA=" Saul was largely responsible for the guest list for the memorial service at the apartment a few days later—there was no funeral—and took care of all of its arrangements. I was unable to attend because my wife had given birth to our son almost simultaneously with Carlo's death, but friends wrote to tell me about the memorial service.

Fania was so distraught that she had to be propped up, but she did manage a few words to thank everyone sitting there, row upon row in the foyer and the drawing room. Then before everybody had left—although many had—Fania suddenly turned on Saul, condemning him for wishing she had died instead so that he could be "Mrs. Carl Van Vechten." Regardless of whatever truth the accusation might have contained, it was a tactical error, and Fania suffered as a result. Saul was certainly in the deepest grief of his own; he had, after all, devoted over twenty years to Carlo and his projects. But once he had disposed of photographic materials in accordance with most of Carlo's wishes, he disappeared from her life.

When three months later I planned a trip into New York, I wrote to ask if I could see her; Fania telegraphed back: "=SINCE CARLS SUDDEN DEATH I REMAIN IN A STATE OF SHOCK AND SORROW FORGIVE ME UNABLE TO WRITE WILL BE HAPPY TO SEE YOU BOTH IN MARCH. THE BABY IS BEAUTIFUL CONGRATULATIONS AND LOVE=FANIA"

Fania had moved down Central Park West into smaller quarters, very elegant indeed, with a view of Lincoln Center from the back and of the park from the front. A lot of things had been disposed of, like the grand piano and the big credenzas, but she'd made an effort to recreate 146 Central Park West on a miniature scale. But the earlier ambience—simultaneously magical and opulent and cozy—was gone forever, not because of the smaller space but because Fania had had lights of such high wattage installed that everything looked garish. The ornate Venetian glass chandelier, for instance, which she'd bought in Venice and brought back in its hundreds of faceted and hand-blown pieces without breaking one of them, seemed somehow vulgar with so much light. Glaring reflections bounced off pictures' glass and oil paintings had blooms of light on them that moved when whoever was looking at them moved.

Mark Lutz, Carlo's lover during the Thirties and subsequently his intimate friend, had come to her rescue immediately, training in from Philadelphia many times, to help her settle in, but when the hour grew so late that he had to stay over, she insisted on locking up at nine PM, and they were prisoners until dawn. Donald Angus, Carlo's earlier lover and similarly an intimate friend afterward, had the same experience when he trained in from Ardmore, Pennsylvania, to help her sort through her belongings. It was virtually impossible to get her to part with anything.

In the fall Fania went on a cruise of the Mediterranean, scheduled to stop at a number of ports, but she returned in a terrible state, exhausted by bad food, bad weather, impossible passengers, and rude stewards. She had not gone ashore at a single stop along the way, she claimed, since she'd been to all of the ports before and why should she bother? She decided at that point to move again and telephoned to say she wanted to give Margaret and me "all my furniture." She was moving to the Century Apartments, and had to get rid of "everything." She couldn't stand the noise of the wind blowing against the glass French doors that opened onto the lovely little terrace fronting her new drawing room.

I took the five hour bus trip from Oneonta, New York, into the city—to approve of the pair of handsomely needlepointed walnut side chairs, the impressive Korean chests, the mahogany cabinet that Carlo had used to store sheet music, some cartons of dishes and trinkets, and a ghastly, oversized, red lacquer oriental floor lamp, hardly "all her furniture" but a nice haul, and I made arrangements for movers to collect it. I'd been home for a day when she telegraphed: "=SORRY I FIND NEED CHAIRS CHEST CABINET LAMP GONE TODAY LOVE=FA-NIA=" As the telegram had no punctuation, Margaret and I had visions of having to pay a sizable minimum freight bill to transport that lamp, but everything except the chairs arrived.

Fania's new apartment was about the same size, far more room than she needed, but she seemed reasonably comfortable, and the long series of unsatisfactory domestics temporarily terminated with Fania's finding Novella, a pleasant and patient African American woman of about fifty. I made the mistake of referring to her as "black" one evening, since circa 1966 "Negro" was losing its acceptable currency. Fania flew into a rage about that, not at me but at the word itself. She had always said *Negro*, darling, and intelligent, cultured *Negroes* preferred to be called *Negroes*. She had never said *Colored Person*, and she was goddamned if she was going to start saying *Black*. Over her shoulder I saw Novella standing at the kitchen door, smiling with her eyes closed and shaking her head at me as if to say she was used to it.

Mark Lutz had been out of the country in the spring of 1965 when Fania wanted to dispose of Carlo's ashes, so that ceremony was delayed a full year. On what would have been his eighty-sixth birthday, 17 June 1966, Fania, Mark, and Carlo's longtime lawyer Joseph Solomon went to Central Park to scatter the ashes in the Shakespeare Garden there, under the oak from Stratford-on-Avon, at sunset. Mark dug a furrow with a silver spoon and they took turns filling it. "A highly emotional woman under any circumstances," Mark wrote to me afterward, Fania "remained remarkably calm through the whole thing." Afterward, he reflected, "I believe it is against some ordinance or other to scatter ashes in the garden, but the fuzz did not catch us."

Fania's ailments increased, most tellingly her sight, for she had always been a compulsive reader. She had little appetite for food and none at all for what her diverticulitus would allow her to eat. She suffered mightily from insomnia, fear of the dark— a holdover from childhood—and she could only walk with a stagger.

Mark died less than two years later. Accepting his help had been difficult for Fania because of his intense relationship with Carlo, but without his regular forays in from Philadelphia she felt abandoned all over again. Having known Mark only briefly, she had at first welcomed his help reluctantly, but soon enough she had realized what a loyal friend he had proven to be. Donald Angus, whom she'd long loved despite his early affair with Carlo, went in to see her when he was able to get away from his job. I saw her whenever I was in town, and I wrote to her maybe once a week. Regina Wallace and Armina Langner and a few other elderly actresses continued to call on her, also Virgil Thomson now and then, also several relatives, but she had been pretty clearly abandoned by most of Carlo's friends whom she had thought of as *their* friends.

A couple of times I took her out to dinner, both catastrophes. By that time we had moved to Lancaster, Pennsylvania, so it was easier to get into New York. At the Russian Tea Room, where Fania had wanted to go, not having been there in years, she was frustrated and caused a ruckus because the romantic lighting merely made the menu unreadable. Next I took her to the Women's Exchange, where things went pretty well until after we'd eaten. Then New York staged one of its cataclysmic rainstorms and I was unable to flag a cab. Fania began to careen and lurch, and she was not acting. In desperation, I persuaded her to take a cross-town bus. At least half a dozen people rose simultaneously to offer her their seats as soon as I more or less carried her on.

After that, we ate in whenever I came to see her, and I am not convinced that she ever again went out to eat. A new succession of cook-housekeepers followed Novella, none of whom proved satisfactory—"three stupid domestic dames in three weeks," she wrote in April 1969—although an enormous white registered nurse aptly named Faith had then taken over, and Fania had seemed finally content to be bossed around because Faith was so mothering about it. Faith's patience, too, in time abated.

Fania had an unsuccessful cataract operation after that, and macular degeneration set in. Her diverticulitis acted up again. She spent a great deal of time in bed, reminiscing about the past, parcelling out to me a dozen or so of Carlo's hundreds of ridiculously beautiful silk neckties each time I called, saying I could only have a dozen so that I'd return for some more. By the fall of 1969 she was "jogging along without any aim, interest or health."

In the spring of 1970, Fania wrote to her nephew Nathan Marinoff to offer him all of her belongings if he would come to help her pack up and move to a retirement home in Los Angeles, where he lived. It would only require about two weeks to settle everything, and he could stay at the nearby Y.M.C.A., she said. At the end of two months, he was still assisting her as she gave away not all but most of her belongings—to other people. I was commanded to come in for some books during this harried period, and on arrival she told me to take anything I wanted but that she needed to see what I was taking. I selected a small stack, most of which went right back on the shelves because, she said, she needed them. She couldn't understand why I didn't want dozens of ancient, decaying French grammars from which she'd learned to speak and read passably well, and when I said they were out of date she grew angry because nobody spoke good French anymore. She couldn't understand why I wanted her copy of Gertrude Stein's *Tender Buttons*. I said I'd never even seen a copy before, at which news she burst into tears and pushed it and everything else I'd selected—plus some others—right back at me.

By the end of the summer, she was ensconced in what sounded like a pretty good place, in "a large beautiful room . . . with space enough for most of the ridiculous amount of trunks, suitcases, etc, etc., that she insisted on taking with her." There were seven patients and seven staff members, Nathan Marinoff reported. "Fania, who as might be expected, requires and has been getting more attention than all the other six combined." She was not fighting him, he realized, but life itself. "In her better moments which are few and far between she tells me what an angel I am to her, then shortly thereafter begins to clip my wings, pulling out one feather at a time, blood and all." Then Fania accused him of bringing her to Los Angeles under false pretenses. Under threat of expulsion from the retirement home because of her recalcitrance, she disowned Nathan Marinoff, dismissed Carlo's nephew Van Vechten Shaffer as her conservator, and demanded that her lawyer Joseph Solomon fly out to Los Angeles to accompany her back to New York and relocate her.

He found what seemed to me an ideal locale. Martha Lorber, a well-known dancer during the Twenties, lived in retirement in a small village in New Jersey and took two paying guests—one in each of the two upstairs bedrooms—in her lovely cottage by a brook. The landscape was beautiful, Fania's room was comfortable, and Martha Lorber seemed genuinely concerned about this *actress* she'd seen in her youth and had so much admired. I drove up to visit Fania in high hopes. We'd moved from Oneonta, New York, to Lancaster, Pennsylvania, by that time, and it was not such a long drive to Martha Lorber's idyllic retreat. But Fania was convinced that the other paying guest—a woman in late middle age recovering from a nervous breakdown who spoke incessantly on the telephone to the dial tone—was trying to kill her. She sent me off with her diaries and packets of family letters, a painting of her as Ariel, a wax figure of her by Hidalgo, some scrapbooks, and hundreds of postcard photographs of her in her various roles in multiple copies, all for me to deliver to Carlo's collection at Yale; she gave my wife and me her portrait by Adolfo Best-Maugard, some silver and linens she'd hauled out to California and back again, and begged me to return to visit her.

A few days later I called to see how things were going and expected pretty much what I heard. Martha Lorber didn't really like her, she announced, loudly enough for anybody else in the house to hear. That other woman was piling books up outside her door so she'd trip on the way to the bathroom. The food was inedible. She was desperately lonely. She was so far removed from everybody who cared about her. Regina Wallace and Donald Angus couldn't come to visit her because they had no cars. Why was it raining all the time?

I asked her if she'd considered the Actors' Fund Home, for I knew that it was one of her favorite charities, but she grew indignant at the suggestion; she was not indigent! I got a long-distance lecture about some of the inmates there she couldn't stand, also a withering assessment of the meals. And then one morning she telephoned me. Oh, was there not some retirement home near Margaret and me in Lancaster where she could stay? She promised not to disturb us, not to make any demands, but perhaps we might come to see her now and then. My tears blinded me, and I could only think of the end of Auden's poem, "Old People's Home," in which he takes a subway to make a dutiful call on a now forgotten woman who once upon a time was glamorous and popular. A visit with her in those days, he remembers, seemed like a cheeky intrusion, not an hour-long chore. He wonders—as I surely wondered about Fania—if it is wrong of him to hope, as he knew she hoped, and I knew Fania hoped, for a mercifully immediate death.

Then Fania decided on her own that she would go to the De-Witt Nursing Home on East 79th Street in New York, a vast, noisy complex of numbered wards. After all, she reasoned, Mrs. Eugene O'Neill had been there. I did not remind Fania that Carlotta Monterey O'Neill was *non compos mentis* at the time, but I did offer to come up to Martha Lorber's and drive her into Manhattan. When she said she was just going to ride along in the moving van she'd engaged to transport her belongings, my eyes widened in a kind of hilarious horror at a vision of Fania propped up between two burly haulers in the front seat of a truck, and I wondered what they would make of her.

She lasted three weeks at DeWitt—just the length of time it took Joseph Solomon to relocate her again—and when I called during the interim she screamed over the telephone that she was going mad, that everybody was trying to do her in, that the food was dreadful, that the noise was incessant, that the clientele was illiterate or senile or both, that the attendants kept waking her up, that nobody came when she rang.

The Dunroven Home in New Jersey, the last stop on Fania's terrible journey down Cemetery Road, could not have been nicer. Fania had a double room to herself, a large corner space with two-way exposures through several large windows to a lovely, rolling landscape. The whole facility and the staff members I met there—including her "personal attendant," for which there was a hefty additional fee—seemed quite pleasant, although Fania bitterly resented being taken out for baths, encouraged to join the other residents for meals, and urged to work with one of the physical therapists. She stayed in bed most of the time and could move about only with a walker, which she refused to use, or with assistance from others.

Her hair had been cropped by that time, short and straight, and snowy, like a feather cloche from her heyday in the Twenties, and she seemed pleased when I said it was becoming. And so it was, although it framed a face now furrowed in grief, and her nearly sightless eyes stared vacantly and could no longer even make out the trunks and containers of relics she still clung to.

The last time I visited her, I brought in some flowers. She always loved flowers, but she could not see them and she could not smell them. She felt my face—my ears, my hairline, my eyes, my mouth, my nose—with her fingertips beating the air like moths, while her own eyes peered into mine and saw nothing. She berated me for crying. She could not hear me apologize until I shouted. She had lost her sense of taste as well. Each of her senses, save touch, had gradually failed during those seven long years she outlived Carlo, and at eighty-four—just the age at which he had died—she begged me to pray for her death.

Soon after that, Fania fell, trying to get out of bed without assistance. Her temperature soared, and she went into a coma and lingered on for three days. She died on 7 November 1971. Armina Langner and her attorney Joseph Solomon were with her, but she was not conscious of their presence. She was buried from Campbell's Funeral Home, where her casket was banked with red roses. Algernon Black of the Ethical Culture Center spoke, as he had spoken at Carlo's memorial service. Then Virgil Thomson mumbled some curious homilies, comparing Fania's warmth to a pot-bellied stove, I think. She was buried in Brooklyn among other Marinoffs.

In her will, Fania left generous bequests to a number of individuals. These included some of her nieces and nephews in the Marinoff, Muroff, and Koral families; Donald Angus, whom she'd known since 1919; Aileen Pringle, a silent film star who'd adored Carlo but who secretly only tolerated Fania; her oldest friends, actresses Armina Marshall Langner and Regina Wallace; and my two children, indeed handsomely enough to defray the costs of their educations. Fania made several further large bequests to a number of charitable organizations, and then the four million dollar residue in trust reverted to the estate of Carlo's brother, Ralph Van Vechten.

It was divided in accordance with his directives, in Cedar Rapids, Iowa, among four recipients: the Masonic Library; Coe College; a home for "indigent white women," which had changed its name and its mission long before; and the Cedar Rapids Orphanage. The latter no longer existed, nor any of its records or transactions of adoptions.

A partial list of Fania Marinoff's appearances on stage and in films: *Cyrano de Bergerac* (Denver and on tour, *et seq*),1894; *Mistress Nell*, 1900; *Carmen*, 1900; *Joan of the Sword Hand*, 1900; *Janice Meredith*, 1901; *La Madeleine*, 1902; *The Hunt for Happiness*, 1902; *The Japanese Nightingale* (New York, *et seq*), 1903; *The Serio-Comic Governess*, 1904; *A Stolen Story*, 1905; *The Sorceress*, 1905; *You Never Can Tell* (as Dolly, American premiere), 1906; *The Man on the Box*, 1907; *The Renegade*, 1907; *The House Next Door* (also on tour), 1909; *Romance of the Underworld* (New York), 1911; *The Rainbow* (out of town tryouts only), 1911; *A Rich Man's Son* (New York, *et seq*), 1912; *Within the Law*, 1912; *Get Rich Quick* (New Haven Stock, *et seq*), 1913; *Wallingford*, 1913; *The Gamblers*, 1913; *Madame X*, 1913; *Forty-five Minutes from Broadway*, 1913; *The Talker*, 1913; *Brewster's Millions,* 1913; *A Woman's Way*, 1913; *The Woman*, 1913; *Little Johnny Jones*, 1913; *A Thousand Years Ago* (New York, *et seq*), 1913; *Consequences*, 1914; *One of Our Girls* (film), 1914; *Arms and the Man*, 1915; *Nedra* (film), 1915; *The Galloper* (film), 1915; *The Money Master* (film), 1915; *The Unsuspected Isle* (film), 1915; *Life's Whirlpool*, also referred to as *The Whirlpool As Life* (film), 1916; *New York* (film), 1916; *The Tempest*, 1916; *The Rise of Jennie Cushing* (film), 1917; *Spring's Awakening*, 1917; *The Assassin*, later retitled *The Heritage* (Poughkeepsie tryout), 1917; *The Walkoffs* (New York, *et seq*), 1918; *Behind a Watteau Picture*, 1918; *The Chester Mystery Plays*, 1918; *Pan and the Young Shepherd*, 1918; *The Festival of Bacchus*, 1918; *Karen*, 1918; *Bruised Winds*, 1919; *Call the Doctor*, 1920; *The Hero*, 1921; *Frank Fay's Fables*, 1922; *The Charlatan*, 1922; *The Love Habit*, 1923; *Tarnish*, 1923; *Spring Cleaning* (Baltimore), 1928; *The Comic Artist* (Westport Playhouse, *et seq*), 1931; *As You Like It*, 1931; *The Streets of New York*, 1931; *The Pillars of Society*, 1931; *The Bride the Sun Shines On*, 1932; *Chris Comes Across*, 1932; *Judgment Day* (New York, *et seq*), 1934; *Times Have Changed*, 1935; *Love for Love*, 1936; *Antony and Cleopatra*, 1937; *The Skin of Our Teeth* (Westport Playhouse), 1946; *The Temporary Mrs. Smith* (New York), 1946.

$\mathcal{N}$INA BALABAN

*I*n the summer of 1956, Barry Fuller, an Australian boy I'd met at the University of Iowa, and I decided to live together in New York until the fall semester began. We were both in graduate school—I in the Writers' Workshop and Barry in the theater department—and had become fast friends earlier in the year. I had no job there, but Barry was a typesetter, assured of employment on the night shift at the *New York Times*, and his salary would get us through until I found work. I was charged with the responsibility of finding a place for us to live, since I had driven East with another friend, Bob Karr, as soon as classes ended, while Barry had to stay on in Iowa City another two weeks, typesetting for the local newspaper. Nobody had much money. Everybody had a good time, during what I came to think of as my Balaban summers.

I found a job—clerking at Marboro Books on West 42nd Street—before I found Nina Balaban's apartment. Rosemary Musgrave, a friend from my undergraduate days at Colorado College who was clerking for the summer at the Marboro Books branch in Greenwich Village, arranged for me to be interviewed for a job. In my memory, Jim Harrison and I were hired simultaneously at the 42nd Street branch. We too became became fast friends, drinking through too many nights at the Kettle of Fish in the Village. He was only nineteen then—a wild boy who could put customers off with his bangs and one eye and exotic features. An insolent Native American, I thought, though in those days we all said Indian, but his forebears were Nordic. Jim had not written anything at that time, but he was convinced that he would become a writer—and look what happened: ten novels and a distinguished body of poetry.

Bob Karr had found an apartment almost immediately for himself and two other graduate students coming on later, the cold-water Greenwich Village flat of the experimental film-maker Maya Deren, whom we'd met in Iowa City when she came through on a tour. But for nearly two weeks I was obliged to sleep on an air mattress in the living room of the small apartment that my undergraduate college roommate Richard Rutledge shared with two other men. They all worked at NBC and slept in three beds in a room designed to hold no more than two; you had to step across them to get into the bathroom, but the kitchen was good, and I earned my keep by cooking for us all.

Meanwhile, Barry had arrived and was staying somewhere in Queens, I think, and had begun his night shift at the *New York Times*. So it was a relief when I discovered 6 West 75th Street through a real estate agent. We were going to have to pay $35 as a commission, but the rent was only $65 a month for a sublease from Nina Balaban, and that was very reasonable, compared to the prices I'd been offered elsewhere. I was ready to take this one sight unseen. It is difficult now to approximate the relative scale of costs, but perhaps these examples will lend some perspective. Three years earlier, I had stayed at the Taft Hotel for five dollars a night. At that time, it cost a dime to get on the subway and a nickel to take a ride on the Staten Island Ferry. I paid $1.75 for standing room to see *My Fair Lady* that summer. My favorite restaurant, the Fleur de Lys on West 69th Street, offered a deliriously good *Boeuf Bourguignon* with potatoes and vegetables for $1.15. For $1.50 you could order *Quenelle de veau à la financière*—one of the best dishes I have ever had—tiny veal dumplings in a rich sauce with mushrooms and olives. The top ticket for the New York City Ballet in those days was $3.95, and partial-vision wall-clinger seats near the ceiling of the Metropolitan Opera House—where you held on to the metal mesh fencing behind you to lean forward and see part of the stage—were $1.10. Wine was maybe about fifteen cents a glass. People didn't drink much wine in those days; we drank beer, about fifteen cents a bottle. All of which suggests that an apartment for $65 wasn't so bad.

The agent called Nina Balaban and made an appointment for me. She was eager to sublet, he said, because she was trying to get out of town for the summer. Bob came along—he was an art history major and intended to spend his summer hanging out in museums and working on his thesis—since his schedule was flexible, and an early afternoon jaunt was a good excuse to escape from the library.

Nina Balaban lived on the fifth floor, although the name on the buzzer was some unpronounceable Russian patronymic. Long afterward I learned that the old brownstone had once belonged to the American playwright Philip Moeller before it was converted into two flats on each floor. The stairs were shabbily carpeted in dark red, clean and well lighted along the way, although they tilted markedly out from the wall, with the steps on an appreciable slant. Halfway up the third staircase I collapsed into a little seat built into the mahogany banister, and Bob took a breather on the steps, both of us panting a little. Barry, athletic and limber and skinny, could have pushed on but he waited for us to recover. From above, Nina Balaban's voice rasped down the two flights between us.

"Be brave, younk mens!"

We went on up and arrived winded, Barry well ahead of us and already chattering in his sunny Australian accent that charmed almost everybody. Nina was in the doorway, managing to look apprehensive, welcoming, imperious, and charming all at the same time. Her eyes struck me first, dancing gray eyes, straight across the bottom and rounded into half-circles, black-rimmed and batting mascara-heavy lashes at us, under mismatched arcs for eyebrows, drawn on in high, single lines. Her teeth were white and even, and her hair was a reddish nest through which an electric charge might have recently surged. She was nut-brown, like soft and weathered leather. At first she seemed to be no taller than five feet, gaunt and wizened, and then perhaps of medium height and as youthful as we were. Was she forty? Sixty? I couldn't tell. She wore huraches on her bare feet and an oversized blue wrapper, and under it a plain, soft blouse and a fulsome peasant skirt. There were gypsy loops with little rocks hanging from them in her earlobes; necklaces of beads, seeds, pods, semi-precious stones dangling from her neck; bangles on her wrists. The bright crimson staining her lips bled into tiny lines around them.

"Good morrrrrrninks, younk mens! Come! Who is Bruce?"

We introduced ourselves and followed her into a tiny vesti-bule, then into a room where two people stood surrounded by battered suitcases, stuffed shopping bags, and corrugated card-board cartons tied closed with flimsy string. She introduced the good-looking boy as Terry, apparently mute, almost as short as Nina but thick above the waist with heavy muscles that bulged through his tee shirt, and a neck as thick as his head. I'd seen very few bodies like that, even in the navy. Forty years ago, weight lifters were rarities in the flesh, appearing more often in grainy magazines that extolled the virtues of good health and sunshine. Terry was driving Nina to Woodstock for the summer, she said, and what else he did I never learned. The young woman, a few years older than Terry, was introduced as Delphine, wistfully pretty, lank-haired, pale, anorexic, "a grrrrrrrrrrrrreat dancer," Nina said.

The apartment's off-white walls were chipped and faded or darkened unevenly into melancholy splotches, but light filtered through gauzy curtains at the tall windows that opened onto part of the building's rooftop. Everything was simultaneously eccentric and inviting: the sprawling cushions in many patterns and colors on a single bed that doubled as a couch, rickety chairs and tables, a small desk, a plump hassock losing its insides that Delphine sat on with her knees up under her chin, a threadbare oriental carpet on the floor and another over a large round table, an upright piano that almost made me weep with joy since I'd be able to play regularly for a change, Russian icons and crosses on the walls along with many strange, impastoed paintings of still-lifes, hollow-eyed women, haphazard vases of flowers, and blocky dancers. There were stacks of books, fantastic ceramics with stones and glittering bits stuck into their surfaces, many decorated rocks, and plants seemingly everywhere, suspended from the ceiling in elaborate woven holders, trailing vines to the floor and other surfaces; some were in bloom, most were simply cascades of greenery. A small kitchen and bathroom were off one end of the room, and a bedroom—just wide enough to hold a three-quarter bed and a little chest—through double doors at the other end. Also, there was a parakeet, and at one point during our interview Nina shut the windows part way and turned her loose. Baby flew freely above us, swooping in great arcs; then she perched on top of the piano, then on the keys, blinking and rotating her head, like a miniature owl. A little later she sat on Nina's shoulder and kissed her ear.

But that was well after the introductions. Nina had to start all over again after we'd met Terry and Delphine. "Sit!" she cried. "I mek tea! Who is Brucie? Who is Berrys?" She floated into the kitchen without waiting for a reply. I hadn't been called Brucie since I was six years old and hit the kid over the head with a roller-skate for his presumption, but somehow coming from Nina Balaban I didn't mind it.

When she returned, the parakeet began to squawk. "Now! Baby! Sealaunsssss! We talk about rentink, yes? Yes!" Nina sprinkled her fractured English with French and Russian; she added a *k* to half her words, an *s* to the other half, and she spoke with her arms, her hands, the lift of her chin, and especially her eyes.

She did all the talking. She wanted to go to Woodstock with her bird to paint, and she wanted to go as soon as possible— that afternoon—and we could help Terry carry her belongings downstairs. Delphine lived somewhere in Manhattan—I never learned where—and would be her liaison. I would send the rent to Nina but pay the utilities bills directly when they came in. We could use her linens and anything else we wanted. In between her volleys of explanations, Nina seemed to have extracted our whole histories and spoke as if we were old friends.

"Here is for me Seventh Heaven," she said happily, "and now is for you too?"

For $65 a month it was beyond my wildest dreams, and from his grin I knew Barry approved too. It was small, but as he worked all night and I worked all day, it wouldn't be too small. It was kitschy, it was *gemütlich*, it was fairly clean, genuinely seedy in a nice way. The kitchen had a dangerous stove and a big refrigerator, and the bathroom had a great shower, which Nina insisted on demonstrating. It wasn't air conditioned—not everything was in 1956—though being so high up, with open space beyond its windows, it promised to be cool.

We had surely lucked out. Already there were side benefits, and more would unveil themselves as the summer progressed. By coincidence, 6 West 75th Street was the first building west of the San Remo on Central Park West. Most mornings after moving in, I waved from the rooftop to Carl Van Vechten at the window of the library in his ninth floor apartment. I'd known him by mail since 1951, and we'd met in 1953, but that first summer in New York marked the beginning of our close friendship. Four girls from the corps of Ballet Theatre lived across the hall and became friendly neighbors. One night Carl—at seventy-six—climbed all five flights for dinner, and friends passing through town stayed for a few nights before moving on. My parents and sister stayed the night en route to some holiday or another, though I cannot recall how we found room to sleep. Barry and I held parties on the rooftop at night, we grew brown there from the steady stare of the sun during the day; Richard Rutledge's cat Gaby tore around its yard-high ledges; one night I dragged some blankets out and made love there under the stars. Nina always called the place "Seventh Heaven." She was right.

"You like Seventh Heaven! I know! I trost!"

"Trost?"

"I trrrrrrrrost you, darlink! You are good pipples, is Berry bery good too! I trost!"

Nina always spoke with exclamation marks, and when we began to correspond I discovered that she wrote that way as well. She was a painter, so the dreamy pictures on the walls were all hers: saints, angels, flowers, fruit, mostly in gouache. The rocks around the room were hers too, covered in her designs, and in Woodstock, she said, she'd find more rocks and other natural debris to see her through the winter, for she made her living, apparently, fashioning jewelry from her discoveries, and selling a painting now and then.

And so we helped carry down her parcels and suitcases and a birdcage with Baby fluttering madly inside it, bags of food, and paints, and piled everything into the back of Terry's little truck. Barry must have made three trips to our one, sprinting up and down and not missing a beat. Then Nina kissed Bob and Barry and me on both cheeks, she and Delphine and Terry took off— Delphine was riding along to keep Terry company on the return trip—and we went out and bought a six-pack and wheezed our way back up the five flights to have a celebratory drink in Seventh Heaven. Then Barry, who was due at the *New York Times* at eleven that night, went promptly to bed.

About a week later, Nina's first card came, an almost indecipherable scrawl, full of squiggles and dots, some of which I did not understand. In time I learned to translate her amazing spellings with more ease, but the pleasure was always there from the beginning. Nothing short of a facsimile could reproduce her strange circumflex accents between letters of words and even stranger acute and grave accents at their beginnings, plus her dots along the way, almost as if she were doodling them while she searched her head for the words she wanted to write. (I have not attempted to duplicate these, and I have bracketed my elipses to avoid confusion between my editorial deletions and Nina's decorative ones.)

Nina.

O, Bruce, Berry! First .once more thank Berry for trÉmendus healp! And . . . I . . . forgat nightgown . . . good not—p . . . . . ce !!!—Give it to Delphine, she will send it to me!!!—Darling! Here is wunderful—I endress 3 times, but can't stay in sun—yet! My cabine is very, very smal, but I do it charming— . . . it is primitif! Baby is O.K—better than I thought she will be! Hope—you both will be comphy and happy in our home on 7th heaven! Love to both, Nina.

When I answered, so did she, at length:

Dear Bruce! I am realy so happy, that you are comphy and loving our place—Seventh heaven! Of course next summer it is your place, if you will need it!—Don't worry about brocken dishes and not replace them, I don't want you spend money! Here, I am in my wunderful woods of green, fields, woods, brook sands, where I collect flowers for my charming smal home. I fixed it—and out of dust, dung and darkness came out a copy, tiny nest for me for baby.—Baby?!! Bruce!!! She is quite married—she has a lover. Duffy, my neighbor gived him everyday at some time over night. You should see this life of them.—Baby because so busy, curius, occupied.. she tears paper, digs holles in the walls, untidies the soape, singing, flying a lover. Duffy is more daffy, he works, he eats.—In the evening they kiss each other in a akward position.— She sitts in the cage—he stands on thresdhold and for hour they kiss, and kiss carressing—Then when he insist to come in the cage <u>she</u> angrily sends him away!!! They are gloriusly happy on the scrined porch end in my tiny room!—What do you think of this happiness?!!! Thank you for the nightgown—I need here because to lundry is a problem. No runing watter! But I manage all and I adore my place.—Sorry you don't see it!—I do work, but not any important painting yet—I am just enjoying everything so much!!! Dear Bruce—my love to Berry—He is a nice person, strong and singing and cultural—Hope you do not too much work for earning, but will do something interesting for yourself!

Write to me, when you have time and desire.—
Love from me. Nina

That letter persuaded Barry and Bob and me to want to drive up to Woodstock for the day the following Sunday, and perhaps even stay the night somewhere in the vicinity. Barry would be wiped out after a night at the plant, but he could sleep on the way, and Bob and I would flip to see who drove up and who drove back. We'd leave early.

Brucy dear! It is wunderful! Come! Hope not rain, because is rain will not be dunn!—Tack a bading suit—We will go to my broock even if sun will be short time!—Tack a New Road to Woodstock ask somebody to show you—it is shorter—tacks only 2 + hours. My address:

smal cottage?! (Ha . . .) Miss Menser—on Ohio Road by
The brook.
Please darling—go to 72nd Street, near Columbia and to <u>pultery</u> shop and buy a roasted chiken—1.65, or so. Ask to cut it on smal parts. I will prepare rice, or corn and desert—So we will have early supper. Russian. [. . .] I got—collecting flowers in the fields, a poison ivy and it is a nueccance! No flowers anymore. Golly. . . . . .
——Duffy and Baby took there bath yesterday—it is Duffy, who

taught her to go in wather! I was so happy!——Hope Bobby will enjoy the trip and my Woodstock—let her [ie., him] tack a jacket for the evening—here is cool all the time!—I am still very tired, it is a result of hard winter, I had, but, general I feel fine—So—it is all—Give love to Berry! To you—embrace—

Your Nin.
<u>Dollars for chiken</u>

In the end we didn't go; Barry got booked for an emergency shift, and Bob begged off because of work, and we never did manage to get up to Woodstock to see Nina communing with nature. The one weekend Barry could have gone, I was scheduled to drive up to Cape Cod with Richard Rutledge. On another weekend, Rosemary Musgrave was going to drive up with me, and perhaps Snooks too, a friend of hers I was dating at the time, although that excursion fell through as well. But Nina's and my letters continued to cross in the mail for the rest of the summer.

With Nina's permission, just before I returned to Iowa, I more or less sub-sub-rented Seventh Heaven for two weeks to Judy Womack, a music student I knew who was desperate for a place to stay temporarily. Nina wanted to stay in Woodstock as long as possible; with somebody in the apartment, her plants would get watered. But both my mail and Judy's mail continued to be delivered to 6 West 75th Street, and more than once that prompted a frantic letter:

Bruce darling! What I did?!!! Mechanicaly I oppened your letter!!! Forgive me!!! <u>Do</u>—change your address in Post office on 69 Street—Amsterdam avenue—[. . .] Got your letter and I was so happy to hear from you and to know you are pleased and loving my (our) place! I trusted you—Bruce from the first moment I know, you will give watter to my plants!

She'd returned from a productive summer in Woodstock—seventy-five paintings, she said—and brought Duffy with her as well. I'd left her an oversized art book from Marboro as a thank you present which, she wrote, "just embarrassed my heart, o, I thank you—dear!" And she proposed to give me one of her paintings in return. Intermittently, then, we wrote until the following year when I took her apartment again, this time alone, in part because Barry had returned to Australia, but also because I'd taught at Coe College during the year, which meant an appreciable increase over my miserly salary as a graduate teaching assistant at the University of Iowa. I'd been able to put some money aside for the summer, and my job at Marboro proved to be not only secure but lucrative. I was temporarily elevated to summer manager—with a little raise—when the head honcho went on his summer vacation, suffered some illness, and didn't come back until I was ready to return to Iowa nearly three months later.

By that time, I had pieced together something of Nina's background from our brief encounters at the beginning and end of the summer, and from artifacts around the apartment. She was born in Russia and escaped to Paris during the 1917 Revolution. She'd written a novel, in Russian—there was a tattered copy of it in the apartment—and married Emanuel Balaban. I knew his name because he'd been the conductor of the New York Musical Society, precursor of the New York City Opera Company, which had staged Gian-Carlo Menotti's *The Medium* and *The Telephone*. But Maestro Balaban had long departed from Nina's life when I knew her. I learned bits and pieces of her biography, too, from her letters—one of them in particular, written in the fall after my first summer:

Dear, dear Brucy! How are you?!!!! I want to ask you two questions—one—What painting you prefered to have you saw through the portfolio—and I don't know—which you would like to have? Second question: I can't find a book—"Fault of Angels" by Paul Horgan—This book is very dear to me—it was written about me and by my friend Paul—It is so important to me to have it. Did you tack it, or Berry [. . .]?
Here is wintery cold, seventh heaven is not heated, and I have cold—Babies and I sending to you Brucy our love.—Straingely I miss you!—
    Your Nin.

I hadn't taken the book, of course; I hadn't even seen it, and I wrote to say so, expressing my concern. By December she had not yet been able to locate it, nor had it surfaced by the time I was about to leave Iowa to move into her apartment for a second summer:

Darling—you will be able to ask here—Judy and your amarata from last summer—possible one of them took to read my book—which is specialy important for me—book of Paul Horgan "Fault of Angels" Light brown cover with black large lines—I would appreciate to find it—it is my precious book for me [. . .]

When I returned to New York, I offered to sleuth out second-hand bookshops for a copy to replace the one she'd lost. No, she said, smiling and crying at the same time, another copy would not be the same thing; it was that particular copy that meant so much to her because she and Horgan had been lovers, and every time they'd gone to bed together they'd made a hole with a thumbtack in the binding. I had a momentary vision of something quite tattered and falling to bits from having kept the record. Then, just before the end of the summer, going through the portfolios in her hall closet to select a painting to take back with me, I found the book, wedged down behind them. The cover was intact, if liberally pocked front and back. I read the novel immediately and then left it for her to find, wrapped up like a present. "Brucy dear!" she wrote, "O thank you, you fond the book—so I possiably put it there and forgatt!!!!!"

After I read *The Fault of Angels*, I understood why it was so important to her. If not the main character, she motivates the actions of the others in this comedy of manners that pokes gentle fun at the pretensions of academics and local patrons during a college music festival. Horgan's central female figure is named Nina, and there is no question about her identity. Here is what Nina Balaban must have been like when she first came to this country from Paris during the Twenties, married to Emanuel Balaban, and fell in love with Paul Horgan. In the novel, Vladimir and Nina Arenkoff have emigrated to the United States. He is a musician, and his wife "has never left New York since coming from Paris. She is very sensitive, can you believe it? She detests America because the people have no heart. . . ." She "is always busy, but always occupied; it is her greatest intelligence. . . . She makes things, so beautiful, sewing, embroidery, and all of the sort. *And*, my dear boy, . . . such an actress! You will see." She then disappears from the novel for several chapters, but when Horgan's protagonist, John O'Shaughnessy, finally meets her, he is hopelessly smitten:

> She stared at the gray bare trees outside, whose branches leaned upon the bay window of her turret alcove. She was not tall, but her body was so exquisitely shaped that she gave an impressive hint of tallness. Her face was really oval, pointed at the chin. Her brow and cheeks were pale with underglows of pearly *café au lait*.

Her eyes were deep and sad and black, with sparkling whites and definitely curving brows that gave a frank mystery to her countenance. Her mouth was small and inconceivably expressive, even in repose. She had rouged it only at its outline. Her neck was magnificent, slender and full and straight. No jewel diluted its loveliness. Her shoulders went from it with a pride of waves.

Horgan's novel was named the Harper Prize Novel of 1934, and he went on to write many other books, but none of those I have read is so bittersweet as this one. That fall, when I went to New York over the Thanksgiving holiday weekend and looked Nina up for a dinner date, I asked her about Horgan. She only said, not sadly but wistfully perhaps, "We do not see each ozzer any more longer."

Nina and I so rarely met, yet I felt a strong affection for her, as if we'd always known each other. I saw her a day or two at a time at most, on perhaps six or seven occasions, no more, and our letters are hardly those of intimates who confide secrets. Even when we talked together tête à tête our conversations were largely impersonal, and, as for that, much of our correspondence seems to have been tied up with utility bills and the annual muddle of rearranging who paid which ones.

Brucinka dear! I gat this second bill and I still not have your . . . reciete of money order!—What shall I do now?! Please let me know—Brucy!

And in the following post, since our letters had crossed in the mails:

Brucy! Your card and cheque just brought to me a glorious feeling of real friendship, honesty, human goodness, which I always believed in you! Thank you my dear friend Brucy! Duffy, Baby, Peevy [another new bird] sending to you there love and mine too!

Some time later:

> Brucy dear! Here the bill. Worring not to hear from you about
> electricity. Who fixed? And how much I have to send you in
> money!?!!!!! Please let me know! Love Nina.

In the fall of 1958, after my third summer at 6 West 75th
Street, Nina wrote about her Woodstock summer and to say that
she feared she was going to have give up Seventh Heaven. Even
the small rent was too much for her meager income:

> I did not do much of painting summer—June, July, part of
> August were not too good for me—weather was awful and I gat—
> from dampness—a severe bronchitis, still have, but lately weather
> was gray, clear, beautiful and I feel much better. I did a portrait
> and sold it, not high price, but that healped me a lot. Write me
> once a while, so that I know about you, your life. I send to you my
> warm regards and Duffy and Baby also—They are quite happy,
> outdoors. They have to adjust themselfs to a new place, new life
> . . . well . . . me too! Love—Your Nina.

But she still had Seventh Heaven the following summer, and I
saw her briefly before she left for Woodstock when I moved in,
and again when I was back in town at Thanksgiving. But in 1960
my life began to change radically. I moved East to take a teaching
job, and fell in love, and got married, and had children, and as all
that did not happen in a hurry I did not get back to New York for
some years but for brief holidays.

I hadn't written again for a long time, I think. Then to renew
acquaintance, I sent her an Alice B. Toklas fruitcake, as I had
some years before. Baking that for the holidays had become an
annual ritual for me, dividing the batter up among a dozen squat
coffee cans—a kind, alas, no longer made by any coffee com-

pany—to send to friends. Weeks later, my Christmas card came back, stamped "no forwarding address" or "not at this address" or some equally maddening variation. I hoped some postal clerk had liked the cake. If I'd ever had a telephone number or an address for Delphine or Terry, I had lost them long before. I wrote to the super at 6 West 75th, and I wrote to the "Miss Menser" on Ohio Road in Woodstock, but got no replies. Nina had simply vanished, and I rued my long silence.

I had never encountered her name or her work since then, until this valentine that I have written to her was already as complete as I could make it. Then I learned through a series of coincidences—they occur so often in our lives that we should never be surprised by them—of her long friendships with the poet Arthur Gregor and the painter Sam Spanier. Through them I learned that Nina was herself a countess, born in 1890; her father had been an advisor to Czar Nicholas II, and she claimed that her mother was a direct descendant of Genghis Khan. After fleeing the Russian revolution in 1917, she married a Baltic aristocrat in Germany and bore him a son, Andre von Gronicka. With her second husband, Emanuel Balaban, she emigrated to the United States in 1925 to settle near Rochester—where she must have known Paul Horgan—and then in 1940 she moved alone into the apartment I later sublet from her during my New York summers in the late Fifties. At the end of our brief acquaintance she had not disappeared at all but only moved permanently to Woodstock. And there she lived to be one hundred and one years old, survived by grandchildren and great grandchildren, and survived, too, by her art, samples of which are in more collections than mine.

For all the years after I lost her, one of Nina's paintings in a heavy, ornate frame has always hung in my study: the decorative head of a strange, ethereal woman who stares impassively to remind me of an all too brief encounter with another of my noble dames. One summer, when Nina was at Woodstock and I was in Seventh Heaven, I negotiated to buy one of her paintings: a large still life of fruits and vegetables, and if that weren't for sale, I wrote, then a small head, or both, if I could afford them. Later I also bought a lovely painting of a vase of flowers, and that too has never been off my walls. Nina had written to me about them, drawing little pen and ink sketches in her letter of the ones she thought I wanted, and she'd been exactly right.

> About paintings! I don't remember the smal head—is that a woman's head, quite oriantal?!! If it is—Brucy—I want you will have it as my present for you—from me—The "still life" is that one? I don't know if 30 dol. will be too much for you—the price usualy—if for large painting hunderd dollars,—you can have it for 30 dol—Please describe me or see—if I am right about the paintings—because few I have to keep as possiable buy of peaples who saw it last season, but, as I understood—those particular paintings are still free. [. . .] I embrace you and my happy babies sending for you much love too.—Brucy is it all answered?!!!
>
> Your Nin.

Fritzi Scheff,
A Curtain Raiser

T never knew Fritzi Scheff, but she seems always to have been somewhere in my life, and without knowing it she surely touched me, if not so deeply as some of my other noble dames deeply enough to have preoccupied me intermittently for as long as I can recall. Fritzi Scheff was a Metropolitan Opera soubrette at the turn of the twentieth century and, subsequently, the most popular musical comedy star in America. Long afterward, Fritzi Scheff's songs hummed in my ears, from the cradle on, because my mother—who retained her own sweet soprano, though not nearly so long as Fritzi Scheff did hers—sang operetta arias around the house, especially "Kiss Me Again."

Perhaps that accounts for my having fallen in love with operetta at an early age. *Naughty Marietta* was the first movie I ever saw, and I think I could still find the seat in the theater where I sat to watch it at the age of four or five. My love affair with voices sweet enough to give me cavities never ended, from Luisa Tetrazzini to Helen Morgan and from Beverly Sills to Barbara Cook, and I have always marched in three-quarter time.

Fritzi Scheff might be identified as the first crossover artist —now a bridge that all too many singers attempt to navigate though not always with satisfactory results—because Victor Herbert stole her away from the Metropolitan Opera to star in operetta. From Wagner's mermaid Woglinde in *Das Rhinegold* to the eponymous hatmaker in Herbert's *Mlle. Modiste* was an unfamiliar swim at the time, but Fritzi Scheff crossed with aplomb and sang unchallenged for well over a decade—a long reign in a frothy monarchy.

I did not consciously encounter Fritzi Scheff again until 1954, when I read Carl Van Vechten's affectionate obituary for her in the *Saturday Review of Literature.* He was a good choice for the chore since he'd heard her sing at the turn of the century in Chicago, when the Metropolitan Opera Company was on tour and then he'd followed her long career to its sad end.

I came upon Fritzi Scheff unexpectedly twenty years later, in a bookshop on Lower Fourth Avenue where a perfect woodblock print of Al Freuh's memorable caricature of the lady turned up. It had enraged her when it appeared in a St. Louis newspaper in 1907, adorably exaggerating her wasp waist and dished profile and little snare drum she played in *Mlle. Modiste.* That operetta had proven to be her greatest triumph, for Victor Herbert had guaranteed her theatrical immortality with "Kiss Me Again." Reports varied on the preposterous number of encores she was obliged to sing on opening night.

Fritzi Scheff made no recordings during her heyday—none at least that anybody knows of, despite rumors, although there is a short passsage from *Faust* preserved with as much scratching as singing on the turn of the century Mapleson wax cylinders. She continued to appear on stage periodically for the rest of her life, and inevitably she always included "Kiss Me Again."

Still another twenty years later, I came to own Fritzi Scheff's own scrapbook of newspaper clippings, reviews, programs, and photographs, through the estate of Joel Sater, a collector of vintage paper as well as an acquaintance. I'd known about the scrapbook for long time and pored over it with pleasure more than once. Later, Joel's widow gave it to me. Fritzi Scheff had kept it, from her debut with the Metropolitan Opera and then through her glory days, until the roar of the Twenties killed off operetta as a popular musical entertainment. Her own inscription on the fly-leaf, doubtless written some years later, still stabs my heart:

> What they saget
> What they say
> and
> What they will say
> Scarcei help me
> Fritzi Scheff

Then I discovered—again accidentally—a chapter of Fritzi Scheff's memoirs in a 1942 issue of *Opera News*. Surely the other chapters must be somewhere, I reasoned, and I spent a long time and a lot of postage trying to sleuth them out. Thanks to the persistence of my friend Lisa Browar, then a curator in the Manuscripts and Archives Division at the New York Public Library, the typescript of Fritzi Scheff's memoirs, from her birth until around 1913, surfaced after a search through the files of the Lincoln Center Library for the Performing Arts, where they had been gathering dust for fifty years.

Then I met Betty Bennett, a retired vaudevillian who had served as Fritzi Scheff's dresser for *Billy Rose's Diamond Horseshoe* during the Forties and known her even earlier. She had not only a cache of extraordinary memories but a number of inconsequential, charming letters that Fritzi Scheff had written to her.

Then I discovered through Carl Van Vechten's photographs of the Stage Door Canteen, that my friend Herbert Coburn had had his picture taken with Fritzi Scheff when he was a young soldier during the Second World War. She sang there frequently, always old songs, always "Kiss Me Again," to the delight of the servicemen, although Herb hadn't known who she was, or, rather, who she had been. But a decade later, he'd been present at the Café Grinzing on an evening when Fritzi Scheff—then well past her prime but still singing—was interrupted in the middle of "Kiss Me Again" by the protests of an elderly man. He was volubly indignant and vocally outraged that a great opera singer had been reduced to warbling forgotten songs in a second rate restaurant. She should have been on the stage of the Metropolitan Opera, he cried, waving his cane and shaking his wattles. The man was summarily ousted by the waiters, and Fritzi Scheff went on with her songs, as she did night after night.

Had death been patient, she would have sung "Kiss Me Again" on the Ed Sullivan television program, *The Toast of the Town*. Obituaries also told me, alas, that Fritzi Scheff had been found a few days after her death by her maid and the apartment building handyman, her ageing Pekingese standing vigil over her body.

Then, latterly, Robert W. Jones supplied me with a recording of a rare 1936 radio broadcast of a brief interview with Fritzi Scheff, during which she confided that she'd just been turned down for a supporting role in Greta Garbo's film, *Camille*, because she looked too young. After that, she sang "Kiss Me Again," abetted by a stentorian radio chorus, her voice no longer fresh but still full-throated, and laced with honeyed charm.

I thought to put all of this material into a biography, but the long intervening silence that followed Fritzi Scheff's great celebrity defeated me: nearly thirty-five years of virtual aridity, interrupted by small oases now and then but not often enough or frequently enough to rebuild a faded career. At first, she retreated for long periods of time to a house she had bought in Connecticut years before, where she lived in apparent seclusion. Then, when she lost that soon after the stock market crash, she simply disappeared in between sporadic jobs until her death. So instead of trying to construct a biography for someone whom time had all but forgotten, I decided that a young journalist had been present at the Café Grinzing the night that Herbert Coburn remembered, helping to oust the indignant old admirer from the premises, and then afterward arranging to meet Fritzi Scheff at her apartment for an interview. The monologue was given two performances in May 2001 by the Theater of the Seventh Sister in Lancaster, Pennsylvania, with Mary Adams Smith as Fritzi Scheff, directed by Gary Smith. Inevitably, its title was *Kiss Me Again*.

KISS ME AGAIN

A Monologue Masquerading as an Interview

Fritzi Scheff's home at 308 East 79th Street is a third floor walk-up flat in a turn of the century brownstone. The room is as crowded as a furniture store or a second-hand shop. At best, it drips with gemütlich, old world charm; at worst it is seedy, a rent-controlled space in which the owners have made no improvements for at least forty years. Probably there is a leak in the ceiling; certainly plaster is coming away from the walls here and there. They were painted white once upon a time but now are dingy, hung with portraits, posters, photographs, and memorabilia, most of them from the early years of the twentieth century. An open doorway, upstage left leads into the kitchen. A door upstage right leads into the bedroom. A low-silled window with glass curtains downstage right. An upright or baby grand piano piled with music is upstage slightly to stage center right. There is a small pendulum clock on the piano. Next to it, upstage right is a tall wind-up Victrola, shrouded in a fraying paisley shawl. There are shelves below for records, the doors closed. Downstage left a mirrored hall tree. A round pedestal table and two unmatched chairs in front of the windows. Two easy chairs and a small table stage center. A lot of plants transform the space into a rather suffocating garden. A small chair, lumpy with age and slip-covered in faded chintz with dust ruffles to the floor, has its back to the audience, downstage left center next to another small table. The "fourth wall" is presumably hung with more memorabilia, and the entrance to the apartment, also on this wall, is to stage left. There is a large, well-worn oriental carpet on the floor.

236

The time is October 1953, when Fritzi Scheff was still singing nightly in a German restaurant, the Café Grinzing, a few months before her death. It is late afternoon when the monologue begins, and thin sunlight has begun to come in through the west windows. During the course of the monologue this light changes to a fuller sunset, bathing the room in pink and orange, then twilight, then evening but with moonlight.

Fritzi Scheff is in her mid-seventies. She is diminutive, her hair is bright red and pompadour, she has kept her figure pretty well, and she wears a faded dressing gown of silk or pongee that seems to be vaguely 1910 but might be any age. She is vivacious, she is pert, she is flirtatious, she has — even at her advanced age — chic. Her accent is heavily Viennese, with a vaudeville comic's dz *in place of* th. *Her syntax and verb tenses are less than secure. She pronounces several words as if they were French; some words actually are French. She is effervescent even in moments of sadness, and she speaks almost perpetually with exclamation marks, some but not all of which appear in the text. She rambles when she speaks, forgets what she is talking about, cheerfully avoids chronology, and returns to it again. She asks questions and never waits for answers. She catches herself in answers to questions that have strayed far afield. She is not without self-deprecation, knows her own worth, regrets little, and she is aware that she is slightly preposterous.*

But when the audience first sees her she is surrounded by silence, and she herself waits for time to pass, and it passes through a series of blackouts, punctuated by the chiming of a clock.

A clock chimes six times. The lights come up. It is morning. Fritzi Scheff is in a frowsty, shabby robe, chenille perhaps, sitting stage center as she sips from a cup of coffee. The lights go down. The clock chimes eight times. The lights come up again. She is standing at the mirror, staring at herself. The lights go down. The clock chimes ten times. The lights come up again. She is sitting at the window, still with her coffee, still staring into space. The clock chimes twelve times. The lights come up. She is standing by the chair, center stage, and with determination removes her robe and replaces it with her pretty dressing gown or negligee, suitable for receiving guests. She bows deeply in a curtsey, then sits again to wait. The lights go down. The clock chimes two times. The lights come up. She is at the mirror, putting on rouge and lipstick. The lights go down. The clock strikes three times. The lights come up. She is now sitting stage center; perhaps she fiddles with an antimacassar. The lights go down. When they come again the doorbell rings, and she hastens to the kitchen to retrieve a tray with a teapot and two cups and saucers, placing it on the table between the chairs, stage center. She hastens to

the door, takes a breath, draws herself up, and throws open the door to the
interviewer. The lights go down. When they come up again, the door is
closed, and Fritzi Scheff is offering a cup of tea to her guest, placing it on the
table next to him. He represents the audience; indeed, he is the audience. He
has a grudging respect for opera but doesn't go often and is secretly suspi-
cious of it; he knows a little about Broadway musical comedy; he is a well-
brought up young person who was reared to be nice to his elders. Fritzi
Scheff answers his silent questions. She speaks also of course to herself, and
to the air, to the past, and certainly to the audience. The paragraphing is
arbitrary and only made to suggest changes in subject. Fritzi Scheff is
actressy, bossy, petulant, funny, imperious, and sometimes almost unbear-
ably sad, but she is never maudlin. Also, she is slightly hard of hearing and
sometimes asks "What?" or "Hmm?" in response to questions from her osten-
sible interviewer.

Now, we have tea, my dear! I am so sorry not for to have more
time for you this afternoon for—what is your newspaper? No,
no, magazine, you said. I hope it wants my picture   *(a self-*
deprecating laugh and a pose).   My pictures are better than my
words for interview. I never know what to answer to so many
questions, and my words fly about like arias and perhaps they
are not translating into your oh, so cold-hearted typing on the
pages. But I try to answer your questions and I try to behave.
Yes?

   (She pours out two cups of tea through some of this chatter and ostensibly
anyway she gives one to her guest by placing it on the corner of the desk near
him.)

   What?   *(her attention drawn to one of the posters)*   Oh, that one
is *Babette*. Wasn't I beautiful? Mr. Herbert made it for me especially. What? Who? *Victor* Herbert! *Lieber Gott!* You are so
young! You don't know Victor Herbert? He was a great com-

poser, darling! He made all of my roles for me especially—well, not all of my roles but some of my roles, my great roles, and— that one? *(another poster)* Oh, you know that one, that one is my—my—you know, my *Kiss Me Again*, my *Mlle. Modiste*! *(She begins to sing it, then laughs at herself; her soprano voice is remarkably clear for a woman her age, a little frayed perhaps but still quite lovely.)*

> Sweet summer breeze,
> Whispering trees,
> Stars shining brightly above. . . .

Twenty-six encores on opening night! Christmas night, nine- teen—*lieber Gott!* 1906! Oh, I forgot the biscuits! *(She leaps up and runs toward the kitchen, but the interviewer's question stops her and she forgets about the biscuits.)*

What? Yes, that's the one I was singing last night at the café when the—incident occurred. It has not before happened to me, and the old gentleman was very gallant to say that about me. But to interrupt Fritzi Scheff! In the middle of *Kiss Me Again* to say that I was a great star and should not be singing in such a common place, that I should be back at the Metropolitan Opera House, that I should be enshrined there—yes, I remem- ber everything he said—even in the middle of *Kiss Me Again*! It is—compliment even if it is coming at the wrong time. I mean—it is being flattering to me, no? To know that I am not forgotten. That some of the people coming to dinner know who I was—no, no, know who I *am*. I am still "the little devil." Pad- erewski called me that once—you know Paderewski!—and then everybody called me that: "naughty little devil" and "good little devil," "the little devil of Grand Opera," but I was not temperamental! Emotional, yes, temperamental, no!

But temperament! Temperament makes an artist! It is—atti-
tude; it is—concentration; it is—*je ne sais quoi*; it is—"Fritzi"!
And those other stories! That I paid an electrician $120 a
week—big money then!—just to keep my name in lights on
my dressing room door! Foolishness! He did it for free! And
they made a big thing of the private railroad car I had on trains.
Why not? Everybody had private cars. But the story that I suspended traffic on a Texas railroad, because the motion of the
train made my bathwater spill over the sides, is ridiculous. I
just asked sweetly for them to slow down until I was completed
in my toilette, and they were so happy to do that for me. Also, I
was making four thousand dollars a week from Victor Herbert!
Four thousand dollars in 1906 was a lot of money!

Now maybe I make four dollars in tips on a good night at the
Café Grinzing, and—   *(a sudden haunt)*   after Café Grinzing
(a quick recovery)   —oh, they don't fire me, they like me—but
who knows? Listen to me, darling, life upon the wicked stage is
very precarious—you know that song?   *(She warbles the line and
again laughs at herself.)*

Life upon the wicked stage ain't never what a girl supposes.

Oh, how I could have played that role, in *Showboat*, you know,
but I was too famous for so small a part and I was too—mature.
And frankly, darling, southern girls do not sound like Fritzi.
I still have a little accent, *ja?* But I know all about Southern
accents because my husband was Southern. Well, *one* of my husbands was Southern. How many? Oh, three. Fritz was German
and George was American and John was Southern. Believe me,
darling, American is very different from Southern American.

I have been married and I have been single and I have been

engaged and I have been in love and—I have been rich, I have
been poor—rich is more *comfortable*—and I survive. At Café
Grinzing the customers remember some of the songs even if
they don't all of them remember me. Oh, you were very sweet to
come to my rescue last night, to help the waiters—escort my—
admirer to the door. But, you know, it was—what is the word?
—shattering? Shattering to me. He remembered me at the Metropolitan Opera House, and I am all the time thinking that
maybe I am the only one who remembers Fritzi Scheff in the
opera. You, my dear, you were not born when I was a prima
donna, a star—over forty years ago. When I was—younger.

Records? *(This is the first mention of recordings, and she is simultaneously dismissive and suspicious.)* What do you mean, records?
You mean the Victrola? Oh, no, no no. No records. No recordings. All that scratching with a needle! No, no, I never *(very
definite)* made any recordings. You hear Fritzi in the flesh, not
in the wax. I never made any recordings. I never—trusted
them. *(A pause)* Well, they speed up and slow down, and
then they get warped and wobbled and everybody thinks that
you wobble. No, no no!

I am so sorry to have only one hour for you now before I must
go to Café Grinzing for the first seating. Hm? Oh, I sing three
times every evening, at six-thirty, at eight-thirty, and at ten-
thirty, and in between the other musicians play and I rest. You
know, the little room when you came afterward last night?
After my—admirer got the heave-ho? I am so pleased because
you are so young. I am so pleased because the music now is so
different, and I think, nobody young was wanting to hear my
old songs. But sometimes they do—sometimes —Oh, you are
wanting more tea! No? So, we go to work. What do you want

to know? What do you want me to say? I am very suspicious of interviews because everything right side up comes out upside down, so you must be very sweet—and accurate. *Nicht wahr?*

The first night? My first night? Oh, the first night of *Mlle. Modiste*! You know, I did not want to sing *Kiss Me Again*. Oh, no, I hated it because it lies so low and goes so high. I have high—like a bird. I sang as high as the stars in the sky in *Bohème*. I was first Musetta, you know! I sang—what? *La Bohème*, darling, Puccini. I sang Musetta.   (*She sings out the first few bars of* Musetta's Waltz.)

> Quando men vo,
> quando men vo soletta per la via,
> le gente sosta e mira. . . .

And Nellie Melba sang Mimi. Puccini teached us himself! And all the time he kept muttering to me, "What a Butterfly! What a Butterfly!"

But Nellie Melba already sang in *Madame Butterfly*, and she did not like so much to hear that muttering "What a Butterfly! What a Butterfly!" After that, always she looked at me with her eyes in slits. Then she got very cold to me because when we did *La Bohème*, first I got an ovation for *Musetta's Waltz* in the second act, and Mimi—I mean Nellie Melba—just has mostly duets and has to share the applause with Caruso. And then at intermission I fell down some stairs and sprained my ankle and we had to cancel. "Why can't Scheff be put in a wheelchair?" Melba hissed at us. "I never cancel!" while my poor little ankle kept getting bigger and I kept getting sicker. You see, in the fourth act Melba had a very soggy death scene to make the audience weep, and she didn't want to miss out on the big applause.

(A naughty laugh and a memory.)   Once she woke up after she was
dead in *La Bohème* and tried to die all over again but the conductor wouldn't let her. Once—in New York—we were singing
Bohème, and in the curtain calls Mrs. John Jacob Astor tossed
from her box her orchid corsage at *my* feet, and in a flash Melba
ran in front of Caruso and Bonci to get to me and swooped it up
as her trophy and blow a kiss to Mrs. Astor and then started
bowing all over again to the audience. But, you know, enough is
enough! One night in my *Musetta's Waltz*, my one and only aria
in the opera, Melba got upset because the audience liked me too
much for her to bear, and so she began to sing along with me!
Not her little obligatto or counterpoint part in the reprise but
my waltz! That was the second act, and I went home in a great
huff during the intermission, so instead of my little part in the
third act that silly woman sang the Mad Scene from *Lucia di
Lammermoor* and everybody had to stand there and listen to
her! That woman had leather lungs. She was crazy, that Nellie
Melba, but she got paid back in the next *Bohème* when Caruso
took her hand and sang, "Che gelida manina, se la lasci risdal-
dar"—that means, "What a cold little hand, let me warm it
up." Then he handed her a hot sausage and she screamed and
threw it out into the audience.

Oh, I am guilty too of bad manners! Once, in Chicago in
Mozart's *Magic Flute*, Cleo Campanini and I sang Papagena
and Papageno. You know, the birds? All dressed up in feathers? *(She sings a little.)*

Pok, pok, pok, pok, pok, pok, pok.

It is great comic relief and darling to hear, and after three hours
of all those Masonic rites, and stately music, and Marcella Sem-

brich as The Queen of the Night—not a nice person to know—
the audience is longing to laugh. And they did laugh, but then
they applauded and applauded and stamped the floor and
shouted out for an encore. Now, nobody took encores in opera
any more. Oh, in the old days—a hundred years ago—singers
sang a lot of encores, right in the middle of the opera, not something new, they just repeated the aria, sometimes four or five
times, but when I was in opera that old tradition was *verboten*.
Anyway, in *The Magic Flute* Campanini and I were so much
applauded that the Queen of the Night and her ladies—Sembrich, not a nice person to know?—came sailing on because it
was her cue, and the audience just applauded louder than ever
for Campanini and me, so off she went and waited a little in the
wings and then came on again, and the same thing happened,
and the audience cried, *"bis! bis!"* This time she walked off the
stage and kept right on walking, back to the hotel in her costume, right down State Street with all her little—little twinkly
lights and their batteries on her head and her magic wand in her
fist. When the applause finally quieted down, the Queen of the
Night failed to materialize. Now the audience began to send up
shouts for Sembrich until the stage manager shoved me back
out to announce, "The Queen of the Night has gone home to
bed!"

(The clock on top of the piano chimes four times.)

But you asked about *Kiss Me Again*—my signature tune, my
musical identification. It was a joke on me: I told Mr. Herbert
my voice was no cello, and for twelve weeks on tour I never sang
Kiss Me Again, and then, when we opened here in New York on
Christmas night I promised the lyricist I'd do it for one performance for—a Christmas present for Mr. Herbert. *(She gesticu-*

lates amazement.)   And then fifteen encores! I've never stopped singing it. Did I say twenty-six encores? Well, maybe I don't count so good. Fifteen isn't bad, *nicht wahr?*

Before that? Before *Mlle. Modiste?* Before operetta? Oh, darling, before the operetta I was a star at the Metropolitan: Musetta, Cherubino, Michaela, Papagena, all those screaming Wagner women—well, not Brunhilde or Isolde, but Eva and Elsa, and then all of those Rings. I mean all of the operas in the "Ring": I sang Freya getting traded off to the giants, and Woglinde swimming around and singing under the water to guard the gold in *Das Rhinegold* and then drowning Hagen in *Götterdammerung*, and Helmwige leaping about in the mountains in *Die Walkure*, and the bird, in *Siegfried*, I was the bird, I was the bird in *Siegfried*. You know *Siegfried?* It is very long and—how do you say it? Static. It is very poetic. Very meaningful. Nothing happens. I mean, the valkyries finished up their "Ho-yo-to-ho's" the night before, and Valhalla doesn't burn down until the end of the next opera. And before the bird gets to sing, Siegfried stands absolutely still in the middle of the stage and sings to himself for about an hour, and then I sing from the wings a little song—to a great many empty seats. People were sleeping, right in the boxes. People going out to smoke, for assignations in the lobby, across the street to Brown's Chop House for a little snack. Mind you, Andreas Dippel was a great tenor but not looking so good like Siegfried, standing still and wearing a bear skin and knobby knees before my bird song.

Pardon? Before the Metropolitan? Oh, I sang in London, Munich, Nuremburg, Vienna. I was born in Vienna. My father was a doctor—a throat specialist, very convenient—and my mother was Anna Yeager, one of the greatest Wagnerian sopranos, so it is no wonder I was born with music in my heart, and I cried on key! Under the piano when my mother came home and practiced scales, and when I was a baby I cried to sing duets with her. As far back as I can remember, I didn't think or talk of anything but music, and if I had not been given the opportunity to sing in opera I think I should have died. Yes, I am sure I should have died. At eight I sang solos in church, and at eighteen I was prima donna.

And in between, in Switzerland for my sixteenth birthday at a charity ball I met the Baron Frederick Wilhelm Gustav Carl von Bardelben. He was—oh, devilishly good-looking, tall and blond and wasp-waist and twenty-one years old—a lieutenant in the Thirteenth Hussars, with silver trimmings on his sky blue uniform that matched his sky blue eyes, and—it was love at first sight. We danced into the night and promised ourselves to each other forever. Oh, life was like an operetta in those days! I did not see him again for months because I was back again at studying and he was off on *manoeuvres* and my parents were furious two times at once, because we were so young, and also because I was too young my mother thought for the scholarship I got to study in Frankfurt Conservatory. But when I graduated and sang there in public for the first time, my mother was singing Elsa in *Lohengrin* at the opera house and I was singing Elsa in *Lohengrin* at the conservatory—you know the one, when the hero comes in riding on a swan and we fall in love and the wedding march plays and everybody lives unhappily ever after? I cried because my mother would not hear me, but then she came backstage just before—in her costume— and there we were, two Elsas, like sisters, and the whole cast bowed and curtsied for the great Wagnerian soprano but also for my darling mother. "Mama, your curtain!" I cried, "You will be late!" "Do not fret, my dear," she said. "Tonight the swan will wait for me."

And then I sang in Dresden, Wiesbaden, Berlin, and in between I see my Fritz when he could get away from his Hussars, and the seasons passed *(Fritzi Scheff is easily carried away)* and—Oh, and in London I sang at a command performance also before the old queen—Victoria.

First come in about maybe twelve men in black knee britches who stand around and clear their throats and look very important, and then come in about six ladies all dressed up for a funeral with high necks and gloomy faces, and then comes a little black—tea cosy with a doily on the top, *ja?* Very small *(she measures about five feet in the air with her hand)* but very big *(she measures a large barrel with both hands)*, and I sang Mozart's *La ci darem la mano* with Alessandro Bonci and Brahms's *Wiegelied* all by myself:

> Weigelied und gut nacht . . .

(She da-da-das the next phrase, encouraged that the interviewer finally seems to recognize something.)

And the old queen nodded to me and looked as if she wished I were singing something else, and she say, "We are very fond of 'I Dreamt I Dwelt in Marble Halls.' It was a favorite of—" and she begin to say "my Albert" but she stop in the middle and say "the dear Prince." And then she folded her hands and prepare to listen to me sing it! I apologized because I don't know this song, so *she* started to sing it, but only a little bit and then she giggled and put her fan up over her mouth and blushed, and then she gave me a beautiful bracelet with rubies and sapphires and her initials, V. R. I., on it and said, "We are very pleased"

—and sailed right out of the room. Very pretty bracelet, but I wished it might say F. S.

That was a long separation from my Fritz—three weeks—because at home all the time for an hour or an afternoon I stole little visits with my beautiful baron. Marriage was of course impossible for us. Fritz was German nobility; I was an opera singer, and his family and his Hussars would never tolerate a performer, not even pretty little Fritzi! And so we had a secret—romance, very sweet, very—chaste! And then one night after a performance I was offered a contract for the Metropolitan Opera House in New York, but I went to America weeping. Also, it was for my mother very difficult. You know, nearly twenty years before, they want to get my mother for the Metropolitan, and she said no because of little Fritzi, and then little Fritzi. . . .

I came here in the fall of 1900, and when we arrived they hurried me to a train—the Metropolitan Opera train, with many private cars on the end, and after a week crossing the Atlantic I spend a month crossing the United States, on tour! *Lieber Gott,* this country is bigger than all of Europe, but I did not know that then.

So: I try out my repertoire for the season, in San Francisco and Denver and Kansas City and Minneapolis, and finally back in New York I made my debut, and, you know, Melba got angry all over again because we were supposed to open the season with *La Bohème* and she would get to die gloriously in the last act, but I got sick, and another opera had to open, but when I did sing I was—a big success. I was then "the little devil of Grand Opera." I was—very popular, and I had a remarkable range. My voice could go to F above high C, and I was—petite, I was tiny, and that was a surprise for the audiences because, you know, the ladies in the opera are sometimes—not so little. In the "Ring" when I was one of the three Rhinemaidens I was always like a minnow swimming around in the river with two trout.

They were happy days except that I missed my Fritz. I went back to London for the summer season and sang Marguerite in *Faust* and, you remember at the end in prison—dear boy, you don't remember!—anyway Marguerite prays for forgiveness and falls in the hay and dies and goes up to heaven and Faust goes to hell. Well, the stage hands thought they were being nice to me and put out fresh straw, but it was very—very—what is the word?—very slippery! I rolled right off and down to the footlights and had to die right there, and my understudy got to go to heaven instead—so: two Marguerites were on stage at the same time, and the audience thought it was just—avant-garde, you know, I was the body and she was the soul, I suppose, because they cheered because we were so—daring.

I went home for the rest of that summer, and my Fritz so desperately in love with me resigned from the Thirteenth Hussars to avoid disgracing his family. It was all mad. He was Catholic and I was Protestant, his family was seven hundred years old and aristocratic and mine was, well, professional but common. I was very famous, and poor darling Fritz was only happy with his spit and polish uniform and his horses, and what else could he do? What else did he know how to do? But who can explain love? We married in the fall, and no two people were ever happier—for a time.

(A pause. She has caught herself off guard; a question brings her back.)

What? Oh, for three seasons I sang at the Metropolitan. Fritz came along when we went on tour, and in New York he bided his time and grew bitter because I was paying the bills. He followed the ponies, you know. If he could not ride them he could bet on them, I suppose; after all, a seven-hundred-year-old name does not guarantee an income to go along with it. That was when I first started to think seriously about offers to put me into operetta. It would pay five times as much, and we needed money. I mean I was a star at the Metropolitan but I was a soubrette. You know, not the heavy, tragic queens for me, not Aida getting buried alive, not Brunhilde riding her horse into her husband's funeral pyre, not Tosca jumping off the tower into the river or Violetta coughing until she dies or Lucia going crazy.   *(Suddenly indignant at the thought)*   Oh! I was not comprimaria! I was star! Comprimaria? Oh, you youngsters don't know your opera. Comprimario is—supporting singer, more than the chorus and less than the star, and even less money than me, and I have a good salary but not—Hmm?

Oh yes   *(a grudging admission)*,   I could have made money from recordings. There were a lot of them then—not me, not me. In the beginning we thought it was some kind of a joke. Oh, do you know how they made them? You sing an aria, and then you sing it again, and then you sang it again, and again, and by the time you have made six or seven cylinders your voice is tattered like an old crow's. You know, Caruso used to number his cylinders, and the lower the number the higher the price because the first ones are fresher. Poor Tini—Ernestine Schumann-Heink—she sang Tosti's *Goodbye* so many times— it was so popular—that by the end of a session she sounded like a turkey with a head cold. What? You don't know *Goodbye?* Tosti's *Goodbye? Lieber Gott!*   *(FS bursts into another sudden fit of singing, this time imitating a dignified contralto.)*

Goodbye forever! Goodbye forever! Goodbye! Goodbye! Goodbye!

Oh, darling Tini! Yes, yes, I know, there were soon the flat discs and one time was enough for recording for them, but somehow I couldn't—I couldn't—Listen! *(She goes to the Victrola, winds it, and puts on an old 78 rpm of Luisa Tetrazzini singing "Qui la Voce," which is badly worn and scratchy.)* You see? You hear? Who wants to sound like an old hen with trouble laying eggs? Luisa Tetrazzini had a great voice, a far greater voice than anybody then, I think. Do you believe me from hearing that? And—and *(she searches through a stack of records)* Caruso! This is the greatest voice in history? *(She plays a few bars of Caruso singing "Celeste Aida," also worn and scratchy.)* Not according to the little dog listening on this label!

(She won't lie, however; she needs to confide a secret.) You know, I was—afraid. Afraid! Darling, my voice was very good but my success was not entirely in my voice. I had a certain—chic, an élan, a—I don't know how to say this. On the stage I was *marvelleuse*, I was magic, but maybe without seeing me they don't think so much magic is there after all. And so I don't—What? Oh, I know, all those rumors about my recordings. That's all they are. Rumors! *(She wants to change the subject.)*

Now, now, now! We must go to work or we never finish! You want to know about the Metropolitan and that was my— *(another secret hidden)* last season. I signed with Charles Dillingham for the fall, to appear in *Babette*, an operetta by Victor Herbert on Broadway, and after our short summer season in London I would return to New York to begin rehearsals. It was very sad for me, to leave the Metropolitan, only for money for us. You know it is the greatest house in the world! The greatest company! We all dream of the Metropolitan. We sing every night and we go to Luchow's afterward, and my darling Tini Schumann-Heink eat enough for both of us, with at least two bottles of beer, and Caruso tickled me under the table, and Bonci flirted with me, and everybody was happy.

But then in London for that last summer, I was so sad because it was the end of opera for me, and Fritz had gone home to Germany to be with his family and his horses and his friends—he so much missed the army—and I was going to become an operetta star to make money for us.

What? Oh, yes *(impatiently),* I could have made money from recordings. Caruso made enough in one year from his records to buy his villa in Italy. Nordica made enough to pay for her cruise to the South Seas.

No, no, no, no, no! Besides, memory is kinder, *nicht wahr?* And Fritz did not any longer so much care about my voice after. . . . *(She is hesitant. She is deeply concerned about confiding here. Does she want to tell a stranger this? The story comes out alternately quickly and hesitatingly, depending on the action described, the asides like jokes and the narrative in great pain.)*

You know, I had a baby and—it—did not live, and Fritz. . . . I don't know. You see, Fritz was very happy about our baby. It meant that the von Bardelben line would be secure—a son. He knew it would be a son. My pregnancy even reconciled his parents to me. After all, their heir apparent had married a performer! But they were satisfied because the succession would then be secure. It was in London, just the Met's short summer season there. We were doing *Bohème*, of course, and I had begun to show enough in front so that my costume was with a great shawl to disguise, but my voice! My voice was never better, and

I sang *Musetta's Waltz* gloriously, and at the end of the second
act Antonio Scotti was supposed to sort of catch me when I
stand on the table for my reprise and then fall into his arms and
he carries me offstage. It was a great effect. And then one night
there was a chair. . . . Tony was so full of fun that evening, and
since I was not very heavy, he swung me lightly to his shoulder.
We were all singing and laughing, the café crowd milling
around, when—somehow there was a chair where there should
not have been a chair. Scotti tripped and fell, and I went flying. . . . And at first I thought only of my ankle again and how
angry Melba would be if she couldn't die in the fourth act! But
I went into labor backstage and they rushed me to the hospital
and . . . the baby was born three months prima . . . ? What is
the word? Prematurely. A little boy, and he lived for perhaps
two days, but he was so small and—I don't know—he—died.
And I think I will never sing again. For six weeks I wanted to
die too, and I did not care. My heart was empty. I was suddenly
grown up. I forgot how to laugh. And Fritz, I don't know. Afterwards, on Broadway, when I was great success and Fritz and I
had plenty of money, he spent more and more time at home in
Germany, and in another year we were no longer—together.
Later, whenever I sang my waltz from *Bohème*— and somebody
always asked for it for—some party, some benefit, because I
was so famous for it—inside for my baby I am crying, every
time.

(*A pause. She smiles in embarrassment. Then a new question diverts
her.*)

What? Who? Oh, John Fox! Johnny! I fell in love again in
time, maybe really in love, and with a man so different from
Fritz and so different from me and so different from all the

worlds I know that I think, it is   *(slowly)*   wrong, wrong,
wrong, but he say   *(quickly)*   right, right, right, and I fall into
his arms with no—no resistance, and he made me feel whole
and happy and—oh! I get carried away remembering John.
John A. Fox, Jr., you know? He was famous, a very famous war
correspondent in the Spanish American war and then the very
famous author of very famous books, *The Trail of the Lonesome*
Pine and *The Little Shepherd of Kingdom Come* and, oh, so many
others. He was a Kentucky boy, you know? Tall and—and—
what is the word?—rangy, and lean and with beautiful eyes like
the skies where he lived in Virginia, and almost no smiles but so
gentle and so affectionate for me. Just a mountain boy with the
voice of the gods in him, and he write such books that all the
country loved him. On tour we have such a good time and I can
forget a little my sadness about Fritz, about the—baby, and my
great happiness about John, when I sing in *Babette* and *Mlle.*
Modiste and *Girofle-Girofla*, and *Prima Donna*, and so many
other operettas —they were not all *wunderbar*, darling, but I
was—and with more money than I could spend, and everybody
loved me! I was a favorite of the New York Four Hundred and I
was a favorite with people sitting in the highest balconies who
could scarcely afford their tickets. And when in *Mlle. Modiste* I
play my little drum, rat-ta-plan, rat-ta-plan, they applauded in
time with me! My photographs were in all the magazines and
the rotogravures, college boys begging for a lock of my hair and
wealthy gentlemen flooding my dressing room every night with
flowers. John of course was at home in Virginia, writing, and,
well, I tell you a little secret—I did make some records for John
to keep him company, but just for him! He persuaded me to
make some recordings just for him.   *(A pause over this contradic-*
tion, then scoffing at the questioner's response)   You really believe

that? You wouldn't have liked them—you know, with your hi-fi
and your ell-pee and your 45 are-pee-em records, even now,
with all your modern equipment, a voice on a record is not a
voice in the theater. We hear with our eyes and we see with our
ears. The voice is alive! Not some—some artifact for posterity!
Memory is kinder, my dear. But you know, for all his—sensi-
tivity, John did not care about my voice, he cared about me, and
he wanted them so badly and I loved him so much, and so we
went to some—you see, John didn't care about me on stage;
he had no interest in opera or theater, but he loved my voice
because it was mine, not because I was Fritzi Scheff, and so he
took me to some private place with just a tinny piano making
squawks at me—oh, not a record company, God forbid!—
and I sang into this great brass horn, just for my darling John.
What? Oh, I don't even remember. I sang of course *Kiss Me
Again*. It was after all my—my—signature. *(She sings again,
this time a little more, and she still sings well, even if her voice is somewhat
worn by time.)*

> Sweet summer breeze,
> Whispering trees,
> Stars shining brightly above,
> Roses in bloom . . . *(She laughs in embarrassment.)*

Oh, darling, I wish you might have heard me then! I sang
like an angel! Not some old record, but me, me, me! I was—
famous! I had my face on sheet music and on a cigar box—
*(A supposed guffaw from the interviewer here, and her response is half-
mocking, half-embarrassed.)* Oh, that was a great honor! Not
everybody was cigar material, you know, but there was Galli-
Curci cigars and Nellie Melba cigars and I don't remember how
many others. But no Queen of the Night cigars for Sembrich. I

was on postcards all over too, with glitter! And pillow covers! And cigarette cards! I had—too much success. Too much money. Too many fur coats. My own carriage, and I even bought a house in Connecticut. Hmmm? Oh, in Waterbury, a little house with an acre or two, and sometimes I would escape there when I had a night or two off. John said, "Why live in the country in Connecticut in a little house on a little plot on a weekend when you can live in the country in Virginia in a big house on a whole mountain in the Blue Ridge all the time?"

That was 1908, I think, maybe 1907. No, no, 1908 because that was just when Fritz and I divorced and I married John. All my friends were astonished that I had fallen in love with a solemn recluse and predicted catastrophe when I went home with John to Virginia. They were right. It was —hopeless. We loved each other so much, but I could not live in all that—stillness. John needed quiet to write, and I needed music to breathe. He was in New York very miserable, and I was miserable in those beautiful Appalachian mountains, and wherever we were he insisted that we live on his salary, which meant no suite at the St. Regis but a pokey little hotel. His family's house in Kentucky was lovely and his home in Virginia was lovely too, but— what is the word?—*rustique*, like a stage set for the first act in *Manon* with all those jolly shepherds. John was—very proud, very Southern, *ja?* His books were famous, but he might make in a month what I made in a week, and that is not so comfortable, *nicht wahr?* And I think—his people wanted to like me, but they really couldn't. One day—soon after we married and went to Virginia to meet his family, John said there would be in the afternoon a base-ball-game and that he would play short-stop and then we would have a picnic. I heard "ball." I did not

hear "game" and I did not know what "base" was. I thought the
afternoon was a strange time for a ball, but—well, it was The
South, and I thought it was just a—some local custom, but
I loved picnics and remembered Fritz and me by the stream
behind his parents' *schloss*, with linen and silver and little sand-
wiches and Rhine wine—it was all so gay. So I dressed in my lavender organdy, with tiny, tiny pleats all over my bosom, *ja?*
And my parasol to make an entrance—like an operetta! All I
needed was Victor Herbert to set the scene to music! I thought.
But all the heads turned when I appeared. John's mother and all
his aunts and his sisters wearing house dresses for scrubbing the
floor or washing the dishes or—for going to a baseball game.
And—they laughed. They were embarrassed for me, but they
laughed. You see, they were mountain people, good people, but
very—unsophisticated. Oh, I did not mind that! I wanted to be
so much one of them for John. It seems now so silly, but their
laughter was to me like the "fate theme" in *Carmen*. *(She sings
the four notes menacingly.)*

I knew in my bones at that moment that it was all a terrible
mistake. I could not belong to John's world and he had no interest in belonging to mine. He never heard me in opera. He did
not very much hear me on Broadway. He was in love with Fritzi
but not in love with Fritzi Scheff, and my dear, there is a great
difference. I think no two people ever loved each other so much,
but I could no more stop singing than I could stop breathing. I
had too long been Fritzi Scheff to begin to be just Fritzi, no—to
be Mrs. John A. Fox, Jr. And so we—parted. It was without ran-
cor, without anger, only regret.

What? The records? Those recordings? Oh, long lost, long
lost. Oh *(an answer to a question)*, I don't remember when we

divorced. It had been such a—drifting apart, and then just at
Christmas time in 1913 I married George Anderson, and that
(now she laughs heartily at herself) was a real mistake! He was an
—actor! Believe me, darling, it was more—foreign for me to
marry an actor than for me to marry a beautiful German baron
or an intellectual American hillbilly. One temperament in the
family is enough, and believe me, if there are prima donnas
there are plenty of primo dons around too. George was in the
cast of *Hanky Panky* with me—oh, I bubbled over with anima-
tion in that one! And we toured very successfully—The Fritzi
Scheff Operetta Company—until the war broke out. The war!
I was not even German, but you have no idea how my accent
hurt to hear, and all things German were frowned on. People
changed their names to sound American. Irving—you, know,
the composer?—Irving Berlin was the only Berlin who didn't
become "Buŕrlin" or "BURlin" or "Búrlin." People took lessons
to lose their accents. The—the *widerstriet*—what is the word?
The antagonism against any performer of—teutonic origin
caused by the war affected every-body, including me, even
though in every town where I sang in if there was a military
camp I went to sing for the soldiers—and they loved me! There
was no question about my loyalty!—and I knitted all the time
scarves and gloves for the Red Cross too, and at home in Connecticut I make into a farm my little acreage—and I am raising
chickens, *ja?* And making crops for food. Fritzi Scheff canning
beans! But even so, nobody dared to eat *sauerbraten oder knock-
wurst*—business fell off at German restaurants. There was a moratorium on Wagner at the Metropolitan Opera. On tour I was in
small towns sometimes booed off the stage, and we only had

debts—the newspapers claimed we had more attachments placed against us than any other road company in history! Some times there were more people on the stage than there were in the audience. We were—evicted from the St. Regis because we could not pay the bill! George fled to some place in Indiana to write a new revue but nothing came of it, and I went to hide in my little house in Connecticut.

After that I played in two or three movies—in the silent movies, you know, nobody could hear Fritzi's accent—and then I got booked again for vaudeville at the Palace, that time with Will Rogers. Ziegfeld announced me for his 1916 *Follies*, but nothing came of it because—what? Oh, why not vaudeville? I have no patience with artists who feel their art is too refined or too subtle for vaudeville. I just sang my songs and the audience loved them. Well, the audience in New York at least knew who I was and loved them. But then, with the end of the war, operetta fell out of favor very quickly. I starred in a new one, *Gloriana*, and everybody loved me, all the reviewers and in the audience people who had loved me with my little drum and my *Kiss Me Again*. But Strauss's wine, women, and song politely stepped aside for Gershwin's bootleg and flappers and jazz, and Fritzi Scheff got soon forgotten.

A long time that I didn't perform. In Connecticut I lived carefully on my savings, sometimes a little engagement here or there. But it was nearly ten years before I appeared again on the stage, and then just a little part in a play about Sherlock Holmes. What part? You think I was the hound of the Baskervilles? No, I was a French maid, and all the reviews said I was just like the old Fritzi, with an impudent swing to my short skirts and a chic they had missed for so long. It gave somebody the idea to revive *Mlle. Modiste*, and after twenty-two years I appeared in the same role, and everybody loved me all over again. My voice was as abundant as ever and so were my red curls—even though they had a little bit assistance from my hairdresser—and my waist was—well, not still seventeen inches, but I still looked sensational! Time stands still on the stage, my dear. Sarah Bernhardt played girls young enough to be her granddaughters. Our distance from the audience and the footlights make a magic that erases our age, and even my little pink spotlight at Café Grinzing makes me—feel young again.

But, you know, the theater is very fickle, my dear. After *Mlle. Modiste* there were no other offers. Life was precarious for me. Some times the Actors' Fund stepped in to help me, and I sang whenever I could. Five years later I was a sort of hostess at a tap-room in the Manhattan Hotel on West Fifty-seventh Street.

I toured from time to time, once with Tallulah Bankhead in a terrible play called *I Am Different*—let me tell you, she certainly was. I had only tiny part, even though I got a long ovation when I entered, and at the curtain call Miss Bankhead snarled at me more than Melba ever did. Sometimes I toured to play the part of an old operetta star in *Ladies in Retirement* and sang *Tit Willow*—you know?   (*She warbles the line.*)

> A dickie bird sat in the top of a tree
> Singing willow tit willow tit willow

And got I strangled for it by the crazy housekeeper.

And then a few years ago I was invited to sing *Kiss Me Again*—what else?—at Tallulah Bankhead's book party. She wrote her autobiography, you know, and everybody came and performed, and Tallulah was just as rude as ever, but after I

KISS ME AGAIN 261

sang she curtseyed and kissed my hands, and then everybody
stood up and applauded and Tallulah called me "a grand old
trouper." I didn't like the "old" so much. That was the same season that I returned to the Palace, in vaudeville, and they billed
me as "The One and Only Fritzi Scheff," but I was preceded by
Fox and White, the Gruesome Twosome, and I was followed by
Ross Harvey and His Dancing Budgie Birds. The old days were
certainly gone forever, *nicht wahr?* Although in the second war I
was three nights every week at the Stage Door Canteen for some
talking with soldiers and a little dancing, and sometimes they
get me to sing. I had a weekly radio program for a little while.
Billy Rose engaged me to sing *Kiss Me Again* in his *Diamond
Horseshoe*, and I wore a black sequin sheath gown, and—the old-
timers in the audience remembered how I used to sing it   *(She
knows what that means, and her voice has broken in saying it)*,   and
there was still from the golden days some magic.   *(A sudden
memory)*   Oh, you know, somebody thought I would be just
right for Jerome Kern's *Roberta* to sing those wonderful songs.
*(She begins to sing "Yesterdays," but her voice breaks after the first few
lines. She cries a little and laughs a little.)*   Oh, forgive me!

  And now I sing at the Café Grinzing, and believe me, darling, I am lucky to have the job. I'm broke. My Connecticut
house went in the Depression. My jewels, my furs, everything.
I make good tips and my voice is on a good night still clear and
strong. I think sometimes of the mistake I made in leaving the
Metropolitan for the operetta. I had a great repertoire, you
know, and perhaps—I think maybe my life would have been
very—different. Who knows? We make choices and those
choices lead to other ones and eventually we end at the same
place, all traveling in the same direction and our lives come
down to our scrapbooks full of mementoes nobody else cares

about. But I made people happy, and that ought to be enough for anybody, and whether Musetta or Mlle. Modiste did that, it doesn't really matter. What they said, what they say, and what they will say scarcely help me. Art—whatever art is—warms the heart for a moment, makes it maybe just a little easier to accept what the head tells us is true—on both sides of the foot-lights. In our—inconsequential span of life, sometimes we sing and sometimes we listen, and maybe that amounts to the same thing.   *(The clock chimes five times.)*

Oh, is it so late? Now you just forgive me, darling. I must dress for the Café Grinzing. You will come to hear me there some time again, yes? I hope so, darling. Oh, I am tired from all this talking! I think perhaps I don't speak so good but you will maybe make Fritzi sound okay when you write about her? When you remember her? Oh, it is too dark in here!

(She turns on a wall switch, flooding the apartment to show its ghastly, faded state, its peeling paint, its shabby accoutrements, and the light should be bright enough to startle the audience. She looks about, appalled, and shrugs. She catches sight of herself in the mirror and shrinks.)   Oh, dear, that was a mistake! All the magic goes away when—the audi-ence comes too close.   *(She turns off the lights, again allowing the light of dusk to stream in through the window, transforming the space into a romantic cocoon. She is almost silhouetted against the moonlight, visibly upset by the truth that the lights revealed.)*

What?   *(She runs to the door and flings it open, moving on to the other side of the room and speaks without looking at her guest but for a hasty glance or two.)*   Now, you will show yourself out, *nicht wahr?* I cannot now—goodbye to you now, young man, goodbye. Come again—to Café Grinzing some evening, and we will speak again if you like, but I must now—prepare. You can see your-

self out? *(She says goodbye only by waving a hand hurriedly, impatiently, and shaking her head back and forth very quickly. She stands
motionless. After a second or two the door closes by itself, shutting out the
light that briefly streamed in from the hall. Then she turns on a small, single lamp, but it allows the audience enough light to follow her actions. She
walks slowly to the Victrola, cranks it, and, with a great sigh, slips on a record which she has located, with no difficulty, on a shelf below. The machine
buzzes getting started, and she begins to move away toward the windows
again, but when the music begins she stops dead, listening with her head
cocked, to the old recording. It is scratchy, of course, but the voice is almost
unbearably beautiful. She listens to the opening lines of the verse without
moving.)*

> Ah, dear one, how often I think of the past!
> Can it be you forget?
> Perchance 'twas a passion too wondrous to last,
> But I dream of it yet!

*(She floats about the room, starts to sing along, although only to the end of
the verse)*

> I see you again as you gazed in my eyes
> With joy all alight.
> So fondly you'd fold me, as softly you told me
> Of love through the star-sprinkled night.

*(She listens enraptured as the refrain begins, but soon her body sags, she
looks around, defeated by what her life has come to. Perhaps she moves about
the room a little, but she stands still for the end of the music, listening, listening, mouthing in joy the last words, and taking again a deep bow before
she must then listen too to the scratch of the needle afterwards until the
lights have faded out completely.)*

Sweet summer breeze,
whispering trees,
Stars shining softly above;
Roses in bloom,
wafted perfume,
Sleepy birds dreaming of love.
Safe in your arms,
far from alarms,
Daylight shall come but in vain.
Tenderly pressed
close to your breast,
Kiss me,
kiss me again.
Kiss me again!
Kiss me!
Kiss me
again!

VASSAR MILLER, SWIMMING ON CONCRETE

*P*aul Bodurtha burst into my office with an anthology he'd received in the mail, thrust it into my hands, and demanded that I read two poems by Vassar Miller. We were in our mid-thirties then, teaching in the English department at a small college in upstate New York. Not long before, Paul had introduced me to Edwin Muir's poems, and to those of a friend of his, R. G. Vliet, both of which had made a strong impression on me, so I was willing to take a chance on anything he had come across. I felt the hair rise at the nape of my neck, when I first read "Defense Rests" by Vassar Miller.

> I want
> a love to hold
> in my hand because love
> is too much for the heart to bear
> alone.
>
> Then stop
> mouthing to me
> "Faith and Sacraments" when
> the Host feather-heavy weighs down
> my soul.

So I
blaspheme! My Lord,
John's head on your breast or
Mary's lips on your feet, would you
agree?

If this
Is not enough—
upon Your sweat, Your thirst,
Your nails, and nakedness I rest
my case.

For the first time, I thought I began to grasp something about organic prosodies and the authority of lines motivated by a poem's content. The second poem was an immaculately turned Italian sonnet, again religious in its implications and nearly as staggering to me as "Defense Rests." It was titled "Without Ceremony":

Except ourselves, we have no other prayer;
Our needs are sores upon our nakedness.
We do not have to name them; we are here.
And You who can make eyes can see no less.
We fall, not on our knees, but on our hearts,
A posture humbler far and more downcast;
While Father Pain instructs us in the arts
Of praying, hunger is the worthiest fast.
We find ourselves where tongues cannot wage war
On silence (farther, mystics never flew)
But on the common wings of what we are,
Borne on the wings of what we bear, toward You,
O Word, in whom our wordiness dissolves,
When we have not a prayer except ourselves.

I can't speak for Paul, but I was not religious nor was my response. The poems seemed to transcend their own subject matter. The anthology's maddeningly unsatisfactory "contributor notes" said only that Vassar Miller lived "quietly" in Houston, Texas, and had written three books, one of which had been nominated for a Pulitzer Prize. Paul and I agreed we'd been hit hard and wanted to see more, so we persuaded the grumpy librarian to order them. When the books arrived, their dust jackets didn't add much information, except to reveal that Vassar Miller was a woman, but nearly every subsequent poem I read convinced me that this poet was writing to me.

When in the fall of 1969 I joined the English department at Millersville University, near Lancaster, Pennsylvania, I learned that Vassar Miller sometimes visited one of her great friends there, Mary Jean Irion, whom I'd recently met. But I learned, too, that people had been disarmed by their encounters with Vassar Miller. She was virtually helpless, appallingly afflicted with cerebral palsy, her arms and legs flailing or contracting awkwardly, and her voice an impenetrable series of graveled groanings and laughings that could not always be distinguished, one from the other. Following her conversation was nearly impossible, I was told. One hand had atrophied. She usually walked with someone at her elbow. She drooled. She went up and down steps, one at a time, from a sitting position. Meeting her, especially at first, could be unnerving.

When I learned that Vassar Miller might be coming to Lancaster again, I wrote to her, first about my admiration for her work and then about my wish to have a reading of her poetry on campus. She replied with a brief letter, undated but flawlessly typed: "I hope to come before too long and will be happy to be at

your disposal in any way that I can." Then she'd signed it, a sparrow's effort to autograph a stone with its claws. I met her at the
Irions' house in February 1972. Despite my having been warned,
I *was* unnerved. In repose and seen from the distance she showed
no clear sign of her afflictions, apart from the pain of the past I
thought I saw on her face. She spoke with tremendous difficulty
—every syllable seemingly torn out of her guts—but she was
not, after awhile, hard to understand, because the precision of
her speech turned out to be well nigh perfect, once I stopped
guessing at the words toward which she lurched.

The poetry reading went well, I thought, including a lively
question and answer session afterward. Two students and I read
most of the poems, but Vassar chose to read three herself. I'd du-
plicated copies of all of the poems for the audience, since, on first
hearing, her constricted voice was nearly impossible to translate.
After thank you notes, Vassar and I did not write again until she
was scheduled to return two years later. I mounted a second reading, once more duplicating copies of the poems. Listening to
Vassar's words, and simultaneously seeing them, persuaded me
that I never again wanted to go to a poetry reading by, say, Robert Frost or John Donne (or even one of those performance poets meant to be heard and not read) without having the words
printed out and in front of me or already firmly in my head.

Vassar had a new book out that fall. Entitled *If I Could Sleep
Deeply Enough*, it was far more confessional than anything of hers
I had read before: poems of direct despair, terror, heavy irony,
sometimes surreal humor. The forms were often freer but still
under obviously tight reign; and the subject matter could be
daring and upsetting, as in "Spastics (*First poem from Handi-
Lib*)":

They are not beautiful, young, and strong when it strikes,
but wizened in wombs like everyone else,
like monkeys,
like fish,
like worms,
creepy-crawlies from yesterday's rocks
tomorrow will step on.

Hence presidents, and most parents, don't have to worry.
No one in congress will die of it. No one else.
Don't worry.
They just
hang on,
drooling, stupid from watching too much TV,
born-that-way senile,

rarely marry, expected to make it with Jesus,
never really make it at all,
don't know how,
some can't
feed themselves,
fool with, *well*—Even some sappy saint said they
look young because pure.

No one would have easily assumed from her earlier work that
Vassar was physically impaired, although elliptical references
were frustratingly untranslatable without that knowledge. "An
Epitaph for a Cripple" from her first book, *Adam's Footprint*, published twenty years earlier, might have been autobiographical;
who would have known? "The Common Core" from her second
book, *Wage War on Silence*, included a couplet that was certainly
arresting and bewildering at the same time: "You weep for your
love, I for my limbs—/ Who mourns with reason? who over

whims?" What did that mean? In her fourth collection, *Onions and Roses*, she was direct as she had not been before, with a poem called "On Approaching My Birthday," a single, staggering sentence twelve lines long that still haunts me:

> My mother bore me in the heat of summer
> when the grass blanched under sun's hammer stroke
> and the birds sang off key, panting between notes,
> and the pear trees once all winged with whiteness
> sagged, breaking with fruit, and only the zinnias,
> like harlots, bloomed out vulgar and audacious,
> and when the cicadas played all day long
> their hidden harpsichords accompanying
> her grief, my mother bore me, as I say,
> then died shortly thereafter, no doubt
> of her disgust and left me her disease
> when I grew up to wither into truth.

Once aware of Vassar's catastrophic limitations, I found that I could unlock a lot of her poems, and that some of those in *If I Could Sleep Deeply Enough* cruelly turned the key all by themselves, as any attentive reader will discover with considerable discomfort:

> The day, damp bird, mopes on its branch where leaves
> still cling with wizened fists above
> the lawns all blanched the color of stale vomit.
>
> The day drops dead, time's tune inside my skull
> droning toward sleep when I lie down
> lonely to lust's one-finger exercise.

When the book was due to appear, Vassar was in the middle of a dry spell: "An unfinished poem is on my desk," she wrote me, "but I can tell when a poem isn't going anywhere. That certain something just hasn't clicked, and in this case I fear it won't." Ordinarily, a poem was pretty well complete in her head before she ever tackled the onerous task of typing it out, she said. She was an expert typist, but she dived at the keys, one at a time.

That's how she'd started, at about the age of seven, when her father lugged the typewriter home from his office for her to play with. Until then she had only crawled about the house, careening as she went, although her mind was quick, and her step-mother had read to her and taught her to recognize words early on.

> I remember my father, slight,
> staggering in with his Underwood,
> bearing it in his arms like an awkward bouquet
>
> for his spastic child who sits down
> on the floor, one knee on the frame
> of the typewriter, and holding her left wrist
>
> with her right hand, in that precision known
> to the crippled, pecks at the keys
> with a sparrow's preoccupation.
>
> Falling by chance on rhyme, novel and curious bubble
> blown with a magic pipe, she tries them over and over,
> spellbound by life's clashing in accord or against itself,
>
> pretending pretense and playing at playing,
> she does her childhood backward as children do,
> her fun a delaying action against what she knows.
>
> My father must lose her, his runaway on her treadmill,
> will lose the terrible favor that life has done him
> as she toils at tomorrow, tensed at her makeshift toy.

The following year, when Vassar was scheduled for another visit with the Irions, I asked her if she'd be willing to do a reading at The Pennsylvania State University Medical College in Hershey. My friend, Joanne Trautmann, who taught there, had suggested this, offering a handsome honorarium. Jo conducted a series of literature courses in a successful program designed to familiarize medical students with the humanities. Vassar and I were sufficiently successful at Hershey to be invited a year later to give a reading at the annual American Medical Association conference in Washington D.C.

Vassar would return to Houston after these forays into the limelight, alternately revived and depressed. Invitations for readings were sparse because of the audience's difficulty in understanding her. I had discovered early on, however, that I needed only to listen to her at her own speed, syllable by syllable, rather than to anticipate or assume what was coming. Most people aren't prepared to do that during readings, even less so, perhaps on a one-to-one basis.

Vassar had a strong social life through her church, or, rather, churches, since she belonged to two and had always actively attended both, the Episcopal Saint Stephen's and a free-wheeling Baptist Covenant. That did not mean that she was an easy parishioner or that her relationship had ever been free of frustration. Religion for Vassar, despite her devout commitment, was persistently problematic. "My Christian faith has always been a wistful hope," she wrote me, "hope, more than anything, but one that I dare not let go of. For only in reference to it do I find myself addressed, judged, bolstered, incited to pick myself up and try a little harder for a little while. I cannot make a psalm of despair . . . or, still less, make cheap jibes at the faith. . . ."

That passion led to some strange alliances and alienations. Over the years, Vassar angered plenty of people, and they angered her too, friends as well as enemies, including her half-sisters and half-brother. She took on one or the other of her church congregations over access for handicapped people. She struck up friendships with a strange assortment of alcoholic priests, gay motorcyclists, drug addicts, semi-literate secretaries, creepy hangers-on, honest as well as dishonest housekeepers, and pleasant as well as unpleasant poets, some talented and some hopelessly inept. Perhaps all those others were poets too.

When I first knew Vassar she was always on her best behavior, but of course as a visiting poet she was given a lot of attention, lunches and dinners, and certainly the pleasure of applause after readings. On her home turf, things were less celebratory, and she could return from a Lancaster trip to loneliness, escaping into cheap novels and beer and cokes.

> The ashes have waited for me in the ash tray,
> but say nothing.
> The towel hanging on the rack that I have longed to see
> somehow says nothing.
> My dogs who have already forgotten how much they missed me
> say nothing either.
>   And O O O O
> I wish I could call my mother
> or eat death like candy.

That's called "Homecoming Blues," from a pamphlet, *Small Change*, published in an edition of five hundred copies, in 1976, and a second pamphlet, *Approaching Nada*, came out the following year, a thousand copies, but they did not sell. Do collections of poems ever sell very many copies? Poets survive by writing fiction or essays, by teaching, even some I've known by manual labor. No poet, not since the nineteenth century at least, has made a living wage on nothing but his poetry—not T. S. Eliot or W. H. Auden or Wallace Stevens or Robert Frost or William Carlos Williams, and certainly not Vassar Miller. Nor was she a likely editor, lecturer, insurance executive, farmer, or pediatrician. She lived on a trust fund, established by her father, in a house he deeded her on Vassar Avenue, which had been named for her mother. But she was often improvident, and in time that took its toll.

Vassar was not a good correspondent, largely because it was such an effort for her to write, and conversation over the telephone was difficult, so we were not often in communication. I did see her in Houston a couple of times between her visits here, when I'd flown down to see my sister and her family, who lived there too. I'd borrow one of their cars and drive over to Vassar's to spend a couple of days with her, staying in the garage she'd had converted into a guest cottage. We'd progressed over a period of about five years from a professional association to a strange affection, and our conversations had grown as intense about ourselves as they had about poetry, especially on long drives out on Texas's arrow-straight highways. Vassar really loved speed.

We did not argue exactly about religion but it was a constant in our equally skeptical faith. She believed in a resurrection of some kind, and I do not; she believed in a God who was aware of her, and I cannot conceive of a God capable of afflicting the innocent. She chided me that her twisted body was not at issue; I did not argue there. Her abiding concern always had less to do with the future than with the present, however. "I'm writing very little, which is discouraging," she wrote after one of my telephone calls. I didn't call often; it was too much of a strain on both of us. "I've been slowing down for the past eight years and I have the strange sensation of surviving myself, at least my poetic self. Being too proud to be content with a private self, I grow depressed." That was over twenty years ago, and her fear proved to be all too true, but not before a good deal of intervening activity.

In November 1979 we boarded a bus in Lancaster for a four-hour journey to Washington, D.C., where we were scheduled to read at that American Medical Association conference the next day. We'd arrived the afternoon before to discover we'd been put up handsomely in adjoining rooms at a mid-town hotel. With the afternoon and evening to play with, I tooled her around in a wheelchair at the East Wing of the National Gallery to see the Matisse cutouts and then we went out to dinner—not easy on Vassar and never easy on squeamish strangers at adjacent tables—and looked forward to seeing Shakespeare's *A Winter's Tale* at the Arena Theater. But the weather turned foul, we could not flag or call a taxi in time for the curtain, and so we returned to the hotel and got drunk on white wine during a long and hilarious and intimate exchange of confidences. By the time we said goodnight we were pretty well oiled. The next morning Vassar had a terrible hangover, but the reading was a success anyway.

On the return bus trip we more or less bonded for life, I guess, when she got stuck in the toilet. We'd sat at the back of the bus for easy access since she navigated with such difficulty, so I had no difficulty in hearing her when she opened the door a crack to whisper, "Bruce! Come on in!"

The people behind and in front of us had stared enough when we boarded, for Vassar even under the best of circumstances was an arresting figure, a slowly advancing marionette dancing in fragile, bird-like hops. They gaped when I wedged myself inside the small cubicle. Vassar couldn't get her pantyhose up and needed some help.

"What the hell, honey," she laughed, "what the hell."

Well, gentlemen don't kiss and tell, and they don't repeat stories like that either, but back in Lancaster Vassar told the story herself to half a dozen startled women Mary Jean Irion had mustered for a lunch party the following day.

As a result of that reading in Washington, D.C., we were invited to participate in a humanities seminar at the University of South Carolina Medical School in Charleston the following spring. It would be called *Poetry As a Healing Art*, and Vassar would be the star of the show. We arranged to meet in Atlanta for a short flight together over to Charleston, but Vassar arrived in a fury. She'd been refused a drink on the plane because the stewardesses had decided that she was blind drunk and stumbling. From then on at my insistence we used a wheelchair to get from one gate to another, taking advantage of the services offered to disabled people. She hated that, resisted help from strangers. That made sense, even if it was impractical sense. In Charleston, we were worked hard. We began with a lecture and poems for illustrations one afternoon at the medical school and had a good-natured argument in front of the assembled medicos. The next morning we met with a creative writing class at the College of Charleston, and then, back at the medical school in the afternoon, a round table discussion about coping with death through literature. There was a formal poetry reading that evening and a poetry workshop for aspiring area poets the next morning. All this was punctuated with convivial lunches and dinners and parties, thanks mostly to Ben Goodman, a genial and sweet-natured M.D. in charge of the graduate program who'd put the whole thing together. I think it may have been the first time that so much activity had been centered on Vassar, and I did not realize until afterward how genuinely nervous with stage fright she'd been through most of it.

Soon afterward, in 1980 I think, Vassar had the first of the long series of physical bouts that plagued her forever afterward, beginning with a hiatal hernia, which meant "beerless and coke-less days." She was physically addicted to Coca Cola, had been for years, but the prospect of a trip east to see an old friend in St. Louis was getting her through, and so was the possibility of a new book. An acquaintance had started a small press and wanted to publish the manuscript that some of the trade houses had rejected. A month later she sent me thirteen new poems, and she'd begun work on an anthology—to be called *Out of the Back Bedroom*—of poems and stories by and about people with various handicaps. It was a busy summer, as she wrote in July that year, soliciting manuscripts and trying to cope with her new publisher. Vassar and a friend drove north to visit him and talk about the organization of *Selected and New Poems*, due out that fall:

> I love the Texas Hill country better than any spot on earth. But [my new publisher], normally an abstemious man, smoked pot the whole damned week-end and he didn't care much about being serious. He and I did talk about my poems. The poems he normally thinks little of he likes when he does grass. Then he gave a party for us where I had too much wine and remember little except a very cute baby. However, my book will probably be out by December and Denise Levertov has promised to write the introduction. Next week I am to go to Tennessee with my R.C. priest, . . . one of my very dearest friends, [who] is perpetually hyper and wears me out. He drinks beer like water and Scotch like

beer. In addition, we will go to Tennessee in an un-air-conditioned car, which won't be so bad if [he] won't bar-hop all night in New Orleans and we can get on the road early. I say if. My hopes are feeble.

But she survived, and that Christmas when I was back in Houston, attending the Modern Language Association conference, I stayed with her. We went out to investigate the chapel at Rice University, hung with huge, dark slabs of canvas by Mark Rothko. We sat in silence for some time; I had no idea what Vassar thought about art and figured I'd let her go first, since I was feeling pretty intimidated by great stretches of the darkest shades of color possible in the spectrum. Finally she muttered, "Looks like a lot of blackboards to me. Let's go." We hit a neighborhood bar she liked where everybody seemed to know her, drove around town to take in some houses she liked to look at, and then I took her along to some MLA sessions, including one where she was introduced as one of Texas's treasures.

Those highs didn't come too often, so it was doubly defeating when a month later her co-editor on the anthology quit, and her *Selected and New Poems* was delayed. This was during "The Year of the Handicapped," so Vassar had hoped to take advantage of the publicity. She wasn't a member of a "chic majority," she wrote me, "because we can't burn buildings and overturn cars and nobody's afraid of us. . . ." Her publisher kept telling her that he loved her, which only angered her:

Well, hell, love hasn't much to do with getting a book published.
I often think a moratorium ought to be declared on the word, love.
The word, God, is out (except, sadly, with the Moral Majority)
and love is in. Both words can be equal cover-ups for Nothing.
I know I sound irascible, and I am. I'm less depressed than

disenchanted. . . . I wish you could come back to Houston. In my current anti-social mood, you're one of the few people I feel like talking to.

Sometimes Vassar included poems in letters—sixty or so— that she didn't ever publish, even when a full omnibus came out many years later. Sometimes they were merely charming throw-aways, and sometimes they hit hard:

> All these years
> she wriggled into her life
> this way and that
> trying to make it fit,
> and never did,
> till finally
> she tore a hole in it,
> fell through to death
> which she found
> a perfect size.

Several years earlier I might have shared mutual friends' concern about Vassar's attempting suicide, but I had come to learn that she was probably the last candidate for that. She wrote about it often enough, and we talked about it as well, and despite the deep depression we frequently shared—by that time I was well into my first year of psychoanalysis and Vassar had been in treat-ment most of her life—we decided that life was preferable even if it wasn't. That made sense at the time—still does, although I'd hate to have to defend either one of us on the issue.

Selected and New Poems appeared at the beginning of 1982, al-though she'd had to help finance it into print and was thinking about putting up some capital to get her anthology published as

well. The new book of poems left out a lot of earlier poems that I
would have included and included a number I would have left
out, but ended with some strong new ones, especially "An Essay
in Criticism by Way of Rebuttal":

> Every white page is
> the threat of infinite snow.
>
> Every descent into silence is
> the risk of never returning.
>
> Every tentative word is
> in peril of being wanting.
>
> Every poet knows
> what the saint knows
>
> that every new day is
> to retake the frontier of one's name.

I'd written to invite Vassar to participate in a year-long series
of programs in Lancaster about handicaps and prejudice when
the book appeared, just at the time that a long, thoughtful, sym-
pathetic essay about her and her work was published in *Houston*,
the city's equivalent of the *New York* magazine. She was deeply
hurt by it because the writer had described her physical appearance, not unkindly but candidly. Her response to it when she
wrote me was painful:

> [The reporter] out of sheer vindictiveness (it's a long story) makes
> me out to resemble the sister of the elephant man. . . . The first few
> paragraphs ruined the whole article for me. . . . I wish I could give
> the talk [in Lancaster] on prejudice against the handicapped, but
> perhaps I am too angry. I know I am too angry. After 20 years and
> more in psychotherapy I am so enraged by that article that I am a

little concerned for my mental health. It isn't really the article
(what do I care what one twerp thinks?). It's that I begin to realize
that many people must see me that way. He makes it sound as
though I look retarded, am a sloppy dresser, a slowly moving
disaster. It makes no difference that he praises my poetry. . . .
Praise from "lay" persons annoys me at worst, embarrasses me
at best.

In April 1982 Vassar was in Lancaster to appear on the panel
about prejudice; in October she was back to appear with Robert
Russell—the blind novelist who taught at Franklin and Marshall College—for a joint reading; and in November a local theater group did an evening based on the manuscript of her still-
unpublished anthology, *Out of the Back Bedroom*. Just before she
flew in for the reading, she sent me some new poems "because
they have some humor in them. . . . Pick what you like but for
Pete's sake pick some of my cheerful poems." She sent along a review of the new book too, angered anew:

> It's favorable, but why doesn't he lay off my personal life? He
> seems to know a lot more about it than he can know. How does
> he know I've had no lovers? And as for having no career—I sort
> of thought writing was a career. I now wish nobody knew I had
> cerebral palsy. I used to think the knowledge could "help"
> somehow, but there's no helping dimwits.

I was always able to wangle enough of an honorarium to cover
Vassar's travel expenses, but the residue hardly paid her bills,
and her trust fund was not bottomless, as her advisors kept warning her. Another collection of poems was published, *Trying to
Swim on Concrete*, much involved as usual with faith and death
and time, some of them passionate and some of them even hilari-

ous, concluding with "Love's Bitten Tongue," an astonishing sequence of twenty-two interlocking sonnets, each final line becoming the first line of the next one. But the book did not sell
many copies. Vassar's meager income from an occasional reading
and a few tutorials at a nearby private academy hardly offered her
a living wage. Even the windfall of $37,000 when the University
of Houston purchased her papers did not entirely ease her growing financial difficulties. More than once her step-siblings tried
to persuade her to sell her house and go into some extended care
facility, which only encouraged her wrath. She thrived on her in-
dependence, her motorized three-wheeler that got her back and
forth to church, the stacks of dinners in her freezer that her longtime housekeeper, Rose, prepared for her, her library, her belongings—including a piano on which she liked to pick out "Amazing Grace," one note at a time. She had people over for poetry sessions, she invited friends in for drinks, and she adored her dogs.
Usually there were two of them, sometimes three, mutts and
mixtures that yapped a lot and loved her, once a stray the size of a
Great Dane but with a pedigree all his own. How could she find
any place that would allow her that much latitude? Meanwhile,
taxes went up, and repairs on the house increased, and her annu-
ity stayed right where it was.

   She tithed with a puritan's devotion to her churches, and her
religion got her through very nearly everything, emotionally if
not practically. She began to take communion twice a week, having felt "literally starved for the Sacrament on a regular basis
for so long that now it is a great joy." She was deeply concerned
about my lack of faith. "You said several years ago that you didn't
communicate because of your doubts. Bruce, please don't let that
stop you." I think I shocked her once when I told her that when I

was a kid we referred to communion as refreshments and frequently ran up to the balcony for seconds after the trays had been passed downstairs. But she laughed. She didn't laugh when I told her—that for me, anyhow—praying ranked right up there with rubbing a rabbit's foot, although I'd never belittle anybody else's faith, including hers. Not even when her alcoholic priest friend gave her communion in her dining room one day when she was ill and hadn't been to church for a couple of weeks. Vassar didn't have any wine in the house, and she was out of beer, so he used Coca Cola and Ritz Crackers. Anybody's faith that could go that far was okay by me, I told her, but I wasn't hungry. Besides, I wrote her, my psychiatrist seemed to be doing me a lot of good just about that time, and maybe I'd even be cured without having to take the veil, if I persisted. "I've been going to a psychiatrist for nigh on to 30 years," she replied, "and I'm still not 'cured.' Psychiatry is a good tool, can help you over some rough spots. But there is no cure for our humanity except the grace of God, and that we have to take on blind faith."

Vassar's faith was put to the test when her step-mother died in 1985, cutting her out of the will. They had had at best a strained relationship for many years, but Vassar was convinced that her half-brother and half-sisters had exerted some considerable influence, and she even suggested that they'd hastened their mother's death by cutting off her oxygen supply during her final hospitalization. Vassar's step-mother had been responsible for teaching her how to read and write, but she'd been bitter over the trust set up in Vassar's name, apparently. Vassar was even disoriented in several letters over all this, so when later blows to her fragile ego sent her off into transports of fury, I was alarmed but not surprised. She struck out against friends, against members of one or the other of her churches. She turned on her doctors, her financial advisors, lawyers she engaged and dismissed, at one point the Houston police department when it refused to consider giving her driving lessons—whoever happened to get in the way. In a sudden fit, she even fired her long-suffering, loyal housekeeper Rose, and then she fired Rose's replacement. I'd seen Vassar's anger in action, visited upon mutual acquaintances, and heard other irrational accusations, but I did not experience any of that myself for another year or so.

Vassar's anthology finally came out in 1985, retitled *Despite This Flesh*, and, somewhat more modest in scope than her initial idea, limited to material about physically disabled people. Whether she or her publishers decided to drop so much of the impressive table of contents she'd originally proposed and submitted, I never knew; she seemed pleased enough with the compromise. Vassar's introduction carried more than one passage with powerful autobiographical implications:

> Perhaps the writer assumes the ancient superstitions: the disabled is magic or superlatively gifted by God. I have often been told, "If you weren't handicapped you probably wouldn't write poetry." What about the myriad other poets who have no visible handicap? The afflicted one is the bait dropped in the waters of chaos to catch whatever fish of meaning may surface to take it and so let normal humanity know that, after all, everything is well. People usually feel guilty in the presence of the handicapped. Even the moderately disabled may feel guilty before the severely disabled. But if the maimed person is that way for a reason, set apart, "special," to use the current silly euphemism, then the rest of humanity can rest comfortably. The blind man, being always wise, should feel favored. The crippled girl, being perpetually sweet, should regard herself blessed. The cliché sings out the hours of darkness while we all sleep snugly.

She had been going through several bouts of severe depression just before and after the book came out, "a living hell," she called one of them. "My mind began playing tricks on me, my memory became bad, and I became unable to swallow even soft food." All of that portended what lay ahead.

In 1988, Ford-Brown Publishers issued *Heart's Invention*, a book of essays about Vassar's work, with contributions from nine admirers, including Larry McMurtry, who'd stirred up Houston and all of Texas, for that matter, about her significance in the state's history. I wrote a piece called "Blood in the Bone: Vassar Miller's Prosody," which she liked because it said nothing about her and concentrated on a single poem, a far more scholarly piece than some of the others. She was momentarily pleased by the whole thing, but it did not ward off her encroaching age and fragility.

She broke her collarbone. She broke a rib. Arthritis began to atrophy her other hand. Going too fast, she had an accident with her motorized bike and had to have stitches in her forehead. Pneumonia put her in the hospital more than once. She fell again and broke an ankle. Over the years, Vassar had learned how to fall without hurting herself, since she fell periodically, especially when she went careening too quickly, but her bones were growing increasingly brittle. So was her patience.

I don't know exactly what set her off against me. She always wrote less frequently than I did, but she telephoned for long sessions, not my favorite method of communication, and so I rarely called back. It didn't matter: in both forms she grew incomprehensible, accusatory, paranoid. Her letters during this period are too terrible to quote from here, and in her telephone calls she ranted incoherently against people I'd never heard of who, she claimed, had taken over her life in unspeakable ways, including theft, fraud, telephone harassment, rape, unnecessary sedation, and deliberate physical pain. Mary Jean Irion and I feared that the massive anti-depressants she was on were seriously affecting her judgment, and that her estrangement from her family had pushed her hard toward a complete psychotic break. There was nothing I could do, and any suggestion I made only seemed to anger her further.

I asked Vassar not to call me anymore, found reasons to hang up fast when she did, and I stopped writing to her.

When her poems were republished in an omnibus volume a year later, *If I Had Wheels or Love*, she sent me a copy, inscribed with agonizing effort in a barely legible script, "For Bruce Love Vassar." I wrote immediately and at length to thank her. The book seemed to me an overwhelming achievement for any poet: nearly four hundred poems, including new ones to suggest that her savagery had found its right vent, and that she was well in command of her faculties:

> If I fall down even as those more lithe
> Must do, for God's sake, hush your lamentation
> For joy that then I'll rest on solid earth
> And not on quicksands of imagination.
> Yes, if my image buckles, blurs its structure,
> Don't cry too long (and who knows, you might cry
> Since everyone adores a pretty picture,
> Yet pretty pictures wear the wary eye).
> And, Hell, you're born too old for idols, dolls.
> In fact, you've scarcely time for growing up
> Before death hauls you down to her and lulls
> You sound asleep upon her rumpled lap.
> So, if I trip, take heart—you'll see me clear,
> Polished upon my each particular.

That one is titled "For Stringless Love," a highly unconventional conventional sonnet. I don't know of any other poet who could bring this kind of sass off so well.

I was ashamed of my silence and said so, asking her to write to me or to call me, but she did not. The next time I was scheduled for a trip to Houston to visit my sister, I wrote to Vassar to ask if I could come to see her. Over two years had passed. The reply came through an amanuensis: Vassar would love to see me, and in preparation I began to write to her again, but now her replies came from a nursing care facility, and they suggested that her churches were overstocked with well-meaning boobies, including the clergy, that her friends paid no attention to her wishes, that her trust fund was down to its last gasp. Vassar had been declared a ward of the state, her house had been sold, her belongings dispersed at a clearance sale, and some of her papers may have been destroyed. An indifferent, court-appointed conservator stowed her away in a public facility and refused expenditures that might have made life bearable—all the while threatening her with the embarrassment of Medicaid. Since Vassar could no longer hold books to read them, for instance, the conservator even refused to have her glasses mended. It was *not* bearable, but Vassar's faith sustained her.

I'd heard about the horrors of nursing homes; I think I'd never believed them before. Vassar's own condition was so shocking that her surroundings did not immediately register. She could no longer swallow solid food because her esophagus had ceased to function. She could still drink water and longed to drink her addictive Cokes, but since her hands had atrophied she couldn't manage unless someone held a straw to her mouth. Even with glasses she could no longer read because she couldn't turn the pages of books. She couldn't activate the television set and she couldn't even manage to press a button to call for help or attention or assistance. Instead, she waited for some friend or other to drop by or until one of the staff members happened to come into her room. Vassar had become an elderly, little bird, moulting toward oblivion. Many of her teeth were gone, her skin had grown papery, wrinkles complicating it like a too small road map, her hair was matted and tangled, and she was in discomfort, huddled in a wheelchair, feeding tubes leading into her stomach, her hands frozen into claws in her lap.

Vassar's bones had grown so brittle that her ankle had broken two years before when a home health person had handled her incorrectly. More recently her femur was broken while her diaper was being changed. She had been hospitalized for uremic poisoning and for pneumonia. She was in moderate pain when she was obliged to lie on the bed or to sit in the wheelchair for protracted periods of time, but urging her keepers to put her in her more comfortable recliner met with indifference most of the time. They had put her in that wheelchair before my arrival because she'd been scheduled to have her hair shampooed—for the first time in weeks—and then they'd simply forgotten about her. I knew how cantankerous Vassar could be and I knew how amusing she could be too, but mentally she was the same. The only change lay in the loss of her wit and the growth of her despair.

In an adjacent bed in the small room, an ancient patient whimpered and moaned and occasionally cried out. For several months, Vassar said, the woman had been in a permanent coma, crying or groaning periodically, incapable of communication. Vassar was absolutely certain that she had been assigned this roommate since she must have struck impatient staff members as equally incoherent. Despite written instructions affixed to the walls by her friends—about her difficulty in speaking—none of the attendants seemed to make any attempt to understand her. One young man came to examine Vassar's bedsores and spoke to me about her as if she were not present. Rather than asking me who I was or asking me to leave the room while he called for an assistant, he obliged me to hold Vassar forward in my arms while he examined her bedsores. Old acquaintance notwithstanding, I was speechless at Vassar's upper thighs and catheter, embarrassed for us both. Two women came to spray with disinfectant and then cursorily to dry-mop a calcified pool of urine under her wheelchair. It had been allowed to dry there over a period of time. They began shoving around the wheelchair to facilitate mopping the floor and ignored Vassar's imprecations that either her catheter or feeding tube was being pinched and giving her pain. I shouted them out of the room.

There was little I could do in Houston but complain to the supervisors at the nursing home. From Lancaster, however, I drafted a report and sent it everywhere I could think of where somebody might take some action—beginning with Governor George W. Bush and ending with a Houston television muckraker named Marvin Zindler and, in between them, Vassar's churches, her doctor, an earlier nursing home that her conservator had decided was too expensive, the Houston Cerebral Palsy Foundation, the Texas Department on Aging, several people who purported to be her friends, the conservator, and the facility itself. I was long-winded, but I covered the whole ugly situation in detail and urged that Vassar's limited funds be utilized for her well-being and not just to hold Medicaid at bay. After all, her house had sold for over $100,000, and there had been benefits and fund-raisers for her "cultural needs," which brought in about $25,000 that was being managed by her church and thus far only paying taxi-fare to get her back and forth to services. I suggested an eye-contact word processor, readers on a regular basis, a VCR, a call button she could manage to activate, or just the cost of training staff members to learn how to listen to Vassar's expert diction (slowly), or even to pay to have someone to turn on and off a cassette player so that she might listen to books on tape, or to facilitate her attendance at support groups for people with cerebral palsy, or to replace her broken glasses—all ways that might have occurred to somebody to ease Vassar's passage through "this long disease, my life," as Alexander Pope referred to his own badly crippled body.

Governor Bush's office telephoned four days later, followed by a letter from the governor himself. Several other letters and calls from other offices as well arrived during the next several months, although the conservator and the churches were both silent, maybe outraged by the interference of a stranger. The state sent down representatives from Austin for a full investigation of the nursing home and put it on probation. Vassar's conservator was fired. By a nice irony, Sue Nash, a psychologist at the University of Houston, who had bought Vassar's house—and had never heard of Vassar before—became her strongest defendant and was appointed by the courts as her guardian and conservator.

But the effort came too late. Vassar had deteriorated so far that she was unable to use the computer supplied her or the headband device for turning pages. She was, however, equipped with a custom-made chair for her comfort, a call button she could manipulate with her elbow, and regular readers. Joanne Avinger, a devoted friend from one of Vassar's churches, continued as an amanuensis, sending notes and responses to letters from friends. Also, a number of students from the University of Houston, at Sue Nash's behest, turned up to take dictation—Vassar was trying to write a memoir, and she said she was still writing poems— but she sent me none after her last book was published. A gifted young poet, Robert Lunday, was her most faithful acolyte though he realized early on that dictating a poem and writing one were very different indeed, and like other writers before her, Vassar discovered that poems came from the head to the hand, not to the mouth.

When I saw her again, two years later, she was back in the hospital because of her esophagus and complications with her feeding tube. She had wizened, a shrunken sparrow waiting with her "wistful hope" that God cared about her. Friends still came to visit, not so often as she would have liked, and students continued intermittently to come in to read to her, but her long-ago fear that she would outlive herself—that is, her poetic self—had come all too true. She could not read and she could not write. Then, in the last year of her life, she was initiated into the Texas Hall of Fame, and—a serious undertaking—she was transported to Austin for the formal celebration. Cold comfort, perhaps, but comfort. No colder, though, than the accolades for her poetry that appeared in her obituaries. Why could all that not have been said beforehand?

In the end, Vassar's body simply stopped "trying to swim on concrete," as she'd put it in a poem some years before. Death's vigil began on Friday, 30 October 1998; she died the following afternoon, no longer waging her "war on silence," having learned to "sleep deeply enough," her "bones being wiser" than ours.

I suppose I have known almost as long as I knew her what she meant by the title poem in her last book, *If I Had Wheels or Love*: wheels to escape from what she was, or love to sustain her since she could never escape from what she was. Vassar had been denied both wheels and love in one way by God or fate or life's strange odds that curse or bless us with indifference, and in another way by the rest of us in too many variations for the length of her long life.

Two years after Vassar's death, I completed a project that she and I had spoken of from time to time over the years, a monologue made up of her poems and of observations she'd made in interviews that might be performed to represent her since—as she was well aware—her own reading put such demands on her audience. Our mutual friend Candace O'Donnell performed it in February 2000, jointly sponsored by the Theater of the Seventh Sister and the Lancaster Cerebral Palsy Foundation. Two of the beautiful golden retrievers, trained to fetch and carry and even open doors and turn light switches on and off for disabled people, were brought in from the Foundation for the evening, and they snored blissfully through some of Vassar's best poems. How she would have loved that.

ACKNOWLEDGMENTS

Selections from Arden Angst Andreas's letters are published by permission of her family. Selections from Amanda M. Ellis's letters are
published with her permission. Selections from Alice B. Toklas's letters and other writings are published by permission of Edward Burns,
selections from *The Alice B. Toklas Cook Book* are reprinted by permission of Harper Collins Publishers, Inc., selections from Gertrude
Stein's writings are reprinted by permission of Calman A. Levin, and
selections from *The Autobiography of Alice B. Toklas* in *Selected Writings
of Gertrude Stein* (1946) are reprinted by permission of Random House
and Richard B. Corley of The Acting Company. Selections from Fania
Marinoff's letters are published by permission of the Estate of Carl
Van Vechten. Selections from Nina Balaban's letters are printed
by permission of Andrea von Rulner. Marguerite Young's letter and
selections from her other writings are published by permission of
Daphne Nowling; this chapter was initially published in a somewhat
different form in *Review of Contemporary Fiction*, 20:2, summer 2000,
and the letter was published in holograph facsimile as *"this casually selected page"* by All Kinds Blintzes Press (2000). Fritzi Scheff's unpub-

lished memoirs, from which I employed some passages as well as factual material, are in the Lincoln Center Library for the Performing Arts; her personal scrapbook is in my possession; no heirs survive her of whom I am aware. Selections from Vassar Miller's letters are published with her permission, and her poems, collected in *If I Could Sleep Deeply Enough* are reprinted with the permission of Southern Methodist University Press; this chapter was initially published in a somewhat different form in *Literature and Medicine*, 19:2, fall 2000.

The photographs of Arden and the author (1932), Mary Alice Hadley (1940), Amanda M. Ellis (1952), and Nina Balaban (1925) are by anonymous photographers; the photograph of Alice B. Toklas (1951) is by Donald Angus; the photographs of Fania Marinoff (1937), and of Gertrude Stein and Alice Toklas (1934), are by Carl Van Vechten and reproduced with permission of the Van Vechten Trust; the photograph of Marguerite Young (1964) is by Vytas Valatis; the photograph of Vassar Miller (1979) is by the author; the photograph of Fritzi Scheff (circa 1896) is by A. T. H. Voight; the drawing of Alice B. Toklas (1983) is by Tom Hachtman; the woodblock print of Fritzi Scheff (1906) is by Al Freuh.

For favors large and small, thanks to Warren Andreas, the late Donald Angus, Desmond Arthur, Joanne Avinger, Joanne Trautmann Banks, Lisa Browar, Gloria and W. P. Cameron, Herbert Coburn, Marilyn Storm Cory, J. Joel Farber, Elaine Henecke Fox, the late Donald Gallup, Arthur Gregor, Keith Gregory, the Hadley Pottery Company, Julie Harris, Mary Jean Irion, Robert W. Jones, Peter Kayafas, Jerald Ketchum, Robert Lunday, the late Mark Lutz, Robert McLaughlin, Bart Murphy, Sue Nash, Candace O'Donnell, Loyette Olson, Suzan Beer O'Neill, Priscilla Oppenheimer, Jay Paul, the late Richard Rutledge, Denise Sater, Gary Smith, Mary Adams-Smith, Sam Spanier, the late Regina Wallace, Patricia Willis, Donald Windham, Margaret Woodbridge, and Lou Ziegler.

Albertson, Chris. *Bessie Smith/Nobody's Blues But Mine*. New York: Columbia Records, C31093.

Auden, W. H. "Old People's Home." *Epistle to a Godson*. New York: Random House, 1972, p.53.

Bentley, Eric. "Notes." *The Modern Theatre, Volume 6*. New York: Doubleday Anchor, 1960, p. 286.

Blossom, Henry and Victor Herbert. *Mlle. Modiste*. New York: M. Witmark & Sons, 1905, pp. 49–50.

Durbin, Al, Joseph J. Garren, and Fred Rath. *Just a Girl That Men Forget*. New York: Jack Mills Inc., 1923, pp. 3–4.

Fuchs, Miriam, ed. *Marguerite Young: Our Darling, Tributes and Essays*. Normal, Ill.: Dalkey Archive Press, 1994, p. 138.

Gallup, Donald, ed. *The Flowers Of Friendship: Letters Written to Gertrude Stein*. New York: Knopf, 1953, pp. 58, 73.

Horgan, Paul. *The Fault of Angels*. New York: Harper, 1937, p. 31.

Luhan, Mabel Dodge. *Movers and Shakers*. New York: Harcourt Brace, 1936, p. 45.

Miller, Vassar. *If I Had Wheels or Love, Collected Poems of Vassar Miller*. Dallas: Southern Methodist University Press, 1991, p. 35ff.

Schaap, Dick. "Hercules in High Heels." *Book Week* 12.6 (September 1965).

Stein, Gertrude. *As Fine As Melanctha*. New Haven: Yale University Press, 1954. pp. 224–45.

———. *Geography and Plays*. Boston: Four Seas Company, 1922, p. 16.

———. *Selected Writings of Gertrude Stein*. Edited by Carl Van Vechten. New York: Random House, 1946, pp. 3ff.

Toklas, Alice B. *The Alice B. Toklas Cook Book*. New York: Harper, 1954, pp. 29ff.

———. *Staying On Alone: Letters of Alice B. Toklas*. Edited by Edward Burns. New York: Liveright, 1973, pp. 3ff.

———. *What Is Remembered*. New York: Holt Rinehart & Winston, 1963, pp. 3ff.

Van Vechten, Carl. *Memoirs by Fania Marinoff* [ghost-written]. *American Weekly Jewish News* 1:7, 1:8, 1:10 (March 1918).

Yeats, W. B. "Adam's Curse." *The Collected Poems of W. B. Yeats*. New York: Macmillan, 1962, p. 40.

Young, Marguerite. *Angel in the Forest*. New York: Reynal & Hitchcock, 1945, p. 42.

———. "The Arctic Explorer at the Stock Exchange." *Tiger's Eye* 1.6 (December 1948), p. 1.

———. *Miss MacIntosh, My Darling*. New York: Scribners, 1965, pp. 430, 692.

———. *"this casually selected page."* Lancaster, Pa.: All Kinds Blintzes Press, 2000.